Invasive Objects

D1616413

WITHDRAWN
UTSA LIBRARIES

RELATIONAL PERSPECTIVES BOOK SERIES

Volume 43

RELATIONAL PERSPECTIVES BOOK SERIES

LEWIS ARON & ADRIENNE HARRIS
Series Editors

The Relational Perspectives Book Series (RPBS) publishes books that grow out of or contribute to the relational tradition in contemporary psychoanalysis. The term "relational psychoanalysis" was first used by Greenberg and Mitchell (1983) to bridge the traditions of interpersonal relations, as developed within interpersonal psychoanalysis and object relations, as developed within contemporary British theory. But, under the seminal work of the late Stephen Mitchell (1988), the term "relational psychoanalysis" grew and began to accrue to itself many other influences and developments. Various tributaries—interpersonal psychoanalysis, object relations theory, self psychology, empirical infancy research, and elements of contemporary Freudian and Kleinian thought—flow into this tradition, which understands relational configurations between self and others, both real and fantasied, as the primary subject of psychoanalytic investigation.

We refer to the relational tradition, rather than to a relational school, to highlight that we are identifying a trend, a tendency within contemporary psychoanalysis, not a more formally organized or coherent school or system of beliefs. Our use of the term 'relational' signifies a dimension of theory and practice that has become salient across the wide spectrum of contemporary psychoanalysis. Now under the editorial supervision of Lewis Aron and Adrienne Harris, the Relational Perspectives Book Series originated in 1990 under the editorial eye of the late Stephen A. Mitchell. Mitchell was the most prolific and influential of the originators of the relational tradition. He was committed to dialogue among psychoanalysts and he abhorred the authoritarianism that dictated adherence to a rigid set of beliefs or technical restrictions. He championed open discussion, comparative and integrative approaches, and he promoted new voices across the generations.

Included in the Relational Perspectives Book Series are authors and works that come from within the relational tradition, extend and develop the tradition, as well as works that critique relational approaches or compare and contrast them with alternative points of view. The series includes our most distinguished senior psychoanalysts along with younger contributors who bring fresh vision.

RELATIONAL PERSPECTIVES BOOK SERIES

LEWIS ARON & ADRIENNE HARRIS
Series Editors

Vol. 43
Invasive Objects: Minds Under Siege
Paul Williams

Vol. 42
Sabert Basescu:
Selected Papers on Human Nature and
Psychoanalysis
George Goldstein & Helen Golden (eds.)

Vol. 41
The Hero in the Mirror:
From Fear to Fortitude
Sue Grand

Vol. 40
The Analyst in the Inner City,
Second Edition:
Race, Class, and Culture Through a
Psychoanalytic Lens
Neil Altman

Vol. 39
Dare to be Human:
A Contemporary Psychoanalytic Journey
Michael Shoshani Rosenbaum

Vol. 38
Repair of the Soul:
Metaphors of Transformation in Jewish
Mysticism and Psychoanalysis
Karen E. Starr

Vol. 37
Adolescent Identities:
A Collection of Readings
Deborah Browning (ed.)

Vol. 36
Bodies in Treatment:
The Unspoken Dimension
Frances Sommer Anderson (ed.)

Vol. 35
Comparative-Integrative Psychoanalysis: A
Relational Perspective for the Discipline's
Second Century
Brent Willock

Vol. 34
Relational Psychoanalysis, V. III:
New Voices
Melanie Suchet, Adrienne Harris, &
Lewis Aron (eds.)

Vol. 33
Creating Bodies:
Eating Disorders as
Self-Destructive Survival
Katie Gentile

Vol. 32
Getting From Here to There:
Analytic Love, Analytic Process
Sheldon Bach

Vol. 31
Unconscious Fantasies and the
Relational World
Danielle Knafo & Kenneth Feiner

Vol. 30
The Healer's Bent:
Solitude and Dialogue in the Clinical Encounter
James T. McLaughlin

Vol. 29
Child Therapy in the Great Outdoors:
A Relational View
Sebastiano Santostefano

Vol. 28
Relational Psychoanalysis, V. II:
Innovation and Expansion
Lewis Aron & Adrienne Harris (eds.)

Vol. 27
The Designed Self:
Psychoanalysis and Contemporary Identities
Carlo Strenger

Vol. 26
Impossible Training:
A Relational View of
Psychoanalytic Education
Emanuel Berman

Vol. 25
Gender as Soft Assembly
Adrienne Harris

Vol. 24
Minding Spirituality
Randall Lehman Sorenson

Vol. 23
September 11: Trauma and Human Bonds
Susan W. Coates, Jane L. Rosenthal, &
Daniel S. Schechter (eds.)

Vol. 22
Sexuality, Intimacy, Power
Muriel Dimen

Vol. 21
Looking for Ground: Countertransference and
the Problem of Value in Psychoanalysis
Peter G. M. Carnochan

Vol. 20
Relationality:
From Attachment to Intersubjectivity
Stephen A. Mitchell

RELATIONAL PERSPECTIVES BOOK SERIES
LEWIS ARON & ADRIENNE HARRIS
Series Editors

Vol. 19
Who Is the Dreamer, Who Dreams the Dream?
A Study of Psychic Presences
James S. Grotstein

Vol. 18
Objects of Hope:
Exploring Possibility and Limit in Psychoanalysis
Steven H. Cooper

Vol. 17
The Reproduction of Evil:
A Clinical and Cultural Perspective
Sue Grand

Vol. 16
Psychoanalytic Participation:
Action, Interaction, and Integration
Kenneth A. Frank

Vol. 15
The Collapse of the Self and Its
Therapeutic Restoration
Rochelle G. K. Kainer

Vol. 14
Relational Psychoanalysis:
The Emergence of a Tradition
Stephen A. Mitchell & Lewis Aron (eds.)

Vol. 13
Seduction, Surrender, and Transformation:
Emotional Engagement in the
Analytic Process
Karen Maroda

Vol. 12
Relational Perspectives on the Body
Lewis Aron & Frances Sommer Anderson (eds.)

Vol. 11
Building Bridges: Negotiation of Paradox in
Psychoanalysis
Stuart A. Pizer

Vol. 10
Fairbairn, Then and Now
Neil J. Skolnick & David E. Scharff (eds.)

Vol. 9
Influence and Autonomy in Psychoanalysis
Stephen A. Mitchell

Vol. 8
Unformulated Experience:
From Dissociation to Imagination in
Psychoanalysis
Donnel B. Stern

Vol. 7
Soul on the Couch:
Spirituality, Religion, and Morality in
Contemporary Psychoanalysis
Charles Spezzano & Gerald J. Gargiulo (eds.)

Vol. 6
The Therapist as a Person:
Life Crises, Life Choices, Life Experiences, and
Their Effects on Treatment
Barbara Gerson (ed.)

Vol. 5
Holding and Psychoanalysis:
A Relational Perspective
Joyce A. Slochower

Vol. 4
A Meeting of Minds:
Mutuality in Psychoanalysis
Lewis Aron

Vol. 3
The Analyst in the Inner City:
Race, Class, and Culture Through a
Psychoanalytic Lens
Neil Altman

Vol. 2
Affect in Psychoanalysis:
A Clinical Synthesis
Charles Spezzano

Vol. 1
Conversing With Uncertainty:
Practicing Psychotherapy in a
Hospital Setting
Rita Wiley McCleary

Invasive Objects

Minds Under Siege

Paul Williams

Routledge
Taylor & Francis Group
New York   London

Routledge
Taylor & Francis Group
270 Madison Avenue
New York, NY 10016

Routledge
Taylor & Francis Group
27 Church Road
Hove, East Sussex BN3 2FA

© 2010 by Taylor and Francis Group, LLC
Routledge is an imprint of Taylor & Francis Group, an Informa business

Printed in the United States of America on acid-free paper
10 9 8 7 6 5 4 3 2 1

International Standard Book Number: 978-0-415-99546-7 (Hardback) 978-0-415-99547-4 (Paperback)

For permission to photocopy or use material electronically from this work, please access www.copyright.com (http://www.copyright.com/) or contact the Copyright Clearance Center, Inc. (CCC), 222 Rosewood Drive, Danvers, MA 01923, 978-750-8400. CCC is a not-for-profit organization that provides licenses and registration for a variety of users. For organizations that have been granted a photocopy license by the CCC, a separate system of payment has been arranged.

Trademark Notice: Product or corporate names may be trademarks or registered trademarks, and are used only for identification and explanation without intent to infringe.

Library of Congress Cataloging-in-Publication Data

Williams, Paul, D.P.M.
 Invasive objects : minds under siege / Paul Williams.
  p. cm. -- (Relational perspectives ; v. 43)
 Includes bibliographical references and index.
 ISBN 978-0-415-99546-7 (hardback :acid-free paper) -- ISBN
 978-0-415-99547-4 (pbk. :acid-free paper) -- ISBN 978-0-203-88822-3 (e-book)
 1. Psychoanalysis--Case studies. 2. Psychology, Pathological. I. Title.

RC509.8.W55 2010
616.89'17--dc22   2009030273

Visit the Taylor & Francis Web site at
http://www.taylorandfrancis.com

and the Routledge Web site at
http://www.routledgementalhealth.com

Library
University of Texas
at San Antonio

Contents

Foreword by Glen O. Gabbard   ix
Acknowledgments   xiii

PART I
Clinical chapters   1

1 Incorporation of an invasive object   3

2 Some difficulties in the analysis of a withdrawn patient   21

3 Psychotic developments in a sexually abused borderline
   patient   47

4 Making time, killing time   71

5 The psychoanalytic therapy of "Cluster A" personality
   disorders: Paranoid, schizoid, and schizotypal   85

6 The "beautiful mind" of John Nash: Notes toward a
   psychoanalytic reading   107

PART II
Applied chapters   145

7 Madness in society   147

 8 The worm that flies in the night   159

 9 "The central phobic position": Notes on André Green's
    "new formulation of the free association method" and the
    analysis of borderline states   183

10 Freud-baiting   207

11 Notes on "notes upon a case of obsessional neurosis"   213

12 Unimaginable storms: Introduction and conclusion   227

    Index   247

Foreword

At some point in the course of a psychoanalytic treatment, patients come to recognize that they have been pretending that they are their own person when in fact they are not. Self-deception is inherent to the human condition. We all live in a social reality that is fundamentally deceptive. We pretend that each of us is an independent person who makes autonomous decisions and has the freedom to do so.

This inescapable aspect of human nature may be more apparent in severely disturbed patients, but it is simply an extreme version of what is a universal truth. As Paul Williams teaches us in this superb collection of essays, disturbed patients are controlled by unseen forces that are legacies of their past. They frequently oscillate between states of mind that reflect the presence of these ghosts and their power over the patient. Renunciation, surrender, protest, and conflict are all part of this internal drama.

One of the common clinical phenomena described by Williams in his brilliant exposition on invasive objects is the struggle involving the confusion between the emerging sense of self and the sequelae of uncontained projections associated with the introjection of the projective activity by the object. Hence there is a fragmenting outcome on the core sense of self that feels like annihilation to the patient. Alas, when one's energies are spent managing a foreign body inside, destruction of the mental space generally allocated to symbolizing activity is the result. Such patients may be isolated in a world without symbols, bringing developmental processes necessary for the creation of a person to a grinding halt.

Williams' quest for the symbolic in human experience leads him on a journey in this volume of essays that is far reaching. He examines the symbolic process in poetry and builds bridges between psychoanalysis and anthropology, his original discipline. Using photographs of evocative masks, he educates the reader about the presence of otherness in each of us. Masks, in particular, occupy a liminal space, an anthropological term denoting threshold spaces that allow for differentiating experiences or which permit passes from one context or level to another. Williams manages to transition seamlessly from primitive states encountered in psychoanalysis, to the ideas of Levi-Strauss, and to the primitive mental life studied by anthropological investigators.

After reading this collection, one is impressed with the synthetic capacity of the author. Williams manages to move from the dyad to society at large, while preserving a narrative thread involving his understanding of Bion and the internal object world that was the cornerstone of his training in the Independent tradition of the British Psychoanalytic Society. He takes on the challenge of the experience of time and provides a compelling critique of Foucault in a penetrating discussion of madness in society. It is Williams' particular gift to be able to shift effortlessly between social commentary and clinical wisdom while educating the reader on both subjects with equal adroitness. He even includes a brief rejoinder to the Freud-bashers, lending ammunition to those of us who are fed up with straw man arguments and attacks based on ignorance.

This book reflects the diverse influences on Williams during his evolution as a psychoanalyst. He has made a consistent commitment to the psychoanalytic treatment of our most disturbed patients, and he credits Murray Jackson as a highly influential mentor in this area. Their co-authored essay on the extraordinary case of John Nash, the subject of the film and book *A Beautiful Mind*, is the best thing I have read on the subject. The authors make a convincing case of the importance of attending to the psychological realm of psychosis, rather than reductively approaching it as a matter of malfunctioning neural transmitters. Another well-written essay by Jackson and Williams laments the loss of the search for meaning in psychosis. The authors argue for an avoidance of "fast food psychiatry" and a return to a recognition that psychotic patients warrant a full biopsychosocial understanding and immersion in a treatment experience that takes into account disturbed processes from the points of view of family, systems, intrapsychic fantasy, and internal object relations.

A reader who spends some time with this remarkable collection will wonder how the author has incorporated so much in so little time. Williams, a modest and unassuming sort, is a psychoanalyst who is as much at ease with society as he is with an individual psyche, equally facile with culture and the analytic dyad, and a clinician equally at home with the neurotic and the psychotic analysand. I had the privilege of working with Paul Williams for 6 years when we were joint editors-in-chief of the *International Journal of Psychoanalysis*. In that capacity I became thoroughly familiar with the intellectual honesty and integrity of the man, as well as his wit and charm. All of these qualities come across in the pages of this volume. I can assure you, the reader, that your guide for this journey is reliable, dependable, and will not lead you astray. His thinking will also enrich your understanding of what it is to be human.

Glen O. Gabbard
Brown Foundation Chair of Psychoanalysis
and Professor of Psychiatry
Baylor College of Medicine
Houston, Texas

Acknowledgments

I am grateful to my friend and colleague Glen Gabbard for his foreword to this book. Adrienne Harris has been an inspiring editor whose collaboration I have enjoyed. I would like to thank Murray Jackson who, since 1980, has helped me to think about psychosis, and Thomas Ogden, whose intelligence and generosity have been of inestimable value. Without my patients, few, if any, of the ideas in this book would have emerged.

Paul Williams
Inis Meáin
Oileáin Árainn
Eire
2009

Part I

Clinical chapters

This book is divided broadly into two parts: clinical psychoanalytic chapters, and chapters deriving from the application of psychoanalysis to social and cultural phenomena. This division reflects the influence of two disciplines: social anthropology (my first discipline), and the discipline I have worked in for most of my life—psychoanalysis. In the early 1980s I was fortunate enough to combine PhD fieldwork in social anthropology with my interest in the psychoanalysis of severe disturbance by joining an unusual team working at the Maudsley Hospital in London. These psychiatrists and psychoanalysts, led by Henri Rey, Murray Jackson, and Robert Cawley, together with a group of nurses and psychotherapists, developed an experimental inpatient unit for the treatment of psychosis using psychoanalytic knowledge as the basis of the psychiatric treatment model. The work was effective and was recorded in the book *Unimaginable Storms: A Search for Meaning in Psychosis* (Karnac Books, 1994). A résumé of the work is given at the end of this book, taken from the introduction and conclusion to *Unimaginable Storms*.

Unquestionably, the striking feature for me of this treatment model was the capacity of the team to arrive at an understanding of the unconscious meaning of the individual patient's illness in the context of the person's life history, personality development, internal object world, and current relationships with staff. The therapeutic benefit of this knowledge, conveyed within the analytic relationship and in various other forms by the staff, opened up new opportunities for patients. Time and again I recall being surprised by the extent to which the analysts and patients were able to converse in such depth and with such honesty. It seemed to me that what appeared at the outset to be a potential for serious misunderstanding, conflicts, impasses, and bizarre behavior by the patients, slowly and gradually gave way to a focused, sane discussion between two rational adults about what it felt like to have gone mad. How such a conversation can occur is,

I suggest, an important question for the practice of psychiatry. It is a form of highly personal engagement, based on elucidation of a mutually agreed, truthful understanding of the nature of the individual's internal world, which is capable of contributing to the healing of even the most serious of disturbances. Today, I believe this to be an even more important question for psychiatry, as we have undergone a cultural change in attitudes towards mental illness during recent years. This trend has led us away from the enduring therapeutic benefit of self-knowledge and a capacity to engage deeply in human relationships, and towards wholesale reliance on psychopharmacology and short-term treatments. These contemporary methods, while helpful for some individuals, perhaps most in the area of the containment of symptoms, too often have the side-effect of colluding with the core psychological premise of much psychotic thinking as a result of the scant attention paid to the need for human relatedness, without which none of us feels human and truly alive. This premise is: *Human relationships have proved to be a source of disaster and unimaginable suffering. I have fallen out of their orbit and need to be reconnected to them if life is ever to have meaning again. I fear that this is impossible as I have become so removed from people.*

It is not difficult to discern from such a state of mind that the amount of work required for the patient to reestablish trust in other people, and thereby in oneself, is considerable. It is, in fact, a Herculean undertaking for patient and analyst, and may take years to accomplish, not weeks or months. Such commitment to the recovery of psychotic individuals, and the patience required on both sides, is no longer fashionable. This does not mean that patients accept this situation. A regular occurrence, at least in my consulting room, is a situation in which a chronically ill individual conveys awareness of his or her plight and indicates that they are willing to try to do whatever is necessary to alleviate their despair. In their honesty and urgency, they underscore Freud's observation that their troubles lie on the surface, and today we know that they are amenable to intervention, despite their crippling complexity. Their misfortunate is that fewer and fewer psychoanalysts are being trained to work analytically with them, so the prospect of receiving the understanding and help they need to recover their humanity is reduced.

In the following pages, I discuss some ideas and ways of working that I have learned during the complex process of trying to understand individuals who are suffering crippling psychotic anxieties. Most of this work has been undertaken in private analytic practice, but a proportion of it has taken place in the British National Health Service and as a clinical consultant to two institutions providing residential psychoanalytic treatment: Boyer House in San Rafael, California (now closed), and Arbours Crisis Centre in London.

Chapter 1

Incorporation of an invasive object*

I shall try to sketch out a way in which symbolic functioning appears to be undermined in certain cases of severe disturbance. The failure I shall discuss reflects a developmental crisis, features of which became apparent to me during the analyses of three patients, two of whom I shall discuss here. Each of the patients, though very different in important respects and brought up in dissimilar circumstances, suffered serious narcissistic disturbances. A characteristic the patients shared was the experience of having incorporated an object with random, invasive tendencies, which at times could lead them to the brink of, or into, psychosis. By "incorporation of an invasive object," I wish to convey a primitive, violent introjection of aspects of an object that creates the experience of inundation by the object that can give rise to serious disturbance in the nascent personality. This form of pathological "proto-identification" takes place in early infancy and is consequent upon precocious interaction between infant and object, including, critically, failure of containment and maternal alpha-function (Bion, 1970).

Under normal circumstances, incorporation is the earliest mode of relating in which the infant feels himself to be at one with the other and is unaware of separation between the two personalities (Fenichel, 1945; Searles, 1951; Sterba, 1957). This experience decreases if development proceeds relatively unimpeded. If development is impeded, the experience can persist, leading to an equation between relatedness and engulfment, in which one personality is felt to be devouring the other (Searles, 1951, p. 39). The impulse to unite incorporatively with the other as a defense against separation anxiety has been widely discussed.[†] All note how physical experiences are a characteristic of processes of incorporation, in contrast to the fantasy dimension of introjection into the ego, which assumed importance in Klein's (1935)

---

* This chapter originally appeared as a paper in *International Journal of Psychoanalysis*, 85(6), 2004, 1333–1348. Reprinted with permission.
† For example, Freud (1900, 1933), Klein (1935), Heimann (1942), Fenichel (1945), Searles (1951), Federn (1952), Greenacre (1958), Laplanche and Pontalis (1972), Segal (1981), and Rey (1994), among others.

thinking and which she discusses in the context of incorporative activity and the genesis of psychosis.

The patients I shall describe manifested incorporative self-states in the form of both bodily and psychological symptoms. I shall suggest that they underwent traumatic disruption to the psyche-soma at a time when their sense of self was barely formed and the psyche-soma had yet to undergo differentiation. A primitive introject appears to have been installed in their minds and their experience of their bodies that was held by them to belong to their own self-representational system. Contradictorily, at the same time, this introjected presence was experienced as a concrete presence of a disturbing "foreign body" inside them.

The experience of something that is not a part of the self, yet is confused with the self, can create not only psychic conflict, but also incompatible or "heterogeneous" states of mind (Quinodoz, 2001). "Heterogeneity" is denoted as the product of a "heterogeneous constitution of the ego" (Green, 1993). This description reflects Bion's (1967) observation that "there is a psychotic personality concealed by neurosis as the psychotic personality is screened by psychosis in the psychotic, that has to be laid bare and dealt with" (p. 63).

Heterogeneous patients present for help because they suffer from their heterogeneity, unlike the majority (Quinodoz, 2001). This heterogeneous quality is implicated in the vulnerability and intrapsychic confusion of the patients I shall describe and seems to have affected not only the way in which these patients related, but also how their thinking developed.

CLINICAL EXAMPLE I: JAMES

James, 27, entered analysis after a series of failed relationships culminating in depressive attacks with suicidal ideation. He possessed an unusually high IQ and was capable of abstract levels of thought beyond his years, and of grasping the nub of ideas and arguments. There was a paranoid tinge to many of his observations and his attention to others' motivation seemed compulsive. James was quintessentially a self-made man. He had failed at school but as an adult had become successful in business. His father, an addict, died in his 40s of a drug overdose. James was a replacement child; a previous son had died, apparently unmourned, 10 months before James's birth, his mother having been advised by her doctor to get pregnant again straight away. James's mother seems to have been an unstable woman consumed by hatred and grievances. He said his parents fought continuously during the marriage over affairs each accused the other of having. He recalled as a child sitting in horror in his pajamas on the stairs while his parents brawled. He left home at 16 and remained unreconciled to them.

He saw his mother again once when she was unconscious on her deathbed in hospital.

I was struck from the outset by the speed with which James seemed to reach the meaning of his fantasies and dreams. He would get there before me, with impressive intuitions, yet without making me feel excluded. He strove to be a "model" analysand. It became apparent that he needed to control the analysis, subtly and diplomatically, and that he suffered intense anxieties when he did not feel in control. He revealed that his controls were, in fantasy, controls over my thoughts. Why he needed to control my thoughts was not clear to him or me. His dream life provided evidence of a serious disturbance of the self. He dreamed repeatedly that he had murdered someone. The body, a male, lay buried under a road; it was a secret, but the police were piecing together clues and were on his trail. He developed insomnia to avoid the nightmares. James's compliant, controlling behavior decreased as he became more depressed and nihilistic during the second year of analysis. In one session he lay contemplating suicide and said, with piercing dejection, "I came into analysis for consolation. I knew nothing could ever come of my life."

I was affected by his comment, which was said with no trace of defensiveness, and my response—an intense sadness—persisted after the session. I realized that I had been struck by, to paraphrase Marion Milner, a "thought too big for its concept."* I wondered whether analysis-as-consolation masked, for James, the site of an experience of annihilation anxiety. This phenomenon, which has been referred to as "a memorial space for psychic death" (Grand, 2000), denotes unspeakable, traumatic events that are felt to always be present, yet must remain absent. Metabolization through language is the means we possess of approaching such catastrophe, yet this is disbarred, as language is experienced as unable to approximate the scale of the events involved.

I shall pass to a period in the third year during which James decided he wanted to quit analysis and his suicidal feelings took a psychotic turn. He had become disillusioned and was prone to long, angry silences. "Is this all there is?" he would complain bitterly, following stretches of withdrawal. He could be abusive, accusing me of keeping him in analysis to maintain the vain illusion that I could help him. If he felt I might be close to understanding what he was feeling, he would lash out contemptuously—for example, "This [analysis] is hypocrisy. It deceives, it lies, it's wanking. It's a middle-class fix. You haven't got the first idea about me or what people like me go through." He told me he felt burned out, disgusted by himself, and hopeless. The nightmare of having killed someone preoccupied him, including during the day, making it increasingly difficult for him to function in his work. As his condition worsened, I became anxious for his safety, as he was

---

* The title of an abstract picture painted by Marion Milner.

immersed in what appeared to be a developing transference psychosis. This situation continued for some weeks. I talked with him about his profound disillusion with me and the unmanageable feelings of despair and rage this engendered.

An event occurred in which James communicated his despair in a way that I felt revealed his having incorporated an object characterized specifically by invasiveness. James had spent most of this particular Wednesday session in tormented distraction at his inability to control his feelings of disdain towards his female partner, who he was afraid would leave him. He described unpleasant scenes between them that left him confused and suicidal. The idea that there might be no change possible appalled him. He twisted and turned on the couch, as though in bodily pain. I told him how afraid I thought he was of becoming more and more like his parents, at home and here with me, and how feelings of growing fear, resentment, and hatred of his partner and me pushed him into a terrible sense of failure. Feeling trapped in hate and fear, like his parents, destroyed his power and hope, turning him into a needy, hopeless child who he hated. The only way out he could imagine, in the absence of anyone to help him, was to kill himself, but even this didn't work as he still didn't have anyone who understood what he was going through. James's writhing stopped and his body relaxed. He appeared to be relieved at having his confusion and fear acknowledged. However, he became more restless and what appeared to be a more thoughtful silence turned out to be not the case at all. He slowly and purposefully got off the couch, stared at me—or rather through me—and shouted with unbridled hatred, "Keep your platitudes to yourself, you stupid fucking moron."

This outburst of violent, narcissistic rage seemed also to embody a psychotic effort to try to rid himself of an alien presence or state of mind, of which I appeared to have been the incarnation. He fell silent, walked unsteadily round the room, became distracted, and eventually sat on the edge of the couch, trembling. I felt assaulted by the attack—fear and anger welled up inside me. I could not think of anything appropriate to say, only a wish to protect myself. I felt stripped of a capacity to contain the situation. James sat for some time holding his head in his hands. I recall the session ended with me asking him whether he felt able to manage getting home. The next day James was in a distressed, confused state.

> I don't understand. I can't remember it clearly … it is like a fog … something just came over me. I don't know how to explain it … I'm sorry. I feel a bit like it now, kind of stunned. My head feels full … there is so much going on that I can't think and my legs feel like lead … like my body wants to collapse. I don't quite know where I am in this. I don't know why I should scream at you like that …

He continued in this bewildered, anxious way that seemed to combine guilt about what he felt he had done to me and confused feelings of dread and relief at having lost control of himself. I said to him that, although he felt a need to apologize, what was striking to me was that he had allowed me to see some of his deepest feelings, including those about me, without camouflage, something that I doubted he had done often, if ever, in his life. He said,

> I don't think I had any choice; it doesn't feel like I did ... it wasn't taking a risk. Something exploded. It was anger but there's something not right about that ... it's not the whole feeling. Something in me could have killed you. I wasn't thinking this when it happened but it makes me think that something in me wanted to smash and smash you and shut you up so I didn't have to listen any more, ever again. As I say this it reminds me of my mother and how I couldn't stand the shouting but I couldn't do anything about it. Maybe I was fighting her ... maybe being her—or being like her somehow—but in another way I was outside it, watching it going on ... or rather, it was happening to me.

He talked about a "blizzard" having descended on him, pains in his head and a heavy sensation in his body. I was led to think that he had been in a psychotic transference. During the ensuing weeks, James experienced much confusion and worsening bouts of withdrawal.

Further attacks occurred, often when I least expected them. They seemed to be precipitated by contact with James's infantile self that he despised—that is, when he felt a childlike need for me or when I said something that made him feel understood, it roused an involuntary, psychotic sadism against both me and him. At times, his withdrawals took on what I thought was a narcissistic, even psychopathic quality. In these moments it was as though I ceased to exist for him—I had been obliterated from his internal world. Although each of James's attacks had seemed to free something in him initially, I became aware that his rages could be accompanied by a malignant, anti-life attitude that destroyed opportunities for his infantile needs to be met. What had been a form of letting go could, at times, resemble a sadistic, narcissistic defense. James's responses to his attacks varied from obliviousness to persecutory anxiety to acute paranoia. Yet, after one outburst he commented, "I feel bad about what just happened. I hate you and you make me furious with the things you say, but I think just now it was out of proportion—my reaction, that is." I queried his feelings and he said, "I don't know how real my hatred of you is sometimes. It wells up ... it is true. But when it happens it feels like an automatic thing ... a gut reaction ... sometimes it doesn't matter what you're saying; it erupts and I have to silence you. You're somebody I have to keep out."

I felt that James was experiencing anxiety at feelings of frustration and rage towards me, but was also confused by a psychotic identification with an invasive object that was responsible for precipitating his attacks in order to try to omnipotently annihilate our relationship, in order to provide delusional protection against dependence on me. Non-psychotic and psychotic aspects of his personality seemed to vie for expression in this way. James's behavior outside the session reflected this confusion, as seen in this example: At home one Sunday he heard a dog squealing in the street. He told me he had "no choice but to dash out to help it." He found a large dog belonging to some drunken youths pinning down a smaller dog by the throat. He dived between the dogs without thought to his own safety, prying open the jaws of the larger dog until the smaller one was freed and ran off. The youths turned on James but James's unassailable resolve caused them to back off, without violence. In his session, he could not account for his impulsive behavior, was not proud of it, and yet he felt oddly better. He showed little indication of excessive guilt or confusion. He simply had to separate the dogs, he said, and he could see that many people would think that what he did was dangerous and crazy. He wanted to know why he had been compelled to act. Later in the session, he remarked, "The thing with the dogs makes something clearer to me. It sounds obvious but it isn't. It does sound mad, but I think I thought that the fight that was going on was my fault, but it wasn't. Everything I did when I was a kid was wrong."

Although I did not say it to him, I had been struck by the desperate quality of his compulsive engagement in this conflict, as though only he could rescue the dog. I wondered about his omnipotence, about a child whose infant self was threatened with annihilation by savage attacks and about his witnessing repeatedly hate-filled fights between his parents.

James's insight permitted work on feelings of "being intrinsically wrong," as he put it, in the eyes of his mother. He conceived of this as:

> Nothing I did was right. It wasn't only about making mistakes or doing things that annoyed her. I got everything wrong, as a matter of principle ... when I was small I thought I could please her and I tried to but by the time I went to school I think I felt defeated. Nothing worked ... she couldn't bear to look at me ... not disapproval exactly, although there was a lot of that ... more that I was a terrible burden she'd had forced on her and couldn't stand. There were times when she could suddenly be nice but this lasted only for a few moments before she changed. I stayed out of her way, but I would forget and got screamed at. It took years for me to realize that the whole thing was impossible ... she was on a different planet. I know that by the time I was 7 or 8, or earlier, I had thoughts that I'd be better off dead. I would feel relieved when I went to bed that I'd got through another day and pray that I wouldn't wake up. For years I went to bed early to blot things out.

A: You feel you died as a child.

P: I do [*cries*] … everything went wrong and I have been stuck with it all my life. I think my childhood was ruined … now I am like her and I ruin it myself.

A: You feel you died and yet somehow you managed to go on; not only go on but do well eventually.

P: I can't explain it. The only thing that comes to mind is that I realized a few years ago talking to my grandmother that my mother must have been delighted that I was born healthy and lived. She must have been desperate not to lose another child. My grandmother said I was doted on—given special orange juice and supplements to build me up. But she told me that the marriage was in trouble and my mother started having affairs when I was born. I do recall different men came to the house from as far back as I can remember. I don't know … maybe I was made to feel special in some way and that gave me a kind of good start. What I've always felt is that my life wasn't my life. I felt I was somebody because of what I did for others.

The analysis focused, in the transference, on his sense of having died as a child and how his attacks and withdrawals defended him from the painful experience that his attempts to live felt unviable and a lie, so damaged and confused was his sense of his own self. Gradually, he became more able to work at differentiating feelings of love and hate on the one hand, and a welling up of a psychotic rage against me on the other, which represented an incorporation of a narcissistic, invasive object. These eruptions were preceded by a visceral sensation, blood coursing through his veins or tinnitus-like ringing in his ears; then came the outburst that bore a resemblance to accounts of his mother's aggression. As these more extreme defenses came under more control (they ceased in the seventh year of the analysis) he told me he had always had a "wild side" to him of which he was ashamed. He felt the same hatred of people his mother had shown, with no justification. He did not evade responsibility for this, but was concerned that it did not represent the complexity of his feelings, even at his most angry. He described it as a "default extremism" or a "scorched-earth policy." James had indicated how frightened he had been of his parents, but the scale of his intimidation at his mother's mood changes (which lay behind his identification with them) only now became apparent. Her attacks had left him profoundly disoriented as a child. He described how his mother's violence was a part of his life from as early as he could remember and how he had been quite convinced that he had provoked it. He began to engage in similar attacks from the age of about 7, he thought, initially on his mother's dog that he had tormented. The need to attack others "when they got close" became something he was unable to prevent.

After much work on the defacement of his personality and his primitive identification with invasiveness, his attacks on me receded and he acquired greater tolerance for his emotions and their limitations. He also began a more articulated grieving process that was paralleled by a reluctance to comply with others' demands. His relationship with his female partner improved and they began a family. The love between him and his baby daughter, though sometimes painful, afforded him awareness of his value to another person, something he had not previously experienced. This helped to offset his sense of loss at what he had missed in his life because of his behavior. In the eighth year of his analysis he said, "I feel I have to pay attention every day to that child I was. It's like visiting someone in hospital or a grave. If I don't think of him or hold his hand, I can feel lost. I will never let him go again."

I felt that James had buried his childhood identity and evolved an impenetrable, seamless second skin that afforded him a false sense of integration (cf. Winnicott, 1960; Symington, 1985). Within this illusory maturity lay an experience of being unrecognized for himself and uncontained in his feelings. When James's true, alive self stirred, he was susceptible to fears of abandonment and disintegration, triggering, among other things, a defensive, imitative introject of an object that could not bear loss (and, hence, life) and which reacted invasively, generating narcissistic rage and masochistic compliance in an attempt to preserve an illusory sense of coherent selfhood.

CLINICAL EXAMPLE 2: MS. B

Ms. B, 49, was diagnosed in her 30s with a paranoid psychosis, although I came to think that she suffered from a borderline personality disorder.* She came into analysis 13 years ago (cf. Williams, 1998). The middle child of a working-class family, Ms. B complained she had had no relationship with her mother who, from birth, passed her on to her father because her mother favored the first child, a boy (her other sibling is also male). Her rage at her mother's rejection of her was unremitting. "She never showed any sign of wanting me—never" was her refrain. The father appears to have been paranoid and periodically incapacitated by his difficulties. Ms. B said that at around 2 or 3 years of age she had retreated into a fantasy world, becoming friendly with creatures from outer space who promised to take her away. She also came to believe that she was a famous actress. She maintained that she and her father had had an incestuous relationship up to her 14th year. She told me she had acquired a manager, a pimp-like figure called the "Director," who controlled many of her actions, feelings, and

---

* This case is revisited and expanded upon in Chapter 3.

thoughts. "He" was to emerge in the analysis as a pseudo-hallucination. After 4 months of analysis, Ms. B reported the following dream: "I am being fed. A hand slaps me across the face hard. Then I am on a terrorist exercise, rolling down a hill clutching a male officer. We fall off a cliff or shelf."

I said that she was letting me know of a catastrophe, a loss in her life that she felt could never be made up, and that she had turned to men and sex to try to compensate. I rapidly became an object of idealization, while her violent, perverse pathology was acted out, mainly sexually. By the second year Ms. B had begun to cut herself; she took a non-fatal overdose and jumped from a moving train, injuring herself. A psychosis asserted itself. This is a dream from that time:

> A minibus crashes through the front of a food store. There is a huge explosion. My older brother helpfully leads people away. There are many dead pregnant women. I touch the stomach of one but there is no life. Tins of food are embedded in people's faces. They are missing arms and legs. The manager says, "We carry on, we stay open." I try to stop him I but can't.

She was unable to consider the themes of murder or dead mothers and babies in this or other dreams. Her behavior became more disturbed and she was hospitalized following attempts to swallow a lethal dose of lithium medication. After a 2-year period in which there was a good deal of extreme disturbance (which I do not have space to describe here), the direction of the analysis began to shift towards a more verbalized, transference-oriented hatred of her dependence on me. The patient moved from a predominantly paranoid position and acting out to one of sadistic, abusive attacks. From having complained of abuse, she became an abuser, of me and the analysis. For the purposes of this paper, I want to illustrate how the patient seems to have incorporated an invasive object that combines characteristics of the patient's projective activity with features of both parents.

In a Monday session during the second year of her analysis, Ms. B complained at length that she was no good because girls don't get love. Love from mothers is "lesbian," she said, and this, she felt, was the most awful thing in the world. The way to get love was to be a boy like her older brother, or like her father. She was a boy, really, she suggested, so she could do anything boys could. She recounted how when she masturbated she fantasized that she was a man and that women queued up to have sex with her. She sometimes strapped a dildo to her waist when she went out to make her feel like a man. She talked further about childhood fantasies of being a powerful boy and how she had changed her sex (although the patient was talking about her fantasies, I was unsure whether she actually believed she was male as she spoke):

A: I can see what you mean about the advantages you felt boys had, but I'm wondering about and remembering that you were born a girl—where is she? What has happened to the longing for love you wanted from your mother that you have told me about? You often tell me how lonely you feel and how much you want to talk to me, especially during weekends. That person seems to me like a little girl who feels her needs are being ignored.

P: [*becoming agitated and shouting*]: Keep out! Lock the doors ... the walls are moving. Lock the doors, shut up, lock them! Keep them out!

A: Something I have said has alarmed you. Can you tell me what's happening?

P: It's the Director ... he's telling me somebody is coming in. They're coming in and they're going to get me ... they're going to kill me!

This intrusion of the psychotic "Director" figure was to happen frequently and exerted enormous influence over the patient. The technical problems associated with interpreting these paradoxical "influencing machines," which purportedly protect but in practice subvert and deny the patient good experiences of objects, are obviously considerable. What I wish to stress here is that these paranoid outbursts revealed, in my view, not only Ms. B's deep-seated fears of the consequences of her own projected destructiveness and invasiveness, but also evidence of miscarriage of early introjective processes. The invasive narrative of Ms. B's "Director" (which always involved accusations of people getting in, breaking in, stealing, and attacking, when not manically advocating sex) displayed elements of concordance with the patient's accounts of her father's powerful paranoid anxieties and of the rejections and indifference she attributed to her mother, which she countered by intensifying her own projective activity. Observations by her about her father and mother over several years of analysis, often inadvertent and spontaneous, were consistent in these respects and were paralleled by ways in which she herself could respond compulsively when in the grip of a psychotic transference characterized by invasive fantasies that defended her against feelings of fragmentation. The "Director" seemed to afford her an illusory sense of agency and ego-coherence when in crisis. "His" underlying objective was, as I have suggested, to influence the patient's ego to reject human contact and pursue a course of withdrawal, reflecting her primary narcissistic crisis, felt (delusionally) to be more reliable.

INVASIVE EXPERIENCES AND THE SELF

To avoid misunderstanding, I want to underscore that I do not propose in this chapter a concordance between this patient's and her father's or mother's personalities, or a linear causality between the external object's influence and the patient's fantasy life. There appeared to be no direct equivalence between her father's projective activity and her identification with invasiveness—or for that matter between the patient's narcissism and the mother's own psychopathology. The same applies to James and to any patient with this kind of invasive disorder, I believe. The intrapsychic situation is likely to be complex, involving aspects of the patient's infantile sense of self becoming confused with the *sequelae* of uncontained projections and with the introjection of projective activity of the object. This is commonplace in many severely disturbed individuals. Identification with the aggressor may be evident, but the impact of the processes I am describing has a primitive, fragmentating outcome linked, I suggest, to threats of annihilation of the core sense of self. Inadequately contained and violently projected part-objects are forcibly installed in the psyche of the infant, generating psychophysical pain, confusion, and chronic anxiety. The process involved comprises massive splitting and projection by the object into the infant, which has the effect not only of repudiating the infant's own projections, but also of overwhelming the psychic reality of the infant by extreme external stimulation. Gaddini (1992) offers an account of how such a crisis could evolve. He reports on how normal imitation or mimicry—an oral introjective activity that takes place prior to identification—may miscarry under precocious conditions of oral frustration, which cause disturbance to the psycho-oral area and therefore introjective mechanisms. Imitative introjections, instead of acting as precursors to normal introjections, may substitute for true introjections and cause internalization processes to fail. Imitation may be used defensively to avoid subsequent introjective conflicts. The child's fragmented personality develops on the basis of these failed identification processes, imitation being substituted for object relating. Weiss (1960) distinguished imitation from identification, stressing that "no simple imitation" takes place in the infant's mind. There is, he suggests, a form of "reproduction" or "autoplastic duplication" (following Ferenczi) in which the organism acquires and modifies its shape and functional parts. A defensive use of autoplastic duplication probably gives rise to the seeming concordance between primitive elements of the patient's disturbed personality and invasive projections. Failure of containment and breach of the "contact barrier" (Bion, 1962), having rendered the individual vulnerable to excessive permeability, sets the condition for impairment of the development of the self through mimetic introjection. Such disturbed early attachment processes can create, as in my patients, a backcloth for an amalgam of projections and introjected elements, expressed both corporeally and mentally. There is no space here to discuss the relationships between fantasy, projection, and introjection in these states, especially the influence of unconscious sexual fantasies. However, the organizing roles of unconscious fantasy and memory, the impact of deferred action (*après coup*), and the reelaboration of psychic reality that follows, would need to be taken into account to properly clarify the complex amalgam of projected and introjected elements. The intricacy of these early object-relations experiences—what might be termed metaphorically as encounters with "fractal objects"*—is identifiable through attention to a range of transference communications, through which it becomes possible to identify, *a posteriori*, introjective patterns that underlie the failures in identification. Such investigation is analogous to identifying the "sensitivity to initial conditions" in deterministic chaos theory, through which one or more variables can come to have an enduring, disproportionately perturbing effect on a complex system.†

If we think of the self as a developmental achievement deriving from the infant's need to mentally represent internal states, using the mind of another, then recognition of the intentionality of the caregiver's mind permits the infant to establish an internal representation of himself as a truly separate, intentional being. The quality of the caregiver's image of the infant as an intentional being is critical for the formation of this representation. If caregiving fails to contain and reflect the infant's experiences and anxieties, a misrepresentation of the infant will be internalized corresponding to the partial or distorted representational capacity of the other infiltrating the fantasy life of the infant. The patients I have described experienced, during this early developmental phase, a pronounced failure to have their projections contained and metabolized, leading to an experience of emotional violence. Assailed by invasive projective activity, the trauma was an amalgam of inchoate external and internal experiences, the residuum or precipitate of which corresponded to the "foreign body" experience lodged in the unconscious and in the body, and which lacks mental representational status. Attempts to repel invasiveness through the counteruse of projective identification would be likely to heighten the intensity of the pathological interaction, as it is the identification with invasiveness (associated with projections by infant and object) that is employed defensively.

The infant's body is implicated in the trauma in that it carries the status of a primary object to which the infant relates and which can become installed as an internal object. Laufer (2002) has discussed how uncontained bodily states due to poor handling of the infant by the caregiver can create adverse developmental conditions. I think that such deprived conditions

---

* A fractal object is a structure that repeats itself infinitely and remains identical whatever its scale.

† I am grateful to Jean-Michel Quinodoz for the observation that "sensitivity to initial conditions" refers to one variable among many being responsible for modifying an entire course of events. It is possible to predict only the short-term evolution of such a system; however, it is also possible, *a posteriori*, to go back to initial events and to determine one or more factors that may have triggered the perturbation of the system. Quinodoz (1997) has discussed this analogical model in the context of psychic change.

pertain to incidences of invasiveness. Indeed, extremely deprived infants may "invite" invasion or at least incorporate avidly powerful projections as a consequence of extreme need.

Those who are compelled to expel unbearable mental states force the mind of the other to deal with what the invasive object's mind cannot. I became aware that, in my patients, once an offending mental state has been expelled, an invasive object ceases to have use for the subject as an object and reverts to a position of narcissism. Perhaps it is more accurate to say that the invasive object returns to a narcissistic state of unconscious fusion with an idealized internal part-object. Developmentally, managing a foreign body inside destroys mental space allocated to symbolizing activity by the ego. Identification with characteristics of invasiveness disrupts processes of integration of experiences necessary for secondary-process thinking. The individual who has incorporated an invasive object is likely to feel unstable, depleted of personal meaning, and occupied or haunted by unidentifiable bodily perceptions. Complaints of feeling controlled, alienated, possessed, ill, or diseased may accompany these self-states. During analysis, the transference neurosis can come to resemble a psychosis, with the patient able to think only intermittently and prone to interaction that reflects the dynamics of invasion. The patient may employ stereotypical ideas and language displaying power without conviction, and if pressed may become disorganized. Identity diffusion can occur and there may be acting out. Such patients are unsure of who they are, and under severe stress communicate by proxy through their bodies.

INTRUSION AND INVASION

Although by definition invasive objects intrude, I have found it useful in my clinical work to distinguish between intrusive and invasive objects. Intrusive objects, at least in my experience, tend to be motivated by a need to occupy or become a feature of the subject for reasons that can include parasitism and sadism. Invasive objects seek to expel unbearable, infantile conflicts using, for the most part, excessive projective mechanisms. Expulsions are compulsive and violent and they do not appear to strive to colonize or become a feature of the subject in the same way, as their aim is to mold a repository for evacuation prior to retreat to a pathological narcissistic position. The identity of the recipient of the projected state is unimportant: securing a mind into which the state can be indiscriminately jammed is the goal. I think of invasive projections as akin to "psychosomatic missiles" that are expelled or "fired" into the other. The dream of Ms. B, in which tins of food are embedded in faces and unborn fetuses are killed, is a vivid image that reflects oral invasiveness. Ms. B's failure to internalize benign representations of her mother induced a developmental crisis of critical proportions at the oral stage, exposing her to uncontrolled envy and murderous feelings towards her mother and brother. Perhaps her gender confusion even contained a wish to *be* her brother as a way, in fantasy, of attempting to resolve her identification problems. She seems to have violently rejected her mother, incorporated aspects of her mother's rejecting attitude, and become consumed by fantasies of invasion also echoing themes in her account of her father's paranoid personality. I thought that a claustro-agoraphobic dilemma in relation to her mother (Rey, 1994) had forced her to turn to her father and assume a phallically omnipotent stance in relation to her objects. Her abnormal superego (O'Shaughnessy, 1999) usurped central ego functions, directing her thinking predominantly around the theme of invasiveness via the psychotic figure of the "Director." The fluidity and confusion of identificatory processes in Ms. B's early life seem to have rendered her vulnerable to feeling inundated and overwhelmed, and subsequently she experienced herself as having little or no core personality of her own. Fonagy and Target (1998b) have discussed how violence in certain patients may be employed in an attempt to establish a sense of who they are, and I think the advent of Ms. B's "Director" probably reflects such a process. Interestingly, after 12 years of treatment, Ms. B reported that she was no longer sure whether sexual intercourse had occurred between her and her father. How true this statement is I do not know, but it made me wonder to what extent it is possible that incorporation of aggressive, sexualized part-objects of the type I have described readily lead a disturbed infant's mind to fantasize, via the somatic dimension of the incorporative process and confusion between inner and outer reality, that sexual contact has taken place.

James, in contrast to Ms. B, incorporated the impact of a refusal to acknowledge his very personality. This derived from what appears to have been projections by a narcissistically disordered mother unable to mourn the death of her first child and who became, in Andre Green's words, "centrally phobic" to the experience of loss (Williams, 2000). James's feelings of authenticity were destroyed and he consigned himself to living out a counterfeit, shame-filled life in identification with this denial of his own existence and his brother's death. It is possible that there are different forms of incorporation of invasive objects. For example, the impact of a projectively invasive mother as experienced by bulimic patients may point to how projected "missiles" can later be reprojected physically as well as mentally (Williams, 1997). Invasion fantasies also feature in the psychodynamics of anorexia (Lawrence, 2002). In certain psychoses, auditory or command hallucinations can reflect incorporated aspects of objects, drawing on unsymbolized sexual and aggressive impulses (cf. Jackson & Williams, 1994). Perhaps the dynamics of rape and the implications for the types of personalities involved merit study from the perspective of experiences of invasion by an object. It seems that invasive experiences can occur under a variety of circumstances and are linked to faulty or over-fluid identificatory processes. What they have in common is forcible introjection and embodiment of pathological internal part-objects that disrupt ego functioning and the evolution of a sense of self. The confusion with which the subject lives reflects multiple axes of relatedness (projective and introjective) to these part-objects—a subject about which we still know relatively little.

The literature on severe early object-relations conflicts touches on issues raised in this chapter. Sterba (1957) and Anna Freud (1951) studied the impact of oral invasion that leads to overwhelming identification with a rejecting object. Heimann (1942) described miscarriages of sublimation linked to experiences of intrusiveness. Rosenfeld (1975) depicted the clinical consequences of introjected part-objects, particularly their "mafia-like" qualities that purport to protect the ego through intimidation while countermanding opportunities for recovery and development. Sohn (1985) identified in sudden, unprovoked assaults, a form of primitive identification with a violent, invasive, uncontaining object he terms the "identificate." Gaddini (1992), Winnicott (1960), and others have made the observation that the primitive self of the infant that reverts to a pathological use of mimesis can experience attempts at integration as a threat to the self if a fragmented history of identification has come to be relied upon defensively, a defense that perpetuates developmental arrest. Bion (1962, 1963, 1977), above all, identified the consequences of failure to contain an infant's projections and how this gives rise to states of terrifying persecution. There is consensus, irrespective of theoretical persuasion, that without the establishment of a "third" position based on a capacity to incorporate the "mother-as-environment" (Winnicott, 1967) leading to the acquisition of "reflective function" (Fonagy & Target, 1998a), "binocularity" (Bion, 1967), or "intersubjectivity" (Trevarthen, 1993), ego capacity is consigned to managing psychic trauma. The examples I give indicate that no "third" position had been established. If characterological disturbances within the parents are projected into the offspring throughout development, leaving no stage of childhood untouched, a third position is probably unattainable. Object-relations disturbances are life-long, starting in infancy and impacting on each unfolding developmental stage (Martindale, 2004, personal communication).

The appearance of invasive objects in treatment is often seen as unpredictable and based on disorganized patterns of attachment (cf. Fonagy, 2000). I think that these invasive assaults, on examination, are often more predictable than they appear, being patterned according to the ego's phobic responses to particular constellations of primitive affect (Green, 2000) that result in the body-ego consequences described. Developments in neuroscience confirm that assaults on the psyche-soma of infants during the first year of life can indicate loss of cortical function in the fronto-temporal areas (Perry, 1997). It seems clear that the long-term neurological and psychological impact of invasive experiences may be significant in understanding serious disturbance in infant development.

To conclude, I suggest that incorporated aspects of an invasive object become confused with the nascent infant's self and are subject to idealization. In psychoanalysis, the prospect of relinquishment of a mimetically constructed, incorporative relationship for one with an ambivalently cathected, separate object can be experienced as catastrophe, as this is equated with loss of the ongoing sense of self. It may be necessary for the patient to endure a period of psychotic confusion as the process of unincorporation and disidentification takes place. Without this, the invasive object remains active in the unconscious. The patient may attack the therapeutic process in order to prevent the experience of catastrophic change (Bion, 1965). This defensive activity is, in my view, a response to the confusion that derives from the "foreign body" inside, which must be gotten rid of if disruption to psychic functioning is to be halted and personality development restored, but which the patient feels cannot be forsaken as it is experienced as a part of the self.

REFERENCES

Bion, W. R. (1962). The psycho-analytic study of thinking, II: A theory of thinking. *International Journal of Psychoanalysis, 43*, 306–310.

Bion, W. R. (1963). *Elements of psycho-analysis*. London: William Heinemann.

Bion, W. R. (1965/1984). *Transformations*. London: Karnac Books.

Bion, W. R. (1967). *Second thoughts: Selected papers on psycho-analysis*. London: Karnac Books.

Bion, W. R. (1970). *Attention and interpretation*. London: Tavistock.

Bion, W. R. (1977). *Seven servants*. New York: Jason Aronson.

Federn, P. (1952). *Ego psychology and the psychoses*. London: Imago.

Fenichel, O. (1945). *The psychoanalytic theory of neurosis*. London: Routledge & Kegan Paul.

Fonagy, P. (2000). Attachment and borderline personality disorder. *Journal of the American Psychoanalytic Association, 48*, 1129–1146.

Fonagy, P., & Target, M. (1998a). Mentalization and the changing aims of child psychoanalysis. *Psychoanalytic Dialogues, 8*, 87–114.

Fonagy, P., & Target, M. (1998b). Towards understanding violence: The use of the body and the role of the father. In R. Perelberg (Ed.), *Psychoanalytic understanding of violence and suicide* (pp. 44–62). London: Routledge.

Freud, A. (1951). *Negativism and emotional surrender*. Paper presented at International Congress, Amsterdam.

Freud, S. (1900). The interpretation of dreams. In J. Strachey (Ed. & Trans.), *The standard edition of the complete psychological works of Sigmund Freud* (Vol. 4–5). London: Hogarth Press.

Freud, S. (1933). New introductory lectures on psycho-analysis. In J. Strachey (Ed. & Trans.), *The standard edition of the complete psychological works of Sigmund Freud* (Vol. 22). London: Hogarth Press.

Gaddini, E. (1992). *A psychoanalytic theory of infantile experience*. London: Routledge.

Grand, S. (2000). *The reproduction of evil: A clinical and cultural perspective*. Hillsdale, NJ: The Analytic Press.

Green, A. (1993/1999). *The work of the negative* (A. Weller, Trans.). London: Free Association Books.

Green, A. (2000). The central phobic position: A new formulation of the free association method. *International Journal of Psychoanalysis, 81*, 429–451.

Greenacre, P. (1958). Early psychical determinants in the development of the sense of identity. *Journal of the American Psychoanalytic Association, 6*, 612–627.

Heimann, P. (1942). A contribution to the problem of sublimation and its relation to processes of internalization. *International Journal of Psychoanalysis, 23*, 8–17.

Jackson, M., & Williams, P. (1994). *Unimaginable storms: A search for meaning in psychosis*. Karnac: London.

Klein, M. (1935). A contribution to the psychogenesis of manic-depressive states. In *Love, guilt and reparation and other works*. London: Hogarth Press.

Laplanche, J., & Pontalis, J-B. (1972). *Dictionary of psychoanalysis*. London: Hogarth Press.

Laufer, E. (2002). *The body as an internal object*. Presented as the spring lecture for the Centre for the Advancement of Psychoanalytic Studies, London, 15 February.

Lawrence, M. (2002). Body, mother, mind, anorexia, femininity and the intrusive object. *International Journal of Psychoanalysis, 83*, 837–850.

O'Shaughnessy, E. (1999). Relating to the superego. *International Journal of Psychoanalysis, 80*, 861–870.

Perry, B. (1997). Incubated in terror: Neuro-developmental factors in the cycle of violence. In J. Osofsky (Ed.), *Children in a violent society* (pp. 124–149). New York: Guilford Press.

Quinodoz, D. (2001). The psychoanalyst of the future: Wise enough to dare to be mad at times. *International Journal of Psychoanalysis, 82*, 235–248.

Quinodoz, J-M. (1997). Transitions in psychic structures in the light of deterministic chaos theory. *International Journal of Psychoanalysis, 78*, 699–718.

Rey, H. (1994). *Universals of psychoanalysis in the treatment of psychotic and borderline states*. London: Free Association Books.

Rosenfeld, H. (1975). *Impasse and interpretation*. London: Tavistock.

Searles, H. (1951/1965). Data concerning certain manifestations of incorporation. In *Collected papers on schizophrenia and related subjects*. New York: International Universities Press.

Segal, H. (1981). *The work of Hanna Segal: A Kleinian approach to clinical practice*. Northvale, NJ: Jason Aronson.

Sohn, L. (1985). Narcissistic organization, projective identification, and the formation of the identificate. *International Journal of Psychoanalysis, 66*, 201–213.

Sterba, R. (1957). Oral invasion and self defense. *International Journal of Psychoanalysis, 38*, 204–208.

Symington, J. (1985). The survival function of primitive omnipotence. *International Journal of Psychoanalysis*, 66, 481–487.

Trevarthen, C. (1993). The self born in intersubjectivity: The psychology of an infant communicating. In U. Neisser (Ed.), *The perceived self*. Cambridge: Cambridge University Press.

Weiss, E. (1960). *The structure and dynamics of the human mind*. New York & London: Grune & Stratton.

Williams, G. (1997). Reflections on some dynamics of eating disorders: "No entry" defenses and foreign bodies. *International Journal of Psychoanalysis*, 78, 927–941.

Williams, P. (1998). Psychotic developments in a sexually abused borderline patient. *Psychoanalytic Dialogues*, 8, 459–491.

Williams, P. (2000) "The central phobic position: A new formulation of the free association method" by André Green. *International Journal of Psychoanalysis*, 81(5), 1045–1060.

Williams, P. (2001). Some difficulties in the analysis of a withdrawn patient. *International Journal of Psychoanalysis*, 82, 727–746.

Winnicott, D. W. (1960/1964). Ego distortion in terms of true and false self. In *The maturational processes and the facilitating environment* (pp. 140–152). London: Hogarth Press.

Winnicott, D. W. (1964). *Maturational processes and the facilitating environment*. London: Hogarth Press.

Winnicott, D. W. (1967). The location of cultural experience. *International Journal of Psychoanalysis*, 48, 368–372.

Chapter 2

Some difficulties in the analysis of a withdrawn patient*

In this chapter, I discuss some of the difficulties that arose in the analysis of a seriously disturbed patient who found it very hard to talk about himself. He defended against awareness of conflicts, ideas, and affects while being tormented and often overwhelmed by them. He seemed to have acquired an inhibited character that was not, however, schizoid in the diagnostic sense. He related to others in a wary, quarrelsome, but passive way. It became apparent in the analysis that his sense of who he was profoundly confused. Attention to archaic fantasies led to the emergence of a parthenogenetic unconscious fantasy involving identification with his mother and the attempted eradication of the mental function of his father. Experiences of differentiating himself from me in the analysis led to extreme anxiety, including a periodic risk of failure of ego functions with the arousal of latent psychotic anxieties. Interpretation of the content of sessions became possible only after several years; until then an understanding of his panic-filled need to prevent contact or change, and the motivation for this, predominated. Some confusing transference and countertransference experiences in the analysis are also described. Disclosure of what we came to call "unofficial" communications by the patient, expressed as lapses by his supervigilant superego, gradually revealed his crises and feelings. These idiosyncratic, muted appeals for help became a vehicle through which exploration of content, its transference meaning, and the beginnings of a new kind of relating became possible. The dependency feelings associated with a new form of relating and emotional growth brought varying degrees of mental pain. Eventually, this pain forced the patient, after 8 years of analysis, to leave out of a fear of decompensation.

Alec came to see me at the age of 29 asking for one 50-minute session per week. With certain reservations, due to what I felt was his questionable motivation, I agreed to see him. As it transpired, he increased his sessions incrementally during ensuing years to five per week. From the outset he

---

* This chapter originally appeared as a paper in *International Journal of Psychoanalysis*, 82(4), 2001, 727–746. Reprinted with permission.

conveyed that he did not have an adequate self-structure or "psychic headquarters" with which to symbolize his experiences. He found being in the consulting room with me anxiety-inducing to the point of dread before sessions, which he defended against by closing down on his feelings. He showed a "thin-skinned" vulnerability in sessions, which led him regularly to feel that he was on the brink of collapse (Rosenfeld, 1987; Bateman, 1998; Britton, 1998). At the same time he found himself in situations in which he would feel helpless and taken advantage of by others. These experiences of victimization could be accompanied or followed by feelings of being "thick-skinned" and special.*

I also want to convey how Alec regularly felt misunderstood and poorly treated by me, and how hard he worked at pushing these feelings to one side in favor of a belief that he and I were somehow fundamentally on the same wavelength, thinking and feeling "as one." I shall make reference to certain countertransference feelings, including how I could often feel out of touch with Alec, isolated and ineffectual, and how I attempted to make some use of these experiences. Passive, narcissistic patients—especially those with a tendency towards masochism, as I came to think Alec had—can be highly controlling of their feelings and interactions in complex and obscure ways, and this can leave the analyst feeling unsure as to what is going on. Alec was such a patient, but there was an additional factor that exacerbated his inaccessibility. He seemed to constrict his scope for thinking and feeling in a generalized effort to inhibit spontaneity, and this gave his demeanor an odd calm that belied his instability. I did not understand this defense but took it to be a type of blanket attempt to "put on hold" feelings and reactions, perhaps to prevent a return of traumatic memories and ideas. Taken together, Alec's defenses made him extremely wary of analysis while, as I have indicated, they were not able to keep at bay his profound anxieties. At times the organization of Alec's defenses reflected elements of a "pathological narcissistic organization" (Steiner, 1993), so pervasive could it become. However, Alec's protection of himself lacked the degree of coherence that gives such organizations their consolidated, "system-like" quality that can prove so difficult to address. Alec's defenses were widespread and powerful, but they could and did break down, leaving him exposed to confusion,

---

* A type of alternating movement first described by Rosenfeld as "thin-" and "thick-skinned" narcissistic states and which has been described and elaborated by Bateman (1998) and Britton (1998). Britton suggests that "these two states, the thin-skinned and the thick-skinned, are the result of two different relationships of the subjective self to the third object within the internal Oedipus situation. In both states the third object is alien to the subjective, sensitive self. In the thin-skinned mode the self seeks to avoid the objectivity of the third object and clings to subjectivity; in the thick-skinned situation the self identifies with the third object and adopts its mode of objectivity and renounces its own subjectivity" (p. 53).

depression, and extreme anxiety. I felt that this kind of vulnerability pointed to a chronic threat of incipient ego fragmentation.

In the clinical situation, I came to realize that Alec oscillated between alternating states of mind that were characterized by two different types of object relationship. On the one hand, he could surrender to the object in a state of conflict. He tried hard to provoke conflict and seemed to feel relieved if he felt me as an oppressive presence to which he must submit. Often these situations were initiated by attributing a particular resonance or meaning to a word I had used in an interpretation. Instead of being able to take in the idea on which an interpretation was based, he would focus on a specific word or component (sometimes invented), or even the tone of my voice, endowing it with a meaning that it did not have—at least not in my mind. For example, on one occasion we talked about a job-retraining scheme that Alec aspired to undertake. I commented on his evident interest but wondered about what seemed to be his anxiety about the idea of retraining, given certain doubts that he had also voiced. Alec replied by saying, "The way you use the word 'training' is like a punch in the stomach. I feel like a minion who could never be allowed to mix with people like you." I had, in fact, not used the word "training," but the effect of this misunderstanding was to provoke a gross, sudden inequality between us and put him on the receiving end of a cruel, arrogant attack. The other aspect of Alec's oscillation was a renunciation of his autonomy. He was determined to agree with me, regardless of conflicts, and to behave as though there was ultimately no difference in the way we thought or felt. He strove to "become" or "be" the object. He seemed to experience a "contractual" or obligatory imperative to meld with the object (by melding I mean the pursuit of an illusory state of symbiosis). At the same time he strove to avoid melding due to the terror that he might merge and lose his fragile sense of who he was, and this led him to oscillate between the two forms of surrender I have outlined. These two methods of relating were intermingled, creating confusion in him and me. A continuous threat to Alec's equilibrium seemed to lie in experiences of differentiation from me. When these occurred he would convey to me a fear that he would no longer be able to go on being. He was then required to make efforts to eradicate distinctions between himself and me—particularly through melding.

HISTORY

Alec is a thin (anorexic-looking) man with a shock of wiry, ginger hair. He speaks softly—so softly that I often cannot hear him. His manner is self-effacing and he moves as though occupying the shadows. Such information as I have acquired about his life arose disjointedly: He comes from a village in the far north of England. His father, a farm worker, retired early due to ill health. Mother was a part-time helper at a local shop. Alec has a brother two years younger than himself. He recalls home life being quiet and dull, and punctuated by occasional angry outbursts from his father whom he sees as arrogant and unfulfilled. He sees his mother as self-absorbed and melancholic. She has taken antidepressant medication for many years, which Alec believes is because she was separated as a child from her mother during the Second World War, and who then died when Alec's mother was 16. Alec's parents divorced when he was 16.* They appear to have gotten on well earlier in the marriage, having been successful amateur tandem cyclists. Alec was close to his mother until he was 2, at which point "everything changed," although what happened is not clear. He had little to do with his father or brother during childhood, preferring to play alone. By 14 he had become an observer of people, often imagining he was filming them. He did well educationally, gaining a place at law school but quit in his second year in protest at its "elitism."† He took a job as a charity worker after spending a few months traveling around the Far East. While away he bought a large copper bowl as a gift for his mother, which he carried around with him until he came home. He has had one heterosexual relationship, with a girlfriend whom he married. He has found this relationship difficult to manage and he told me that for a long time he feared that "if he breathed, it would collapse." They have twin daughters, aged 4, whom they appear to have a certain amount of difficulty loving. His wife is a highly valued partner in an advertising agency. She earns more money than Alec and travels extensively, while he spends more time at home looking after the children. She has opposed his analysis.

ANALYSIS

At our first meeting Alec complained of feeling that he had been pushing a boulder uphill all his life and could no longer continue, but did not know how to stop. He was reluctant to elaborate on his request for help and ignored my comments; he insisted, "I want one psychotherapy session a week, and I want it now." I felt I was being presented with an urgent

---

* This was the first information I received from Alec indicating the extent of his identification with his mother. The identification is also expressed in his failure to internalize the paternal object and to assume the secondary role of child within the hierarchy of the family. An effect of this was to dilute his masculine identity, enforce his passivity, and latterly make it difficult for him to be a father.

† Why Alec quit law school was never clear. From the comments he made I thought at times that graduating would have brought into closer focus his identification with a failed father leading to excessive guilt, or that he feared that succeeding might mean becoming homosexual. Later I was persuaded that it was the acknowledgment of difference, including intergenerational difference and competition, that was anathema to Alec. Becoming an adult meant destroying his symbiotic tie to his mother.

situation about which I was meant to say or do nothing. I said to him that he gave the impression of being in great need, barely able to cope, and yet seemed to find the prospect of help intolerable. He became agitated; his irritation turned into persecutory anxiety, then to mute fury, and finally he slumped in his chair as though there were no point in speaking. I was to find out that anxiety, indignation, and collapse were routine responses to interpretations, and that he seemed to need to undergo these reactions as a prelude to being able to listen to me. In particular, Alec experienced a severe reaction to interpretations of conflicted feelings towards me. He would be overcome by indignation but then by extreme anxiety and distress, followed by negative therapeutic reactions, including threats of termination. It was difficult to know what to make of this, although later he did tell me, "I can't think when you say these things. I get taken over and just react. I have to just shut you up because it feels like you're driving me mad." I thought that he was trying to control me and what he thought might be my intrusiveness and aggression, but the force with which he needed to silence me suggested something even more threatening. I wondered whether Alec feared that he might disintegrate when he experienced transference interpretations that were, to use Ferro's term, saturated with content or emotion—unmanageable "electric shocks." The ego, unable to integrate the content of the interpretations and the contact they create, succumbs to powerful superego intervention to avoid psychic pain (cf. Ferro, 2001).

Alec's phobic reaction to "saturated" interpretations led to an increase in tension, punitive superego activity, and a difficulty in elaborating any idea or thought. When this happened I could feel, in the countertransference, a sense of responsibility for not grasping what was going on; that I had lost touch with him, and that I was being cruel in putting him through all this. The sense of losing touch made me think that he might feel that he was losing me at these moments, and he confirmed this to be the case: "It's like everything goes to pieces. There's a storm in my head and I can't think. It's a disaster … I feel hopeless that I'll ever be able to do this." A similar reaction could also occur when an interpretation made sense to him (which was rare) and he felt helped; he seemed to then feel that emotional contact would be followed by total loss, and this led to extreme anxiety. "No! If I let you in, things will only go wrong. You'll let me down … it will be the end. The absolute end," was how Alec put it. I surmised that he might be threatened by unmanageable narcissistic rage at these moments, but the most I could sensibly deduce was that his dread was linked to feelings of separateness and emotional contact brought on by interpretations. Unthinkable anxiety (Winnicott, 1958), nameless dread (Bion, 1967), and organismic panic (Pao, 1977, p. 221) are terms used to convey a level of anxiety in which one's sense of ongoing being is imperiled. Pao, referring to patients with schizophrenia, describes "a temporary, unbearable tension for which no relief is possible due to the absence of a containing object"

(p. 221). Alec is not schizophrenic, but Pao's description reflects the scale of the alarm Alec seemed to feel as his ego was overrun by separation anxieties of psychotic proportions (cf. Jackson & Williams, 1994; Williams, 1998). At these times, I felt myself wanting to calm him (I was eventually able to connect this to the apparent calm Alec displayed, which he communicated to me via projective identification). Alec seemed to be signaling to me in the transference that separation-induced psychic pain that was uncontainable. In order to give a sense of the control Alec needed to exert over the sessions, especially in the early stages, I shall give an extract from a mid-week session about a year into the treatment.

[Alec arrives on time, lies on the couch and is silent for a few minutes. He sighs heavily. There is a further pause of a minute or so.]

A: Your sigh makes me think that you have something on your mind. *[Alec remains silent but becomes more motionless. The atmosphere of tension in the room seems to increase. He eventually sighs several times. I imagine his state of mind to be anxious and despairing and that he is trying to calm himself. My feelings are of frustration and irritation that he is treating me as an enemy with no justification. I feel controlled by him and by the session being stuck. After a further 8 or 10 minutes (making a total of about 13 minutes' silence), he speaks.]*

P: *[anxiously]*: I don't like the thought of what you will say. *[Short pause]*

A: You don't like the thought of what I will say. *[Short pause]*

P: No.

A: You have the thought in your mind that you know what my response will be if you speak. It will be an unpleasant one. If this thought were to turn out to be the truth—in reality—it would make sense to be silent as this would be the safer option. *[Alec moves restlessly on the couch, breathing heavily, and eventually becomes motionless. There is a further pause of maybe 5 or 6 minutes. I feel interested in his reaction and somewhat expectant, as though my interpretation has touched him.]*

P: *[resigned]*: It's not that ... I don't like silences. *[Short pause]*

A: Perhaps you are now feeling misunderstood by me. That I have ... *[Alec groans, as though in pain, interrupting me. There is silence for a few minutes. I feel that it would be inappropriate for me to speak—that I would be bullying him into responding. Eventually I decide to speak.]* You seem to need to silence me, and to make sure you experience me as lifeless. Perhaps this is what you mean when you say you don't like the thought of what I will say. Because you can't be sure of what I might say, anything I say feels as though it might harm you. This makes it important for you to try to keep me under control.

There is then silence until the end of the session. The atmosphere is oddly calm. I have the sense that Alec feels strangely secure, having defused the threat of contact between us. I feel isolated and rather hopeless. What is evident in this session is the imposition of pauses and silences, and this was typical. If I tried to reduce these by intervening it could have the opposite effect of driving Alec deeper into silence. If I did not intervene he was also capable of remaining silent, sometimes for the rest of the session. Was I to speak, or wait? If the latter, for how long? At what point would Alec construe acceptance of his silence as retaliation? I became aware only after repeating this sequence many times that Alec was attributing liveliness and a capacity for thought to me, whereas he clung grimly to stasis. Eventually—much later—this became possible to interpret, but for a long time I was required to tolerate the apparent standstill. In so doing I observed and learned about Alec's ways of controlling me. I gradually became aware of small, often minute differences in behavior, over which he appeared to have no control. Attending to these shifts enabled me to perceive certain patterns that appeared to be cyclical. One such cycle involved Alec not being able to stifle his demeanor following a lightening of his mood. This improvement led him to allude to failings in his colleagues or family. For example: "My father forced me to do my homework by saying he'd beat me if I didn't," or "The whole place [his home] was a dump. I found ways of getting out of it from the time I was four." Following these accusations he would become flat and dead, signifying a retreat into silence. I commented on the sequence, saying that I thought that when he felt safer, critical thoughts could and did enter his mind. Because they arose in my presence, he became frightened of revealing them. He replied, "I do have criticisms of people, but what's the point? Talking about them doesn't change anything." I said that I thought that he needed to ensure that his anxieties didn't get the better of him. He wanted to tell me about himself but this made him realize that we are two separate people and that he couldn't predict his effect on me; this felt like a loss of control. Alec said, "I am sorry. I try to talk to you but I don't know whether you realize how hard it is. I constantly think you are going to attack me or something will happen to ruin everything." I said that I could see that if things were to turn out as he said, any move to allow me further into his life would be a disaster. By drawing attention to processes through which Alec tried to communicate with me while distancing himself, and how such a contradictory way of relating kept some of his anxieties at bay, this prevented him from rejecting my interpretations outright. There surfaced, over a long period, and alongside Alec's "official" withdrawal, an "unofficial" line of communication that took the form of veiled curiosity about relationships. It was a gradual response to my observations and interpretations of his changing mood states and my emphasis that these states were taking place in the context of our relationship and that this had meaning, even if we weren't always able to discover it.

Notwithstanding gradual, complex movements in Alec that were to signal certain changes over the long term, the early stages of Alec's analysis indicated that he had little interest in talking about himself, in identifying his feelings, or in addressing his problems. Mental processes concerned with self-reflection, self-representation, a capacity for individual thought and curiosity in others seemed to be muted, and often missing. This abject situation stood in contrast to his manifest torment for which he demanded relief. An example of his ambiguous position was the way he arrived for sessions: he would often lie on the couch as though ready to talk, only to succumb to inner turmoil that rendered him speechless. The effect was to make me feel initially interested, then confused, and, finally, rejected. If he spoke it was to voice despondency or to try to "get inside" my mind to establish a sense of narcissistic equilibrium, but mostly he was inaccessible. This led me to think that Alec's dread of separation and his need to meld might represent a way of maintaining a sense of identity in the face of unmanageable anxieties, in particular, experiences of differentiation. Speaking spontaneously would be an act of differentiation; the demands of individuation would be a constant threat. In order to maintain his integrity, he needed to split off and project, or else inhibit, processes that augmented the scope of his mental functioning. I was minded to think along these lines, as I have indicated, by Alec's behavior in the transference and by my countertransference feelings. Alec's controlling, self-destructive attitudes could induce in me feelings of drowsiness, futility, and resentment, but I also experienced feelings of sadness and regret when he was hopelessly lost. These feelings drew me closer to him, but if I interpreted his painful isolation I was met by rejection. I came to think that I was being made to feel a concern and compassion for him that he himself could not experience, as to do so would mean acknowledging the losses he had suffered. I also came to feel, after Alec had increased the frequency of his sessions, a recurrent gloom about the analysis, particularly when he was at his most withdrawn and controlling. I interpreted at one point, in response to his despair, that he must sometimes feel quite hopeless about the future, and he replied sharply, "I'm not going to think about that. You can if you want to, I'm not. Anyway ... if it's true, what's the point? Why go on?" It is possible that this is a reference to suicidal ideation, but I thought that he was telling me that feelings of failure resided in him but were intolerable, hence their projection into me.

When not muted, Alec voiced woe. He told me that he thought he would be accused of being homosexual by being in therapy. He had breathing difficulties, suffered pains in his hips and groin, and felt that life held out no hope for him. He could become suddenly excitedly flustered, exclaiming anxiously, for example, "Your eyes are the same color as that vase," or "It's your look that makes me feel funny." These statements had a "this-means-that" quality of narcissistic equivalence, so that when he spoke he indicated that no reply was expected. I interpreted how anxious he became when he complained: He experienced himself and me as separate—two people with different minds and ideas—and this threatened his sense of control over our relationship. The tenor of the sessions early on was one of resistance and anxious recriminations. One departure or "unofficial" slippage from his "official" withdrawal consisted of telling me of the first dream he could remember.

He was a small boy high up in a tower with his mother. She wore exotic clothes and danced like a film star. He followed her around proudly, excited and happy. On a table was a goldfish bowl in which a single goldfish swam round in circles.

He did not associate to the dream and tried (too hard, I thought) to recount it as though it were of no consequence. Later in the session he told me, again in passing, that he was the most important person in his mother's life. This dream was to prove helpful in my attempts to think about Alec. I felt that he had raised it in a fleeting, low-key way so as to leave himself feeling that he had not said anything important, while finding a way of imparting something that he felt was extremely significant about himself.

After a year Alec asked for a second session, and a few months later a third, without being able to account for why he wanted them. I was disconcerted as I could see little evidence of movement to justify the increase. Neither did I have a basis upon which to analyze his intentions. I had identified certain patterns of communication and I had come to know something of his desire to meld and his fear of separation, but I could not detect in the transference much beyond this. After taking up the third session he recounted a dream in which there were three or four diving boards at different heights. He could only jump off the bottom board. When he climbed up to the others he panicked and had to come down again. He had difficulty associating to the dream but did say how he had been a good swimmer as a boy but lost interest as he grew older as he didn't enjoy swimming competitions. It had long been apparent to me what a struggle the analysis was for him, and I thought he might be trying to force change by increasing the frequency of sessions rather than face up to how difficult they were. I also thought that he was anxious that neither he nor I could make the therapy work, no matter how often we met, and that he was telling me this through the dream, without wanting to become conscious of the fact. I put this to him and, predictably, he collapsed into silence. He mumbled, "I don't know what to say," but within 10 minutes asked, "Why did you say what you said?" I said I was glad to answer his question but wondered whether he had any thoughts about it. He was quiet and then said, "I'm not sure what it means. I'm not trying to be difficult. I don't understand what you said but there's something about it that sounded right. It was when you spoke about forcing change. I recognize that. I think I have an idea that just by deciding to do something I can make it happen. Is this right? Could you tell me what you meant?" This comment may not in itself seem important, but I was struck by how he had "recovered" from my interpretation, and was demonstrating unusual curiosity. There followed other examples of a capacity to "regroup" which followed the increased frequency of sessions. The phenomenon persisted leading me to think that he was perhaps feeling more contained as a result of meeting more often. In this light, requests for extra sessions could be seen as his attempt to contain his separation anxieties during the times between sessions. I put this to him in several different ways. He indicated that it was probably the case, saying,

> I don't like saying this to you because you'll take it the wrong way but I feel a bit safer coming more often. I don't know why. I suppose it's because I don't know about life. I know that. I want to know about life: That's why I have to put up with being here.

During ensuing weeks and months Alec brought several dreams or parts of dreams, always as though they were substitutes for anything to say. I felt he was beginning to use the sessions to enable me to catch glimpses of his internal world in a way that did not openly offend the severe superego injunction to avoid dependence on others. After several more months Alec asked for a fourth and then a fifth session. Again it was difficult to discuss this with him. I did wonder whether I had unwittingly encouraged him to come more often by imparting a level of hope that was not justified, as a result of my persisting with the treatment and agreeing to the increased frequency of sessions. At the same time I had observed the structuring effects of the sessions and had come to appreciate Alec's very limited ability to internalize interpretations. I inferred that the containment provided by the analysis had moderated somewhat his worst anxieties around melding and separation. At around this time, Alec confided in me why he had come into analysis. "The truth is … I don't know what truth is …" he said,

> I have no choice but to do analysis. Not to do it would be worse, so there is no option for me. I didn't want to come … sometimes I did but I didn't really … it frightened me too much. I knew that if I didn't do something things would never change, so I had no choice.

I took up this feeling of no choice. He told me he feared he would carry on being stuck all his life, never knowing how to be with people. "The worst thing," he said, "is the kids. They play, want to draw or have stories and things like that. I'm not interested. I can't do it. And when they shout or nothing satisfies them it's impossible. I just want to lie down or leave. I hate that." I thought that, transferentially, Alec was indicating his need for containment of his depressive anxieties and despair, and that he grasped the scale of his developmental crisis and how it haunted him.

SPLITTING, PROJECTIVE IDENTIFICATION, AND PROBLEMS OF TECHNIQUE

At times Alec appeared to derive gratification from the obstacles and impasses he imposed on the treatment, arriving punctually as though settling into a routine of inaccessibility. However, he had imparted in the transference a sense of his anxieties about separation and I had noticed a constant, low-level scrutiny of me, which provided some idea of his concern about his mother's proximity, distance, and state of mind. The increase in the frequency of sessions had exposed facets of his inapproachability, notably fluctuations in mood states, and these had helped me to become aware of points at which he was likely to withdraw. He began to make irritated and at times sadistic remarks, and these often occurred at the beginnings and ends of sessions or weeks. They might be criticisms of his wife or acquaintances, derisory comments about something he had seen or read, or long-suffering frustrations at the endless obstacles he faced in getting through daily life. During the middle of the week he frequently slipped into what I thought were manic states in which ideas could become sexualized and contempt laden. These were often expressed through a preoccupation with an idealized woman friend, with whom I was contrasted. "She understands me, she's so sensitive ... she just knows how to listen and how to be on my side. She doesn't try to analyze me or tell me what to do, she just is there for me ... for me!" was a typical statement. This use of splitting was more blatant when he referred to my "heavy handedness" or, worse, "pig ignorance" in contrast to her sensibility. Later on he linked these failings to my being a man, and he saw them as irredeemable. I thought that he was splitting me and the internal parental couple into idealized and denigrated aspects, in order to sustain his union with an idealized maternal figure. I also thought that he was defending himself against feelings aroused through closer contact with me, including growing reliance on what he felt was my capacity to understand him. His use of projective identification was pervasive and these interpretations often foundered. "It could be, I suppose," he might reply, or, witheringly, "Your faith in psychoanalysis is touching." Following more manic and contemptuous states of mind he could become persecuted and paranoid, and splitting and projective identification would lead him to feel that I was enraged with him. Despite—or because of—these splits and projections, he continued to let slip allusions to his underlying concerns, including at one point to his need for extra sessions. He told me, to my surprise, "It was for your benefit that I came more often, not mine."* This followed an interpretation of his

---

* I experienced this communication as important, although I did not properly understand it. The transference-countertransference led me to think that Alec was probably sacrificing himself to me out of primitive devotion. His requests for extra sessions were motivated, it later transpired, by concern for my narcissism and well-being. Perhaps more masochistic patients than we realize increase their sessions for this reason.

punctuality, which contrasted with his difficulty in taking anything from me. I asked him what he meant and he replied that he had had what seemed to me to be a genuine thought that I might be ill: "What I mean is depressed … overburdened … I think you do too much." I tried to explore this, with limited success: he then stayed away for two sessions and found it difficult to speak for about a week. When I tried to refer to this extreme reaction he insisted, "It's of no significance. There's nothing to talk about." Such disruption of contact between us again generated concern in me about the justification for continuing the analysis. However, he was determined to persist using a mixture of reticence, withdrawal, and lapses of vigilance that denoted his true states of mind. I was not convinced that my reading of these lapses was always correct. I wondered whether they might not be "bait" reeled out to replenish my narcissistic supplies as an analyst, in order to prevent me from losing interest. Were this true it would not necessarily preclude genuine communication. When Alec did impart a truth only to then vanish in the session, the effect was powerful. I felt left in a vacuum, so ruthless was his severance of contact from feelings and from me.

My concerns about the viability of the analysis continued until about the fifth year. Reliance on my countertransference feelings to interpret Alec's fluctuating states had been helpful but not sufficient. Feeling inept, moved, that I was being bullied (or else being a bully), held to ransom, or that the analysis was destined to fail, and observing Alec's behavior in the transference, I had been able to identify the oscillation between Alec and his internal objects described earlier, as well as the shape of certain moods. I was then helped by an unexpected experience that at first I could not understand at all. This was the disquieting feeling of being soothed by Alec. He developed a habit of punctuating the sessions with sighs and murmurs that seemed designed to comfort or console me. Then, when he did speak, it was as though he was resuming an intimate chat (like pillow talk), following a break in contact in order to attend exclusively to my needs. The effect of this pseudoconcern was to make me feel both drawn to and distanced from him at the same time, and also controlled. Perplexed, I discussed this, and my contradictory feelings of being a powerful failure in relation to Alec, with a colleague. We reflected upon the material of the analysis in the light of the primitive nature of Alec's submissiveness and the possible psychotic anxieties that underlay his narcissism. I had noticed how Alec's more "lively" masochistic defenses (associated with provocation of conflict and persecutory anxiety) collapsed under the imperative to meld (this is, I think, what gave his withdrawal its immutable quality). Challenges to the melding risked the threat of breakdown, due to stimulation of Alec's dread of loss of the object. It then struck me that Alec's bizarre, consoling behavior was a parody of "mmm" sounds I occasionally made when listening to him, only appropriated and distorted by him in the service of fusion. The word "ominous" came to my mind, and as I reflected on this with my colleague she remarked that the meaning of "ominous" is "without beginning." Two further thoughts arose: First, that damage to Alec's self-representations and ego development had, in all probability, occurred prior to the onset of infantile amnesia, and this was a reason for my difficulty in apprehending early relational patterns and obtuse defensive strategies. Second, Alec had not acquired an authentic sense of self, but was identified with aspects of his objects (external and internal), not with whole objects. These representations, or part-object identifications, were his way of articulating himself in the absence of knowing who he was. His parody of me was one way of establishing a narcissistic mode of relating on a part-object basis.

In the light of Alec's restricted mental functioning, which was the outcome of splitting, projection, and projective identification of unwanted and unmanageable aspects of himself, I decided to pursue my emphasis on the processes preventing contact between us. I thought that by continuing to make links between his states of mind and those he disavowed, the process of withdrawal of projections—though difficult—might be facilitated. When the opportunity arose, I interpreted ways in which another person—myself—could experience his states of mind, particularly when he withdrew, and how these experiences were brought about. I do not mean that I revealed "wildly" my affective responses to Alec. I am referring more to an "analyst-centered" approach to interpretations (Steiner, 1993) through which I tried to clarify and interpret the emotional content of his communications. For example, when he was masochistic and paranoid I sensed a mixture of power, boundless rage, and contempt being attributed to me and I described the experience, raising the question of how this could come about as it did not represent my view of him at all. I placed my comments on a notional coffee table between us, for his consideration. Similarly, when his thoughts were sexualized, his tendency towards manic thinking could produce in me feelings of stupidity, failure, and a sense of shame. I suggested that he split up his emotional experiences to try to avoid pain, locating the most difficult aspects in me. During his more manic thinking he forced me to experience unpleasant feelings at points when he could not tolerate the depression and pain associated with his and his parents' sense of hopelessness. My aim in doing this was to try to build some kind of a bridge between two planes of violently split and projected experiences. My comments did not overly menace Alec, and once or twice they interested him. Gradually he began to tell me how he experienced powerful feelings in relation to me, but had no ideas of his own about what they meant and didn't know what to do with them. His thoughts, he said, were variations of his parents' attitudes, and this made thinking about things I said almost impossible. He cited a voice in his head, similar to his father's, which reacted to things I said in a derisive manner, which made Alec feel powerful. He described an upsetting feeling of passive, depressed self-loathing, a condition in which everything was "too much," which he associated with his mother's defeatism. Although these disclosures contained only limited emotion, he was drawing closer to the disavowed world of his affects, and I thought that very gradual steps were probably the only way he could ever achieve this, so painful was the experience.

At around this time complaints about lack of progress in the analysis began to surface. These were followed by a preoccupation with troublesome neighbors whom he described as "thugs who don't care," and this lasted for three months. Attempts to relate this to his feelings in the transference met with limited success, but the pattern of his moods did appear to be altering once more. They began to alternate between his familiar, hopeless martyrdom and new, openly scornful attacks on acquaintances, members of his family, and on psychoanalysis. Somehow he managed to keep me dissociated in his mind from psychoanalysis, at least for a time, confiding in me as though I agreed that psychoanalysis was a sham. As the sadistic feelings grew, and he was able to be more openly critical of others (not me), so the strength of his persecuted responses to things I said eased. The displacement of his aggression and contempt was obvious, but interpretation alone did not alter this. He needed, as always, time to become accustomed to having his feelings, while I needed to sense the maximum transference content he could tolerate when I spoke.

I should pause at this point to say that, when Alec had increased his sessions to five a week, and prior to being able to discuss his feelings, he had fallen virtually silent for about a month. This was a dramatic situation that seemed more or less unamenable to interpretation. His withdrawal was complex. I felt pushed away and ignored. He appeared to experience isolation and relief while looking guilty as he shuffled in and out of sessions. At one point during this "absence" he said, "Full analysis is my aim." He knew someone in analysis who had improved and he wanted this experience for himself. I had no idea what "full analysis" meant to Alec. A fantasy of the beginnings of a creation of his own? An omnipotent, narcissistic illusion based on identification with his friend or what I might think?* An attempt to meld? Much later, when we were able to talk about this, he said:

> I don't know what I really think or whether any thoughts I have belong to me in the end, although sometimes my mind is so full I think I have all the thoughts I can cope with—too many. I didn't know what else to do but be silent. I can see that it's not helpful from your point of view, but it was just something I needed to do, like I had no choice. It was like I had nothing to lose, in a way. I'm not trying to say I was deliberately messing things up, I don't mean that ... there was just nothing else left for me to do.

---

* I connected the notion of "full analysis" with his feelings of being full or empty inside. For example, he felt "full" when proudly situated at the top of the tower with his mother, and in relation to the goldfish bowl—the fish via identification with the third object, or else the bowl representing fullness via identification with the bowl's containing function (see Discussion).

I remain uncertain about why he needed to be so silent. Although the aggressive, controlling aspects were not lost on me, I take his word for it that it probably represented some kind of inchoate attempt to assert himself and what he needed. Having put to Alec how aspects of his internal world manifested themselves and how he split up his emotional experiences, locating unacceptable aspects in me while holding on to others, he hinted to me of disturbing feelings he didn't understand, saying they frightened him whenever he thought of them. In one session he said, "I can't imagine myself having feelings at all. I know this sounds stupid because I do have feelings—I know I do. Feelings feel to me as though they belong to someone else—what's in them doesn't reflect me." As he was telling me about this he interjected, "I think I'm going to vomit. I'm going to have to leave the room." I took this to be an expression of psychotic anxiety created by the object-relating taking place between us, and told him so. He alluded to a yearning to be looked after properly and an abiding resignation that nothing good would ever come of his life. I interpreted his unmet need to feel loved, his feeling of responsibility for me, and his horror of being demanding. He elaborated over several subsequent sessions how his thought processes underwent a kind of involuntary scanning which cleansed them of content that might distress me. This rendered dialogue unnecessary, as it meant that he always "understood" me. If I introduced thoughts or ideas of my own, he no longer knew where he stood. This, he said, was why he had reacted so violently to my speaking to him. At these moments he felt that he no longer knew who he was, only who I was, and he felt he was disappearing. He added that he wasn't completely sure who it was who was disappearing. He hated it when I engaged in "real talk" (meaning interpretations of his feelings and experiences), which, he said, was "reckless." He had to stop me as he thought I had no idea of the consequences of what I was doing. "You need to understand that I can't think in the way you do," he asserted. I thought that Alec was reiterating the imperative to seek fusion and how this was threatened by experiences of differentiation. I interpreted this, stressing his unmet need to find a way of being himself without the fear that I would lose interest in him or judge him. This led to a discussion of his confusion about how people relate while remaining themselves—something he could not conceive of, he said. "Everyone can influence me," he complained. "I become what they want." He referred fleetingly to sexual confusion by saying that he liked and disliked sex. It felt right when he needed it, which was when he was stressed or upset. He might get his wife to give him sex or else masturbate; the aim was to feel better. He was embarrassed at telling me this, but I was struck by his unusual frankness. I felt Alec was letting me know that our "unofficial" relationship had acquired a momentum, and that he was using it as his way of becoming an analytic patient.

I have demonstrated some of the difficulties presented by Alec's withdrawal, and have described a point in the analysis when Alec was becoming more able to talk to me. I would now like to provide extracts from three consecutive sessions in which there was more talk than silence. These are taken from a period when Alec provided a clear indication of his problems of identity and passivity, during the summer term of the seventh year of his analysis and shortly before the summer holiday break. I shall conclude with a more recent session indicating developments in his fantasy life that permitted greater communication of his feelings, but that also heralded untoward, negative consequences. The first session is Monday.

Monday

Alec had left a message at my consulting room the previous day, saying that he was having difficulty coping at home. This was the first time he had contacted me outside the sessions. He came to his session a few minutes early and was obviously distressed, with none of the "thick-skinned" defenses I had seen previously. He lay down and began speaking immediately.

P: [*distressed and tearful*]: K [*his wife*] got drunk over the weekend at work and didn't get home until late on Friday, leaving me to look after the kids. I couldn't manage. The worst thing was Saturday: I went for a walk with the girls to the local cemetery and I saw my stolen bike! [*Three months earlier he had left his new bicycle unlocked outside a shop in central London and it was stolen.*] There were three blokes and one of them had my bike. I explained to the one who had it that this was my bike. I showed him the marks. I had the frame number in my wallet, but they had filed it off. He said he hadn't stolen it, he'd bought it from someone. He seemed friendly, saying that if it was mine then I should get hold of the police and sort it out. His friend had a mobile phone and said he would ring them and the police said they would send someone along straight away. After half an hour they hadn't come so he rang again and they said they were on their way, but they still didn't arrive. The kids were getting impatient and I said let's go to the police station, which wasn't far away, and we set off, but the bloke with my bike just rode off. I was frantic. I ran after him asking him to stop but I couldn't catch him. Later on I realized that they hadn't been phoning the police at all. I rang them when I got home and they said they'd had no call. They would have been there within two minutes if they had. I feel such a fool, a wimp; I think you, everybody, can see I am a fool. I should have grabbed the bike and held on to it, but I couldn't. I think of what you've said that I have difficulty accepting that it's hard for me to assert myself. I wanted to trust the bloke. As soon as he was reasonable I sympathized with him. I just walked up to him and said this is my bike, thinking I was being my father's son. If I'd stopped and thought, I wouldn't have done it. I'm not scared of being hit; I don't know what I am scared of. I think I'm being assertive and then he just rides away. I'm not scared of being hit.

A: I think you are telling me complex and important things about yourself that require careful thought. One of these things seems to me to be how confused and betrayed you feel by these other people and by your own reactions, and how angry it makes you, but also how afraid you are of your feelings getting out of hand—for example, you might want to hit someone.

P: I didn't even shout at the guy when he rode off. In my mind I shouted at him, but I did nothing except to say it was my bike. Yesterday I spent all day in bed. There was an awful noise coming from next door's garden. They were having a party, but they were arguing. Jim, my neighbor, told them to shut up. I couldn't bring myself to do that. I can't accept the situation with my bike. I try to work out how I could be like Jim, but I can't do it, and I can't accept that I can't do it, that the things I say are gift-wrapped. I think that if I try harder I can be different. If I stopped trying I would have to walk around feeling scared. I think I am scared. I know I'm scared.

A: I think you do feel scared of men and I can see how you might have copied your father's attitudes to cope with your fear, but I also feel it is the case that you don't know what to do with men or how to relate to them in a way that doesn't involve conflict. This is one reason why talking with me is so difficult. I think that you probably feel more comfortable with women, even though they cause you great problems.

P: I know where I am with women. All the time you speak I keep thinking I should be like a man. I wanted to come and see you today. I don't always see you like my father. I can see you are different, but it doesn't stop me feeling you want to criticize me about the way I handled the business with the bike. I rang B [a female friend] yesterday after I couldn't get hold of you and she said she would come round if I wanted. She did and I felt a lot better; she told me she appreciated me and how sensitive she thought I was. It made me want to be with her, not you. I don't like you. You and this bike bloke are the same in my mind. All sorts of things add up in my head. K took the day off and I'm meeting her afterwards. I want to be with her, not here with you. I mean this. It is easier to say it this way than to say that I am scared when I am with you. To be opposed to you is very hard.

A: It makes sense to me that you feel frightened of me. What I am about to say might sound like a strange idea, but in the light of what you've said, and what you've conveyed in the past about your intense closeness to your mother and alienation from your father, I wonder whether sometimes you don't feel confused about the fact of being a man, and whether you might even have preferred to have been a woman.

P: When I was younger I wanted a girl's body, always. I thought it would make everything easier, that I would feel better if I was a girl. I'm not really a man, I've never felt like one. Last week I was looking in a bookshop and bought *Portnoy's Complaint*. The main character was like me, only angry, whereas I'm not. It's a good book but I couldn't carry on reading it. So I read a book about women by Doris Lessing set in the offices of a fashion magazine, and it was much more interesting. I've never been able to read anything by Updike either; it's all about men. I feel that I don't want anything to do with you. I just want to be with K or B, or B's mother who I get on with. I like K's girlfriends, too. In *Portnoy's Complaint* all the stuff about masturbation was overt. I felt like that, a long time ago. [*Pause*] I now think you don't understand about my wanting to be a woman, even though it was you who just raised it. I feel comfortable with K and her mother who talks about her mother, and I feel close to her. I have a need to masturbate. I've got a penis, but sometimes I don't want it.

A: I am interested in the fact that you feel better with women, and that you wanted to be a woman when you were younger. At the same time I also know that you want to feel that you are a grown-up man, and it must therefore be difficult for you if you experience the feeling of being understood here in your analysis by a man.

P: [*anxious, abrupt*]: I won't have it. What you say won't stay in my mind. I want to be with women. As soon as you said what you said a voice in my head said, "He's like your father, a macho bastard who thinks he knows everything." I can't listen to you.

There are numerous points that could be taken up from this material, which is rich compared to months and years of reticence. Obviously this session did not arrive *ab initio* but was part of a gradual increase in communication. I was struck by two aspects. I felt that Alec was telling me, in the transference, about his relationship with his father (possibly his brother, also) and how his attempts to identify with his father had failed. His reference to his wife's drunkenness I thought could be an allusion to his mother's depression and how at some point Alec did turn to his father for help, without success. The bikes and bicycle riding may also be associated with the "tandem marital couple" that Alec failed to internalize in a meaningful way. One outcome of Alec's failure(s) of identification is that boundaries and proper behavior between generations are not something Alec understands. In life and in the sessional material he feels betrayed; he deceives himself; there is no proper help; the police do not come and no adequate superego function is established. I think he is ashamed of his reactions as he feels himself to be identified with those who mistreat him. When I made my interpretation about Alec feeling understood by a man (me) he reacted sharply, partly I think, because at that moment the maternal transference was dominant and he felt rejected.

However, he managed to tell me about his identifications with women and how his relationships have proceeded on a narcissistic basis.

Tuesday

The following day Alec arrived again early and spoke about his negative reactions in the previous session. He was less anguished, but more openly depressed and miserable.

P: I kept switching backwards and forwards in my feelings yesterday, in the session and afterwards when I'd left. It was confusing: I felt angry but also interested in what you said. There was a part of me that didn't want to listen at all. I kept thinking that if I carried on listening to you and talking, you would drag me into some place where there was no return. [*Pause*] I didn't want to go at the end. I don't like coming but I don't like leaving either. When the holidays come round it feels terrible. I don't think I miss you or anything like that; it's just like everything collapses and I can't move. I don't know what to do. [*I felt concern for him and considered whether to say to him that allowing himself to need me was extremely painful because it made him feel how much he had missed. As I was thinking how to put this, given that he could reject expressions of concern, he rejected his feelings himself by becoming powerful and triumphant.*]

P: [*angrily*]: I couldn't stand my father. I thought he was an idiot. In the end he was irrelevant; he could frighten me, though. Did I tell you he threw someone down the stairs once? He never got on with anybody, and I didn't miss him after the divorce. When I was a child I felt I could do anything, really, I didn't need him. I remember a couple of times us trying to do things together in the shed but it didn't work. My mother loved me and we didn't need anybody else. He didn't mean anything. [*There was a pause, during which he seemed to recover from the outburst and become calmer. He resumed in a more thoughtful way.*] I like you sometimes. You're not like my father, at least not completely, but I can't give way to that because it would mean betraying my mother— and K. Everything I had is bound up with her—my father hasn't been involved, except to discipline me.

A: I think that your relationships with your mother, me, and your wife feel confusing. You have made a pledge to your mother and she to you. As a child you must have felt uniquely special to her. Maybe you even fantasized that you had the biggest or the only penis in the world. But the problem with this pledge was that, to remain a knight in shining armor on his tricycle, you had to stop growing up. You couldn't allow yourself to love your father or brother because you and your mother had taken possession of each other and couldn't separate. Perhaps in the end you felt that there was no difference between your mother and yourself. Your relationships with men have become threatening, and this has made it painful to need me to help you in a fatherly way. Your childhood prize—a needy, depressed woman who demanded emotional and psychological support—has left you burdened, with no one to turn to for help. Meanwhile you and your mother were obliged to maintain the fiction that you were a golden couple in need of no one.

P: I made a pact with my mother. You know, we understood each other, meant everything to each other. She used to tell me her dreams of the future and I promised her that I would make them come true. She would tell her friends about how I was going to make her happy and look after her. It embarrassed me but the main feeling was that I was important to her. Men behind the counters of shops would smile at me and I felt they knew how important I was to my mother—I was her little man. One of the things my mother wanted was to travel. She also wanted to own a red sports car and I promised her that I would make her dreams come true and buy her one. I can see that this is an impossible situation for me to be in, but it didn't feel like that. I felt I had all the power in the world.

My main observations from this extract were (1) Alec's unusual expression of dependence upon me and its attendant risks, (2) the brief "thick-skinned" defensive eruption about his father following his statement about needing me, and (3) the rapid resumption of a more reflective attitude, including confirmation in his last comment of my interpretation regarding the shared parthenogenetic fantasy.

Wednesday

Alec had left a further message saying "my back has gone" and that he was having to come by taxi but didn't know if he would make it. He arrived and lowered himself slowly onto the couch.

P: It was very difficult coming here. I bent down this morning to pick up a cup of coffee and my back gave way. I couldn't help feeling that something was conspiring to bring me down. It was awful—like a knife going through my back. I realized that I had to move carefully because if I tried walking normally there was excruciating pain. I didn't know whether or not to come. I wasn't sure whether I wanted to, either, but then I thought about the weekend and the summer break, and I decided I wanted to come. I rang K to ask her what I ought to do and she said I should go to our GP [local physician] instead, but I decided to come and called a cab. I think I might have slipped a disc like my mother did years ago; I massaged it for her.

A: Even a slight change of position—like deciding for yourself that you wanted to come to your session with me because you needed to—could be extremely painful.

P: It wasn't as bad as I thought it was going to be. The taxi driver helped me into the cab and he didn't mind taking his time; without that I wouldn't have made it here. He didn't drive fast and he didn't talk a lot on the way either; I appreciated that.

I felt that the session, from which this is a brief extract, was complicated. He had declined his wife's advice, and appreciated a taxi driver who didn't rush him. He was expressing, transferentially, his dependence on me. But who I am in the transference is not clear. I felt that Alec was needing me to understand how terribly painful it was to change his position to one of dependence, either on a non-narcissistic mother or a caring father, and that the transference figure in whom he was confiding probably contained a mixture of maternal and paternal elements.

TRANSFERENCE DEVELOPMENTS

In the year following these sessions, Alec continued to bring ideas and feelings, through a gradual libidinization of wishes and fantasies, and "unofficial" comments became more frequent. He noticed, for example, that he believed that it was normal to not talk and was puzzled by his interest when we did talk. I interpreted how this contrasted with the threat dialogue posed to his need for symbiosis. More talk provoked his sadomasochistic tendencies, not least as a need for and great resentment towards his father and mother grew in the transference. A good male object materialized in the shape of a former schoolteacher who had taught Alec art—a man who had encouraged his pupil to draw and paint in his own way. In the transference this figure was not strongly differentiated and seemed to be of indeterminate sexual orientation—not homosexual but neutral, as though in "draft" form. Alec began to divulge envy and jealousy of his parents, of his brother, and of me, and the role of envy in his negative therapeutic reactions became more apparent. His shame and guilt at his failure to individuate were touched upon and this was painful for him. He became preoccupied by what he called his mother's and his "mistake," by which he meant their snobbism towards poorer neighbors in their home village. He recalled how his neighbors were decent people and he felt ashamed at having colluded with his mother's airs and graces. It was his own family that was in trouble, but this had been ignored by all of them, especially his mother who had maintained that everything was fine. Alec said he could see what had to be done if he was to get well, but he was not sure he could do it. Alec's attitude to me seemed to have undergone a change. I had the impression that dialogue was possible, even though its point and meaning could prove elusive. When I collected him from the waiting room he looked like an unhappy, frightened animal, fearing yet wanting contact with me. He was no longer the resistant, pseudopatient I was used to. In a more recent session he suffered a prolonged bout of stomach rumbling which led him to the idea that he saw his emotional needs as being the same as eating me. "I can't stand the thought of needing you or eating you," he said, "I prefer my needs to eat away at me, it makes me feel like a hero." He was proud of being able to feed himself but also acknowledged that he was incensed at having to cope alone. He accused me of being a predator feeding off his mind: "I have this picture in my mind of the top of my head being removed by my mother or you and my brains being scooped out and eaten. The more I reveal, the deeper your talons sink into me." I interpreted the appalling state I would have to be in to want to do such a thing—to have him sacrifice himself as a martyr to rescue me from psychological collapse. He did not reject this interpretation. His resistance to interpretations of his identification with what I thought of as his mother's narcissism and cannibalism had reduced. He had also developed an awareness of how he could project his needs into me, and found the discovery of this process disturbing and interesting. A recent series of primitive, devouring fantasies involved Alec being a *Tyrannosaurus rex* biting and tearing at me, and this frightened him. What was noticeable was an absence of masochistic or perverse gratification. Aggression, guilt, and anxiety accompanied his oral impulses and this, in my view, indicated a growing distinction between ego and object that had previously been absent. He had come to realize that I possessed ways of thinking that did not entail annihilation of his own. This had helped to bring about a starting point, albeit a precarious one, for resumption of his arrested development.

DISCUSSION

The psychoanalytic literature on narcissism and masochism is extensive (cf. Hanly, 1995) and I shall not attempt to address this here. I shall comment briefly on Alec's passivity and how I have understood it. Alec's capacity for generalized inhibition was, I felt, a secondary defense of a kind described by Fonagy, Moran, Edgecumbe, Kennedy, & Target (1993).* His submission, however, was, from one perspective, an echo of his relationship to his father

---

* They state that the analytic process may be difficult or impossible to establish with patients like Alec because the infant may have shrunk the capacity for mental process such that whole classes or categories of mental representations appear to be missing. Such situations stem from an attempt by the patient as a child to protect his mental functioning from painful mental representations that are too central to be isolated from the core of the representational system that may become part of consciousness. The patient attempts to disengage mental processes that generate particular categories of mental representations. Alec's "involuntary scanning" of his thought processes in order to disengage from unwanted ideas may have its origins in this type of inhibition.

as Freud describes in "A Child Is Being Beaten" (1919). The image of the child being beaten by the father undergoes repression and therefore cannot be properly addressed. Recurrent conflicts with me in the transference over questions of power and control reflected, I thought, his ambivalence towards his father, as did, I suspect, his lack of explanation of requests for more sessions. His relationship to his mother in the transference was conflicted by anxieties of an extremely primitive kind. These required Alec to seek out and meld with the object, deepening his passivity to the point of relinquishing his autonomy. He would submit to others not only out of pursuit and fear of conflict, but also to maintain a narcissistic form of relating without which he felt extremely anxious. His impulse to meld with the object reflected an identification with what I thought of as a cannibalistic dependency in his mother as an internal object which needed to be "penetrated" for her to survive. Another way of putting this might be to say that Alec was identified in a fusional manner with a female object felt to contain phallic power. However, this object seemed to be essentially weak and manic in disposition. It is also possible that the parents are, for Alec, a "combined object" (symbolized by the tandem riding) with which he is also identified. Klein (1952) wrote, "The infant's capacity to enjoy ... [his] relation to both parents ... depends on his feeling that they are separate individuals" (p. 79). Alec did not see his parents as separate, either from him or from each other. He sought fusion with his mother to whom, in my view, qualities of both sexes were attributed. The parental couple was collapsed into one combined figure. At the same time his parents seemed in reality to have repudiated differentiation and triangulation. A lack of differentiation, reciprocity, or experience of generative sexual intercourse may account for Alec's scorn of couples and of relationships, including at times his relationship with his children. I had repeatedly noticed a disdainful repudiation of generative sexuality. I do not think Alec felt himself to be born out of his parents' sexuality; instead, he reproduced in relationships an identification with a fused/fusing mother/couple. Pregenital sexuality of this type might suggest a homosexual character, but I had no evidence for this and thought it more likely that Alec possessed a poorly differentiated sexual identity. In other words, he was neither homo- nor heterosexual.

The archaic substrate of masochism remains a matter of debate (cf. Cooper & Sacks, 1991). The two sub-groups delineated by Kernberg (1988) and Simons (1987) emphasize the depressive-masochistic character and the sadomasochistic character, respectively. The former is characterized by guilt, self-punishment (through obsessive ruminations), and inhibited aggression, and the latter by less conflict over aggression, provocation of punishment by the other, and emotional coercion. Alec contained elements from both categories but tended more to reflect the former. Cooper (1988) stresses the centrality of narcissistic injury in masochism that accompanies difficulties in relinquishing infantile omnipotence associated with separation-individuation and this is, I think, fundamental to Alec's difficulties. In serious narcissistic injuries, a masochistic stance can also be a means by which the structural cohesiveness of crumbling self-representations is maintained (cf. Stolorow, 1975). Describing the dynamics of the narcissistic fusional tie with the mother, Deleuze and Sacher-Masoch (1989) suggest that these primitive crises can lead to "contractual" fusion with the object. Fantasy is the central motivating force for and prerequisite to the establishment of a "binding contract" between the narcissist-masochist and partner, and this is the basis for the continued viability of the subject's depleted narcissism. There is asymmetry between sadism and masochism, in that sadism stands for the active negation of the mother and inflation of the father, whereas masochism proceeds by a twofold disavowal—a positive, idealizing disavowal of the mother and an invalidating disavowal of the father (by expelling him from the mental representational system). Masochistic passivity seeks to secure a narcissistic solution to the impact of the superego on the ego through the creation of a new ego-ideal in the form of a mother who lacks nothing, including a phallus, thereby affirming abolition of the father and the rejection of sexuality (Deleuze & Sacher-Masoch, 1989). Alec's separation-individuation crisis produced, in my view, a pathological narcissistic resolution of this type. Identification and compliance with his mother precluded surrender to a state of infantile dependence. Disavowal, thrall, and the self-negating security of fantasies of fusion and parthenogenesis were substituted for the inauguration of an alive self. As a result, the growth of that part of the ego that leads to a sense of personal identity never properly proceeded. Alec's narcissism was originally a rejection of the object but it was also a means of retaining it in fantasy.

Alec's goldfish bowl dream could be said to reflect this situation. He is an imprisoned goldfish going round in circles in identification with his mother's narcissism, submission, and cannibalism. He is identified in fantasy with a (contained) goldfish and, by reversal, with a (containing) bowl, the two inseparable and codependent. I discussed the goldfish dream with Alec later in the analysis. His remarks indicated that he had taken possession of his mother in identification with her and later had appropriated his father's role. He became a big fish in a little pond. Efforts to understand the negation by Alec of his brother led me to think that the goldfish in the bowl also signaled, ominously, the arrival of the new baby inside mother, an event which occurred at the time of Alec's withdrawal from life. It is questionable whether the arrival of the child, for which Alec was completely unprepared, produced unmanageable envy and jealousy. Interpretations of envy and jealousy had little effect for a long time, because Alec disavowed psychologically the very existence of his brother. To feel envy and jealousy one must first register that the other person exists. For Alec, the presence of his brother was of physical but no psychological significance. I felt that the goldfish dream and the image of the bowl he bought for his mother on his travels pointed to a prior crisis that precluded reaction to his brother, but also included it. Did Alec, faced with a developmental vacuum, embrace and avow the pain of his and his mother's emptiness in order to endow life with meaning, including by creating, among other things, an "empty/full" symbol of his predicament, reflected in the image of the bowl and his omnipotent, "thick-skinned" and collapsed, "thin-skinned" states? The versatile image of the bowl could conceivably represent a shell-like defense or elementary container for the parthenogenetic fantasy authored by Alec and his mother, in that it became a counterfeit emblem of wholeness used to help forestall the threat of psychic dissolution.

The compelling feature of Alec's analysis has been my need to attend assiduously to countertransference experiences and to the slow piecing together of transference communications concealed by a veil of defenses, particularly splitting and projective identification. It was necessary to endure prolonged periods of confusion and uncertainty for psychoanalysis to become possible. At the point when genuine, sustained dialogue was established, Alec underwent a further serious negative therapeutic reaction, which, at the time of writing, remains unresolved.* The degree of difficulty in making contact with Alec raises important questions regarding our theory of technique in the treatment of patients who suffer primitive disturbances of the ego leading to chronic withdrawal. Enquiry is needed into the forms of fantasy that dominate the ego's unconscious relations with the object, and the consequences of this for affective experience, deformation of object contact, and developmental arrest. Only with this detailed information, and under appropriate conditions, can these patients realize their unconscious aim of negotiating with internal objects a sense of their separateness.

---

* Alec's self-destructiveness asserted itself unexpectedly and more powerfully than at any previous time when, after becoming much more able to talk to me, he found himself being drawn into a debate with certain friends and his wife over whether or not psychoanalysis actually worked. Coincidentally, his wife had been offered the prospect of relocation to another country to take up a highly paid position with an international advertising agency. This situation created a painful conflict of loyalties in Alec. The circumstances combined to lead him to feel that, in order to deal with the confusion, he "must" somehow end his analysis and encourage his wife's career move. Without discussing it with me in any great depth, he enacted his decision and stopped coming. However, after a year he subsequently contacted me and returned, in a very distressed state, to talk about how unhappy he had felt. But he has not resumed his analysis. It remains to be seen whether he will be able to overcome this latest crisis, in which I am left holding the baby of projected curiosity.

REFERENCES

Bateman, A. W. (1998). Thick- and thin-skinned organizations and enactment in borderline and narcissistic disorders. *International Journal of Psychoanalysis*, 79, 13–25.

Bion, W. (1967). *Second thoughts*. London: Maresfield Reprints.

Britton, R. (1998). *Belief and imagination*. London: Routledge.

Cooper, A. M. (1988). The narcissistic masochistic character. In R. A. Glick & P. I. Meyers (Eds.), *Masochism: Current psychoanalytic perspectives* (pp. 117–138). Hillsdale, NJ: Analytic Press.

Cooper, A. M., & Sacks, M. H. (1991). Sadism and masochism in character disorder and resistance (panel report). *Journal of the American Psychoanalytic Association*, 39, 215–226.

Deleuze, G., & Sacher-Masoch, L. (1989). *Masochism: Coldness and cruelty* (J. McNeil, Trans.). New York: Zone Books.

Ferro, A. (2001). *From the tyranny of the superego to the democracy of affects: The transformational transit in the psychic apparatus of the analyst*. Paper delivered at the European Federation of Psychoanalysis Conference, Madrid.

Fonagy, P., Moran, G. S., Edgecumbe, R., Kennedy, H., & Target, M. (1993). The roles of mental representations and mental processes in therapeutic action. *Psychoanalytic Study of the Child*, 48, 9–48.

Freud, S. (1919). A child is being beaten: A contribution to the study of the origin of sexual perversions. In J. Strachey (Ed. & Trans.), *The standard edition of the complete psychological works of Sigmund Freud* (Vol. 17). London: Hogarth Press.

Hanly, M. A. (Ed.) (1995). *Essential papers on masochism*. New York: New York University Press.

Jackson, M., & Williams, P. (1994). *Unimaginable storms: A search for meaning in psychosis*. London: Karnac.

Kernberg, O. F. (1988). Clinical dimensions of masochism. In R. A. Glick & P. I. Meyers (Eds.), *Masochism: Current psychoanalytic perspectives* (pp. 61–80). Hillsdale, NJ: Analytic Press.

Klein, M. (1952). Some theoretical conclusions regarding the emotional life of the infant. In *The writings of Melanie Klein, vol. 3* (pp. 61–93). London: Hogarth Press.

Pao, P. N. (1977). *Schizophrenic disorders*. New York: International Universities Press.

Rosenfeld, H. (1987). *Impasse and interpretation*. London: Tavistock.

Simons, R. C. (1987). Psychoanalytic contributions to psychiatric nosology: Forms of masochistic behavior. *Journal of the American Psychoanalytic Association*, 35, 583–608.

Steiner, J. (1993). *Psychic retreats*. London: Routledge.

Stolorow, R. (1975). The narcissistic function of masochism (and sadism). *International Journal of Psychoanalysis*, 56, 441–448.

Williams, P. (1998). Psychotic developments in a sexually abused borderline patient. *Psychoanalytic Dialogues*, 8, 459–491.

Winnicott, D. W. (1958). *Collected papers*. New York: Basic Books.

Chapter 3

Psychotic developments in a sexually abused borderline patient*

Prior to referral for analysis, Ms. B, age 40, was assessed by an experienced analyst in whom she confided her crippling, lifelong feelings of depression and loneliness. During a painful assessment the analyst made a simple statement that has stayed with the patient: "You seem to have no people in your mind." By this I believe the analyst meant that no good object of either gender had been internalized. Ms. B's subsequent analysis has shown this to be largely the case. This chapter seeks to show how Ms. B's capacity for sustaining object relationships has been severely compromised by unresolved immature identifications, the origins of which lie in her early relation with her mother. It also shows how an ensuing, profoundly damaging incestuous relationship with her father was constructed on the basis of her disturbed identifications with her mother. I shall describe Ms. B's borderline pathology and the significance of anorexia nervosa in it. Ms. B has been diagnosed psychiatrically as suffering from a paranoid psychosis, to which she remains vulnerable. A pathological narcissistic organization (cf. Rosenfeld, 1964, 1971), to which the patient has given the name the "Director," and through which her psychosis found expression, has controlled much of her mental life leading her to try to take her life on a number of occasions. The difficulties involved in analyzing the transference in such a disturbed patient led to certain modifications in technique, which I shall describe. Finally, I consider whether the patient's shifting identifications and difficulties in distinguishing between fact, memory, and fantasy constitute a discernible pattern or syndrome.

In trying to orient myself in a mass of complex material, I was influenced significantly by the work of Henri Rey on double-identification in anorexia nervosa and claustro-agoraphobia. This work, a development of Klein's observations on projective identification, refers to a type of fixation in the mother-infant dyad which leaves the adult prone to regress in relationships

* This chapter originally appeared as a paper in *Psychoanalytic Dialogues*, 8, 1998, 459–491. It was awarded the Rosenfeld Clinical Essay Prize by the British Psychoanalytical Society. Reprinted with permission.

in such a way as to experience him- or herself as both a baby relating vora-
ciously to a mother, and at the same or other times as the mother exposed
to the baby's attacks. A turning in fear and frustration from the mother to
the father occurs in early life as a consequence of this fixation, and this is
expressed symbolically as a failure to differentiate breast or nipple from
penis, leading to associated disturbances of function (cf. Rey, 1994). Prior
to her analysis, Ms. B had exploited her psychotic pathology in an unusual
choice of career. She was an operational member of a branch of military
security. She was frequently required to pursue and confront dangerous
males and to witness scenes of mutilation and carnage. In carrying out this
work she has had little hesitation in placing herself at risk of injury or even
death. Her abilities were held in high regard by her senior officers.

HISTORY

Ms. B is the middle child of a working class couple from the North of
England. Her parents are, at the time of writing, alive in their 70s. She
has older and younger brothers by 18 months and 5 years, respectively—
Ian and Anthony. She described her childhood as bleak and affectionless.
She feels she had no relationship to speak of with her mother, who was so
enamored of her first child that she rejected Ms. B, pushing her onto the
father. The father appears to have resented the attention paid by his wife
to their son, Ian, whom he treated badly. The boy suffered a depressive
breakdown in his teens. Ms. B's impression of her mother is of a fragile,
narcissistic woman, and of her father as alternately paranoid and ill-tem-
pered and charming. Ms. B's hatred of her unavailable mother conveys the
quality of an *idée fixe*—a consuming, unremitting grievance unamenable
to interpretation. The atmosphere at home seems to have been one of con-
trived normality and emotional impoverishment. The children were told
that they were loved and that theirs was a happy family. Ms. B appears to
have had some happy moments with her father. She has memories of walks
in the countryside with him as a little girl. No criticisms were permitted
at home, especially of mother, and any fuss was, according to Ms. B, pun-
ished by the father who beat the children. During Ms. B's first 3 years of
life, her father, a builder, spent time working away from home. This left
Ms. B, her mother, and her brother Ian alone together. Ms. B feels that she
was excluded by her mother and Ian from the start, and took to playing
on her own while clandestinely studying them. At some point she began to
experience them, and others, staring and laughing at her. At such times she
wished she could turn to her father. Her mother then became pregnant with
Anthony and Ms. B took to hiding in the under-stairs cupboard space ("to
get away from their stares," she said) where she developed an elaborate fantasy life. She has disclosed that since making the under-stairs cupboard her

"home" as a child, she has experienced uncertainty as to whether people she speaks to are real or are part of her fantasy world. In her isolation, she constructed a grandiose fantasy: a family romance in which she lived on a country estate adjoined by another. Her parents had been killed in a car crash. Her upper-class neighbors had two sons, Peter and David, who were her friends. They shared adventures such as horse riding, rambling, and "special assignments" in which she accompanied Peter on missions to free hostages or capture bad people. These forays could make David jealous. On her missions, Ms. B could be male or female or neither. Two further fantasies arose as she became, I think, more isolated and psychotic. She developed friendly relations with creatures from outer space who promised her they would come and take her away. This gave her hope, but she could not allow herself to go with them as she didn't know where they would take her. At this time (she was aged 5) she complained to her father of a high-pitched ringing in her ears. After several weeks of this she was taken to the doctor who found nothing amiss, physiologically. The patient wanted to tell the doctor, but was unable to, that the noise was, in fact, the creatures trying to make contact with her. A final, more pervasive fantasy has been that she is a famous actress managed by an ominous, protective, pimp-like figure who was to feature prominently in her analysis as a pseudohalluci-nation—the "Director."

On the basis of Ms. B's account and my transference and countertrans-ference experiences, which I shall describe, I came to a view that Ms. B may well have been sexually abused from about the age of 5, at or around the time of the birth of the third child although I could never be certain about this. It seemed possible that the father, feeling excluded by his wife caring for a newborn baby, took Ms. B into his bed and persuaded her to masturbate him. This occurred irregularly, from Ms. B's accounts, and was interrupted by her father's trips away. These absences left Ms. B feeling abandoned. By the time Ms. B was 7 she recounted that she was masturbat-ing and fellating her father in his living room armchair while her mother was out with baby Anthony. If Ms. B did not feel like obliging her father, she said that he persuaded her with flattery, or if this failed he became angry and occasionally hit her until she complied. She has confided that he inserted the handle of a hairbrush into her vagina when she cried, to make her feel better. The father is said to have attempted vaginal and anal intercourse without success, but from what I have learned full intercourse may have occurred at around 10 and could have continued perhaps until the age of 14, at which time Ms. B, fearing pregnancy, insisted that sexual contact stop. When feeling abandoned by her father, or when lonely while he was away working, Ms. B has indicated that she would masturbate with a fantasy of her father, or of a queue of men, waiting to have sex with her. As an adult, intense affects associated with loss have been erotized and infused with violence, and until recently she has been compelled to find men to masturbate or to mistreat her sexually. At school, Ms. B was passively aggressive and withdrawn, teased, and occasionally bullied. She has said she was overweight and by puberty seems to have developed a pronounced anorexic tendency, dieting, wearing a large coat, and refusing to shower naked with other girls. She insisted on wearing a towel in the shower to avoid being seen. She was deeply confused and ashamed by the changes taking place in her body. By 16 she was masturbating schoolboys, an activity which made her feel wanted, and by 18 a pronounced anorexic-bulimic cycle had set in. Academically, her achievements at school were negligible when contrasted with her intelligence, which is high.

Relations between Ms. B and her parents deteriorated progressively in her teens. Having broken off sexual contact (whether real, imaginary, or both) with her father, she believed he became extremely strict, opposed to her seeing boyfriends and controlling her life because he could not tolerate the thought of another man having a relationship with her. At the same time, relations with her mother were so estranged that when Ms. B thought of her it brought to mind images of her mother with her older brother and these ignited unmanageable jealousy and hatred. For many years she was excessively protective of her younger brother, maintaining a fantasy that he was her baby by her father. Occasionally she lost her temper and beat him. Ms. B left home at 18 and went to France, where she worked in cafés and restaurants. She had sadomasochistic relationships with uncommitted or aggressive men until she fell for Antoine, a car mechanic, who seems to have cared for her. Her schizoid functioning made Antoine's demands for emotional intimacy intolerable, and after a few months he announced that he was to be engaged to a girl from his village. Ms. B, distraught and relieved, returned to England where she took a job as a security guard, work that bore a resemblance to her childhood daydreams. She then applied for a position with the armed forces, was accepted, and was eventually placed in intelligence fieldwork. She was effective in tracking down political and civil lawbreakers, commanding a certain awe, if not respect, from her colleagues for her fearlessness. It was not unusual for her to be confronted by guns or explosives, or to witness woundings and deaths. During her work Ms. B became friendly with a minor criminal whom she married. The relationship deteriorated into sadomasochistic brutality, with Ms. B being assaulted and beaten. She has told me that she required her husband to hit her in the stomach, "to kill the crying baby in there," as she put it. They produced no children, although she arranged for the abortion of two pregnancies early in the marriage. They divorced shortly after she entered analysis.

Accounts of a seemingly objective history such as this one, provided by extremely disturbed patients suffering florid fantasies often of a hysterical type, are extremely difficult for the analyst to verify, to say the least. Can one believe anything such a person says, and if so, to what extent and in what sense? Only over a prolonged period can the consistency and detail of the accounts be assessed, and even then, distinguishing between fact and fantasy remains, in my view, an ongoing, ultimately unresolvable problem. In Ms. B's case I was eventually left in little doubt as to the essential truth of many of the facts reported here, but the overriding "truth" of her statements laid, for me, more in the transference and countertransference experiences of the sessions that depicted her traumatic internal situation.*

ANALYSIS

My initial meeting with Ms. B was unsettling, as she was anxious to the point of incoherence. She wore dark, masculine clothes (the same as, I was to discover, those "worn by the Director") and large sunglasses. She stood before me shaking, clipped a beeper to her belt and asked, "Where do you want me?" I replied that she was free to talk from wherever she liked. She could stand, or use the couch or the chair, but as she seemed to be feeling anxious, perhaps the chair might feel more comfortable. She responded compliantly and told me about herself, as though reading from a newspaper article. Her isolation, unhappy marriage, and feelings of helplessness were recounted with no trace of emotion. A moment of apparent distress overtook her when she let slip, "My father kissed me once." She quickly dismissed the statement, saying that what had happened with him was a harmless lapse. Towards the end of the meeting she again momentarily appeared to drop her falseness, becoming aggressively seductive: "They are all men in my unit," she remarked scornfully. "I am the only woman. I can handle men. Women are scared of me." Transferentially, I thought that this display of tough independence might have something to do with her being about to leave; otherwise, our first meeting was intense, enigmatic, and disconcerting. So split and massively projecting did I experience Ms. B to be that I felt that interpretations that went beyond acknowledging her initial, extreme anxieties might be felt as an assault likely to persecute or excite her. In the early stages of the analysis I proceeded by trying to establish an atmosphere in which a space might be created for tolerance of the fear and latent violence which beset her, and which might facilitate her telling me something about herself.

---

* In attempting the extremely difficult task of distinguishing between fact and fantasy, I think it is important when dealing with schizophrenic or borderline patients to study the precise, even uncanny ways in which they select their object or part-objects, into which they proceed to projectively identify. To separate the behavior of the object who is doing certain acts or responding in specific ways, from the alike projections into that person becomes a highly complex problem. It is analogous to dreaming—only when we wake up is the reality of the situation restored, or at least we hope so. In psychosis it becomes difficult if not impossible to separate delusions and hallucinations from reality. Addressing this confusion in Ms. B has been a central problem in her analysis.

I think it is important to stress that Ms. B did not behave at any time in the way one might have expected an analytic patient to behave, until perhaps comparatively late in the analysis. The ideal working model of "interpretation-response" cannot be achieved with such a patient (perhaps not with any patient) for a long time, if ever. My comments went ignored, at least outwardly, for years. Most of her dreams remained unexamined, comprising as they did unmediated expressions of primary process about which she could not think. And acting out dominated the treatment. The sessional material from which I shall quote represents certain moments of more candid engagement. More often I was reduced to confusion and silence by her dismissals of me, and to querying in vain her transferential state from seemingly incomprehensible utterances and my own chaotic experience of sitting with her. Any *post hoc* coherence this paper might convey should not minimize the perplexities and confusions that suffused the analysis, which, at the time of writing, is in its 7th year. One might legitimately ask: Why consider such a patient for analysis in the first place? Despite many misgivings, both the assessor and I felt that her request for help was serious, and more importantly that her distress was accessible. However, I had little confidence in our prospects, although as things have turned out the patient has done better than one could have expected. How and why this has happened became important for me to understand.

During the first 3 months of analysis Ms. B talked in her newspaper reporting style, and I learned a good deal of what was conveyed as fact. This was interrupted by what I took to be a number of references to sexual abuse, although it would be 3 years before I would succeed in any serious exploration of these with her. For example, her analysis was to be kept a secret from work. Her superior officer must not find out as she would be sure to be discharged (even though her employers in real life accepted that she was in analysis). She felt nervous about having analysis with a man. It made her want to cry. On hearing that she had entered analysis, her father had taken her aside and said, "Your illness might have something to do with what happened between you and me when your brother was born." There were further statements on the theme of the need to keep secrets concealed. Alongside these arose, immediately, severe difficulties with weekend and holiday breaks. Ms. B's initial solution was to write me innumerable letters assuring me of the value of analysis. Attempts to explore this behavior proved futile. They abated only when more serious acting-out supervened. She experienced my statements about her separation problems as either narcissistic demands or as rebukes. She was unable to regard me as capable of empathic understanding. Unconsciously, her dependence on the analysis and outrage at its frustrations had drawn her into acting out, and this became increasingly masochistic (e.g., missed sessions, excitedly placing herself in danger at work, etc.).

After 8 months or so she reported the following dream: "I am being fed. A hand then slaps me across the face hard. Then I am on a terrorist exercise, rolling down a hill clutching a male officer. We fall off a cliff or shelf." It was possible to briefly discuss the dream with her, which was unusual as she was unable to think about her dreams despite dreaming prolifically. Her associations were to feelings that something catastrophic was going to happen, and to the excitement she felt when on dangerous military exercises. I felt that she was communicating, in the transference, a sense of loss of the breast, followed by an incestuous solution. I said to her I thought that for her to take something from me in her analysis gave rise to feelings of disaster, which simply had to be prevented. Although I thought she needed help, and that was what analysis was for, she had little or no hope that her needs could be met. For several minutes her anxieties seemed to abate and she appeared to think about what I'd said. She told me calmly that she had never relied on anybody and that to do so was bad. Her anxieties then returned and she appeared to no longer be able to think. Two further themes became prominent at this time. One was a complaint that her mother had given her elder brother Ian more food when they were children. Her tone was one of unspeakable injustice. The other was an expression of triumph as, for example, when she told me of an army psychiatrist with a Welsh name who had been drafted in during an assignment and with whom she had worked well, once she had shown him the ropes. I felt that her principal injury—deprivation in her primary relationship—and its incestuous, sadomasochistic solution had, transferentially, surfaced in earnest. From this point on she no longer missed sessions. I became an object of curiosity and idealization, while her violent and perverse inner life was acted out. She instituted a divorce against her husband, apparently seduced men, and took such operational risks as to provoke reprimand by her superior officers. She had once told me how, in her childhood fantasies, she, Peter, and David had used special code words to organize their adventures. Now, on a recent real-life assignment, she had become temporarily confused between her private fantasy codes and the real-life military operational codes, creating near-disaster for herself and her colleagues.

By the middle of the second year she had become convinced, on the advice of the Director, that she was being trailed by assassins and that the woman who lived next door to her hated her, "because I [Ms. B] am an individual" (meaning a person with her own opinions which could not be tolerated). For several days she brought to her sessions—in reality—a disabled friend whom she insisted was in a suicidal state and installed her in the waiting room, while Ms. B, in tears, angrily assured me of her own sanity and goodwill, and that she desperately needed her analysis to succeed. This is an extract from a session at the time:

P: You don't understand. My mother never understood me. When my grandmother was dying, she was very old, I tried to give her the kiss of life. I was breathing into her. I was trying to get her heart going. My mother thought I was hurting her. I wasn't. I wanted to keep her alive, not die. She didn't understand, she just didn't understand. You don't understand. [*Cries, pause*] You're trying to kill me. [*Angry*]

A: I think you may be hearing a voice that tells you that I will collapse and die if you make any demands on me. This makes you afraid that if you and I carry on with your analysis something terrible will happen, even perhaps that we will both die.

P: [*Pause, calmer*]: But it is true, isn't it? People don't like people, they don't, do they? Nobody wants an individual. They can't cope with an individual. That is what happened to me. I wasn't an individual. It's the only thing I know. [*Long pause*] My mother didn't understand me. [*Pause*] You're going to stop my analysis. I know it. [*Shouts angrily*]

P: I think that something in your mind is telling you that I can't stand you, and that I will reject you like you have told me your mother did. I think you are upset and you want me to understand how afraid and angry you feel, but you are being prevented from telling me about it. All this makes you feel confused.

P: I feel confused. [*Pause, cries*] I don't feel well. The Director tells me I'm fine. I don't feel fine. I want to be in the hospital. Everything's going wrong and I don't know why. What's wrong with me? I don't know what to do. Please help me.

A: I realize that you need help but the Director in your mind says that your needs don't matter, and that if you show me how unwell you feel this will destroy me because I am weak. So you push me away, even though you need to talk to me.

P: I think I know what you mean. He says that I don't need help, I'm fine. I feel sick ... I want to vomit. [*Pause*] There's no other way. [*Pause*] When people get too near I want to vomit. People take you over, you see. I don't want you to misunderstand me. I know you understand me. You do understand me.

A: I wonder, when you feel that I do understand something about you, you feel that something bad is happening inside you, which you must stop.

P: That's sexual. It's wrong. I'm sorry. I don't want you to misunderstand me. [*Cries*] I worry all the time that you might misunderstand me. Nothing must go wrong this time.

One way of understanding these anxieties is as an expression of depressive guilt leading her to self-destructively act out in order to protect me from her overwhelming impulses. She feared that emotional closeness would destroy me, and thus her. Yet what interested me about this and other, similar sessions was a discovery that when the psychotic voice which influenced her was interpreted in a simple way as an autonomous, frantic outbreak of concern (no matter how destructive), which erupted in the transference without warning at times of acute paranoia, seemingly to protect her from the consequences of having her needs met, Ms. B felt relieved and momentarily coherent, prior to being re-advised by her psychotic personality of my unreliability and malevolence. This way of understanding and interpreting her transference anxieties had certain implications for technique, which I discuss below; the principal of which was the need to understand that the thoughts of the psychotic personality present when Ms. B was in my room were distinct from those of my patient. Her understanding of my final comment as being sexual seemed to relate to her experiencing making emotional contact as the same as engaging in sexual activity. At other times contact could be equated with a threat of death or as the death of me or of someone else. Shortly after the above session Ms. B began to cut herself lightly on her arms. She took a nonfatal overdose and a month later jumped from a moving train as it entered a station, injuring her leg. This behavior was a prelude to a period of highly destructive acting out as her paranoid psychosis asserted itself, and which could not be contained by interpretation. Certain dreams drew attention to the crisis:

> There was a baby bird in a nest with its beak open. It was starving. Nobody came to feed it. I watch it die. I am crying.

> A minibus crashes through the front of a food store. There is a huge explosion. My older brother helpfully leads people away. There are many dead pregnant women. I touch the stomach of one but there is no life. Tins of food are embedded in people's faces. They are missing arms and legs. The manager says, "We carry on, we stay open." I desperately try to stop him but can't.

> I am lying on a bed surrounded by cut-up fetuses. I can't look at them because they are parts of the devil.

> I am waiting in a doctor's waiting room. There are other patients waiting. You come out, look around smiling and call me into your consulting room. You take your trousers down and tell me to suck your penis. There is shit on the end, but I have to do it.

Ms. B was unable to associate to these dreams. It is probable that what is being depicted in them concerns an extremely deprived child, perhaps with a mother who was unable to contain her child's murderous aggression (lacking in Bion's alpha-function) and there is portrayed a perverse experience with a man. Yet their meaning is far from transparent. The dream data are close to primary process. The condensation of imagery (e.g., conflation of penis-breast-anus) and absence of symbolic elaboration, together with little or no secondary process, confirm that they are psychotic experiences. In the first dream, how identified has Ms. B become with the person who does not intervene, as well as with the starving, dying bird? In the food store dream, is she communicating confusion between reality and fantasy, as well as murderous wishes against siblings? She believes her projections destroy people, yet a store manager is saying, "We carry on, we stay open." Does she think he is undamaged by her attacks, or is he denying terrible suffering? What kind of person does she think her analyst is? Affective contact seemed to be felt by her to annihilate a vulnerable and rejecting mother-analyst—a situation felt by the patient to have been omnipotently created by herself. At the same time murderous, perverse, and suicidal fantasies consumed and persecuted her. This impossible conflict gave rise to manic states in which, in reality, she attended religious or other public meetings and denounced them in favor of psychoanalysis, until she was thrown out. She tried to give away her life savings, and to buy her local village hall to turn it into an orphanage. She attempted to visit orphans in Romania. She bought baby clothes, took to waiting outside nursery schools, and on one occasion was overwhelmed by an impulse to abduct a child and was deterred only by the arrival of the child's mother. The weekend breaks from analysis were experienced as too long, leading to instructions by the Director to kill herself. In view of the increasing self-harm, I encouraged her to see her GP and area hospital psychiatrist with a view to receiving appropriate medication so that her analysis could continue. A hospital bed was to be made available should it prove necessary in the future.*

Her basic functioning improved with the containment provided by medication, in this case lithium. Whereas Ms. B had for 18 months sat in the chair, she now expressed a wish to use the couch. She experienced panic that "a man will see through me" or that she would be attacked with a knife. She covered the lower half of her body with a rug and held her head, as though anticipating blows. Intermittently she brought into sessions a pillow, towels, toys, a kitchen knife, and razor blades. The references she made to these indicated that they served as either comforters or protectors.

---

* I was fortunate in receiving the support of Ms. B's GP and her psychodynamically oriented hospital psychiatrist who provided inpatient treatment when needed, as well as outpatient care. Without their involvement the analysis could not have continued. This kind of support is, I believe, a prerequisite for the psychoanalysis or psychotherapy of a severe borderline or psychotic patient. However, even though I felt that no alternative to medication presented itself in the case of Ms. B, I am unsure in retrospect if the decision to propose it to her was a wise one. Medication given to help the analysis can have complex consequences over and above any pharmacological benefit. Patients may become convinced that the analyst cannot stand their pathology, and therefore has to resort to medicines. The pills are then taken ultimately for the analyst's benefit. More seriously, pills given to help can be turned into weapons of death. Such abuse can constitute a devastatingly destructive attack on the analyst and the analysis. Soon after commencing her medication, which helped her, Ms. B embarked upon a series of very serious self-destructive acts using her pills. I am unsure as to whether the suggestion of medication acted as a provocation to a part of Ms. B's mind, which then seized upon the opportunity to attack the analysis, or whether the ensuing acting out would have occurred anyway.

This was not simple to understand, as the knife could be experienced as a comforter due to the promise of relief offered by cutting and suicide. Notwithstanding these fears, she was able to tell me of past times with a schoolteacher who had shown kindness to her, and of some happy moments with her grandmother, in addition to her customary, harrowing accounts of persecution. Her benign memories generated anguish and she found it difficult to finish her sessions. She complained, "My bleep goes off outside," and "Men touch me up when I'm not here." A dream seemed to depict the dangers of dependency:

> I am walking along a country lane. A mangled baby, half-human, half-animal, is lying dying in the lane. I see a beautiful woman in a garden and go and ask her for help. She can't hear me. I go back to get the baby but suddenly a huge, black lorry comes towards me, filling the lane. I don't make it to the baby.

Her associations to the dream indicated a yearning for a good mother, which she believed could never be fulfilled. In addition, she thought that the baby she could not reach might have been herself or one of her brothers. She felt that she had died as a child. I said that I thought she felt she had never been allowed to have a mother. She now felt the same with me, that she could never have me, and this made her feel frustrated, angry, and desperate.

THE "DIRECTOR"

Overt communication by the "Director"—the executive expression of her paranoid psychosis—emerged as problems of separation became intolerable. Initially I was told of his influence outside the sessions. For example, he told her that she must sit immobile on the floor of her bathroom at weekends and neither eat nor go to the lavatory. By assuming a catatonic posture, the woman who lived next door would be stopped from coming through the walls and killing her. She hallucinated bulges in the walls. The Director said they were the neighbor trying to get in. She associated the bulges to the shape of a pregnant belly. The Director, located in the same room as the patient and experienced as some feet away from her, eventually appeared in the consulting room as a pseudohallucinated figure standing by the door or sitting in the chair at my desk, issuing compelling instructions. These were, for example:

> "He (your analyst) is rubbish. Chat him up and have sex."
> "You (Ms. B) are a famous actress. Everything is wonderful."
> "They want to take you over and kill you. Swallow all your tablets now."

Depending upon her anxiety levels Ms. B could feel overwhelmed and sub-sumed by the Director, forced to obey him like a compliant child or respond as to a lover. She could not resist his communications. In one sense I had no patient to talk to, but rather a set of shifting identifications over which she had little control. This posed technical problems: I came to realize that if Ms. B was to be able to understand my interpretations of her psychotic pathology, it was necessary for me to understand that the Director figure appeared to function independently of my patient's thoughts or wishes. His paranoid-schizoid responses controlled her thoughts and behavior accord-ing to specific, concrete wishes. His statements were automatic, immediate, totalizing, omniscient, and required no thinking on my patient's part. They were symbolic equations of pure economy. This psychotic organizer pro-vided instantaneous, unfailing responses whenever Ms. B engaged in human relating, an activity which "he knew" with fundamentalist certainty was irrelevant. "He" ensured that she adopted his views by insisting that she would be destroyed by other people if she didn't. Compelling scripts were repeated which immobilized her thinking and evoked ritualized behavior leading to isolation and, ultimately, despair. The scripts were also trans-ference communications of her incarceration. The patient's difficulties in using transference interpretations necessitated the communication of *both* her psychotic and nonpsychotic transference states to her in any transfer-ence interpretation.

As a result of this work with Ms. B, and with other severely disturbed patients, I have come to appreciate the significance of separating analyti-cally these two phenomena—the psychotic personality, which acts asym-bolically, and the personality capable of symbolization and thinking. Often, the psychotic personality is so influential as to be assumed to *be* the patient's personality, a confusion that can reduce the patient to despair. In Ms. B's case, analysis of these personalities and their relationship in the transference led to her gradually becoming able to think about and express verbally the meaning of her psychosis and its impact on her sanity. For example, on the occasions when she was able to tolerate and observe an upsurge of psychotic disparagement of me, a space might be created to explore its meaning, aims, and methods. This was for a long time the only way it was possible to interpret psychotic paranoid anxieties in the transference. Later, as splitting and projective activity decreased, more con-ventional transference interpretations became possible. The Director's out-bursts were recognizable as ruthless interventions purporting to guarantee Ms. B safety in the face of perceived threats to her life, even if saving her necessitated suicide. Close scrutiny revealed that what was in fact taking place was a repeated convulsion of outrage by a psychotic mind violently opposed to any activity different from its own. Ms. B's psychotic person-ality intervened in anything *not already reduced to a symbolic equation*, the aim being to assert a psychotically conservative *status quo* in which an illusion of self-sufficiency was maintained through the use of fantasy objects. For me to have made transference interpretations that required Ms. B to subsume her psychotic transference anxieties via a superordinate ego or rational self, would have been to make unrealistic psychological demands on her leading to compliance. This would also have rendered transference interpretations meaningless.

The coexistence of psychotic and nonpsychotic personalities has been described by a number of analysts, Bion in particular. In my opinion, these coexisting personalities in the psychotic person need to be analyzed as distinct phenomena, if impasse is to be avoided. To try by interpretation to reduce one to the other or to pursue premature attempts at integration can give rise to annihilation anxiety, unconscious guilt, and severe negative therapeutic reactions, not to mention a conviction that the analyst is insane and in need of the patient's help. I believe that the psychotic organization itself is not, in and of itself, modifiable, regardless of how much analysis is received. What seems to alter over time is its relationship to the patient's nonpsychotic personality, as a result of change and development in the latter. When the gulf between the two systems has been reduced and the patient's capacity for thinking can be reestablished, a nonparanoid interest in the status of the psychosis and of the patient's affective states may prevail. Ms. B seemed, in her own way, to be aware of these problems. She talked, brought dreams, and gave rudimentary associations in an effort to provide what she believed the analysis required, but was under continuous pressure from the Director to remain oblivious to their significance. This meant that she felt she had no alternative but to resort to attending to my apparent narcissistic needs, which seemed to mirror the loss of her relationship with her mother and her turning to satisfy her father's sexual and emotional demands. She would recount in a detached manner dreams that were vivid and often difficult to listen to. Occasionally their impact would reach her and she would clutch her body in pain, but generally she remained unable to think about them. The following dreams indicate some of her preoccupations after starting to use the couch:

A small male faun is lying on a bed, tied down. A telephone wire runs from its mouth through its body and out of its anus and limbs. Blood is spattered on the bed. I (Ms. B) am in the clouds, an angel looking down. The faun cannot be touched because it would cause too much pain.

My genitals are covered in maggots. Only my legs and the bottom half of my torso exist. The rest of me is missing.

A man comes up to me in a gym and talks sexily. Suddenly he becomes violent and sticks his fingers up my anus, threatening to kill me.

Ms. B found these dreams, which refer among other things to fears of sexual abuse, especially difficult to think about or talk about due to the degree of violence they evoked in her. A further obstacle was a fusional identification with an idealized mother-analyst. Acknowledgment of difference or separation generated unmanageable pain and hatred, which the Director advised could be resolved only by committing suicide. This was suggested when she thought reflectively or made emotional contact with me. His most frequent suggestion was that she cut her throat, in order to stop speaking. Any notion of progress in the analysis seemed to me to occur at moments when she was able to grasp, in the transference, that I was alive and remained interested in her. Depression and confusion followed these experiences. Unpredictable acts of sanity also occurred from time to time, including admitting in full her psychiatric condition to her employers, ceasing to drive her car for fear of killing herself or someone else, requesting a review of her medication as she felt increasingly ill, and confiding in me aspects of the sexual abuse. At the same time, alterations in her defenses could also be included in a broader, omnipotent fantasy of control over the analysis. After deciding to use the couch Ms. B explained, in stages, the Director's function, which was to protect her from being taken over and destroyed. She feared merging above all, a state of mind in which she was overwhelmed by the near-delusional experience that the other person would get into her food, face, legs, and stomach and want to eat or murder her. The Director would signal when he perceived these dangers. When the coast was clear he would invite her to enjoy manic and perverse gratifications as alternatives to object relationships. His scripts, reminiscent of her childhood fantasies but reworked for contemporary use, often included a dangerous person who would be vilified or destroyed in fantasy. The "famous actress" would be evoked and told to give a performance culminating with an imagined or enacted seduction or exhibitionistic act. Such theatrical confusion reflects how Ms. B evolved from a lonely, imaginative child into a woman with a hysterical psychosis in which fantasy could take over reality. The scripts ended according to the law of talion, with Ms. B retreating into a persecuted, claustrophilic state in a corner of her house contemplating suicide at the invitation of a solicitous Director. The Director's exhortations reached a peak 2 years or so into the analysis when, for about 12 months, Ms. B became increasingly psychotic. At weekends and during breaks she took airline flights to different parts of the world seeking out men for sex and female prostitutes whom she paid to cuddle her overnight. After these trips she would arrive at the consulting room confused and paranoid. On one occasion she recounted how she had consorted with the criminals she was employed to apprehend, although how true this was I do not know. After a trip during which she had "sought out a lady in Brussels who gave me an ice cream when I was little, but I couldn't find her," she returned home so depressed that her internal voice told her to kill herself. She obeyed, taking a near-lethal dose of lithium. She had sufficient sanity before passing out to phone for an ambulance, was taken to hospital, and thanks to the prompt action of the staff her life was saved. It was during this period that I was made to experience something of the violation of boundaries that I suspect Ms. B may have suffered as a child. So overwhelming was the Director's influence that I despaired of alteration to her core pathology. I felt I had no option but to continue to interpret to her that I thought she was trying desperately to preserve our relationship while being instructed to destroy it, in order to prevent a worse catastrophe, and that we were being prevented from talking about any of this. There were times when I felt convinced that I could no longer help her. I had no reason to believe that anything of value could proceed from this crisis, and I often feared for her life. I did not realize at that time that by continuing to interpret, I was responding to an unconscious need in her to make me bear certain primitive, infantile projections, particularly her partly-denied feelings of despair, in order that she could begin to work her way towards the construction of a mental space in which she might internalize the rudiments of dependency on an object. The genuineness or otherwise of this nascent internalization was of ongoing concern to me. Her psychotic personality dealt with feelings of abandonment and loss by slick adaptation. However, following this period there occurred only one further, mild overdose, which caused her to panic and rush to the hospital. Also, The Director's influence gradually seemed to alter, taking more the form of a war of attrition with Ms. B's infantile needs and depressive anxieties, rather than violent acting out. In hindsight, I had the impression that the influence of her psychotic personality had not decreased so much as had become proportionally less effectual as her identification with me and the analysis that had begun to develop.

In the ensuing and rather confusing fourth year of the analysis she seemed to become more able to think about and work with interpretations, while being assaulted by frequent attacks of psychotic anxiety. I attributed this development to her having experienced a certain amount of containment of her basic transference anxieties. The malignancy of her paranoia and its relationship to envy and jealousy began to be seen by her. Families, including fantasies of my own family, women with babies, and images of her mother with her older or younger brother evoked massive envy and murderous jealousy, which she began to talk about. The birth of her younger brother, which had precipitated her sleeping with her father at the age of 5, was at one point refracted through a memory of having been given a scarf by her father, which she wore continuously as a child. She recalled how she used to tighten it round her neck to induce a sense of being strangled. In her later sexual life strangulation had become a *motif*. As these paranoid and depressive anxieties became more conscious, impulses to steal, fears of being intruded upon, and other manifestations of her own invasive wishes emerged. She became preoccupied with break-ins—to houses, cars, and my consulting room, and to her mind and body. There occurred an increase in her sense of guilt and shame, particularly in relation to her envious, murderous, need-filled fantasies. An odd period of lying occurred when she attempted brazenly to manipulate her sessions. She declared that she had only ever said that she loved her brothers, denied saying things she had said minutes before, and stopped bringing dreams, insisting she was cured. Interpretation of her fear of exposure to her need for love, her greed, and the humiliation these could create gradually led to disclosure of a long-standing fantasy in which the Director assured her he could satisfy all her needs without exposing her sad or, above all, her loving feelings to anyone. Ms. B did not object to me knowing about this fantasy. In fact, she seemed to feel relieved whenever I interpreted the spurious aspects of her contact with me, even though to do so gave rise to further depressive anxieties. It was as though a desperate, sane part of her had remained alive and was saying, "This is all I can do. Please understand that and continue to try to help me."

The Director's overt involvement may have abated somewhat, but verbal outbursts of sexualized violence continued to be bellowed when he decided that merging threatened. Between these, low-level mutterings were designed to maintain an atmosphere of chronic suspicion. Ms. B began to make a number of more direct, heartfelt rejections of object relatedness, and these revealed unalloyed envy, fear, resentment, and anger, including towards me. The hatred she harbored against her mother became more conscious. For a time she became extremely upset that her former husband did not want her, even though they had been apart for years. It seemed that a weakening in her identification with her abusing father had begun to threaten her with isolation and despair, as the catastrophe of her primary attachment came to the fore. She suffered a recrudescence of anorectic symptoms and extensive bouts of eczema, in particular during breaks. Her ambivalence toward me increased markedly. As I became increasingly identified with her "bad" mother, so she instituted a mental search for her father. A dream illustrated this conflict:

> I was walking through thick mud with my mother. I left her to go to my father who was looking for his lost child. I get to a house, but the mud on my shoes is too heavy, and I can't walk up the stairs to my father.

We were able to begin discussing the hatred she bore against her mother and her turning to her father, and in so doing, the horror of the psychological murder of her mother and of her siblings, and its paranoid consequences, virtually overwhelmed her. Nightmares portrayed her and others as dead or paralyzed in wheelchairs. She dreamed of being murdered by gangs in retaliation for her badness, or of being turned into a skeleton or a rotting corpse. One day, in the midst of this torment, she expressed a tentative wish to talk to her mother, whom she had avoided for years. Over a period of several months she took to spending an hour or so with her at weekends, and her mother prepared meals for her. A dream followed:

> I am in a house like my own house with another woman. I think we like each other. I suggest that we go for a walk in the middle of the road, which is empty of traffic, each of us wearing our separate space suits.

She associated to a need for, fear of, and feelings of contempt for her mother and how confused these made her feel. Depressive feelings followed and gave rise to a series of nightmares in which she was stabbed in her stomach by her ex-husband. Although this violence terrified her, containing as it did her own projected rage, it did not prevent her from producing further dreams in which talks, walks, and arguments with her mother (or another woman) took place, often culminating in Ms. B trying to climb inside womb-like spaces. A further occurrence was an awareness of her isolation, and of her inability to do anything about it. It seemed that the bare beginnings of a perception of separation anxiety on a whole object basis had brought about an awareness of intense loneliness and need. The need for dependence on her mother and a reduction in the necessity for absolute compliance with the Director brought about a further period of extreme despair. This she endured without serious acting out. Her sessions seemed to comprise repeated attempts to articulate her infantile needs, only for these to be dissipated by destruction of her thinking, leaving her exhausted, depressed, and often driven compulsively in search of sex. I thought that the effects of the Director, although less violent, seemed to be more pervasive in that he now advised at every turn against having feelings or needs met, and I interpreted this as her transference response to needing me.

It had become fairly clear that she would be unable to continue with her military security work, as part of an overall regressive collapse—or perhaps, a progressive collapse of her falsity. Her employers agreed to her taking a desk job. Her demeanor became more timid and depressed and she experienced regular suicidal impulses, although these remained at the level of ideation only. Her transference behavior exposed more detailed splitting of her objects. A yearning for an ideal mother offering the physical and emotional contact she needed was contrasted by a dread of "lesbianism," which she felt would be the outcome of contact with another female. This was interwoven with familiar fantasies of usurping, abusing, and murdering her mother, her brother, and anyone who stood in her way. She could no longer find significant relief in perverse fantasies. She began dreaming of exposing an adult male psychopath to the authorities who would be shocked by his misdeeds and ensure that justice was done. This enabled me to talk with her about her growing recognition of her hatred for her father and her psychopathic tendencies projected into him (an ideal container for them) and into me. A confusional state regarding her parental objects prevailed, and as her depression deepened, conscious fear of loss of her objects grew. Past infantile defensive behavior reemerged: For a time she hid in corners and in cupboards. She tried to make contact with creatures from outer space by staring out of windows. She bought a quantity of second-hand shoes to comfort herself (the cupboard she hid in as a child contained the family's shoes). Nonetheless, her outward appearance had improved. She looked more ordinary and relaxed, although very distressed, compared with the gaunt, sinister figure I had first encountered. She was sleeping better and had begun to read, something she had avoided for years for fear of being taken over by the story (a concrete, almost literal fear of being consumed or eaten by a person, place, or thing illustrates the psychotic, as opposed to borderline, quality of her thinking). She had resumed contact with her brothers, and had become better able to deal with her new work colleagues. She also viewed the patients who came and went from my consulting room in a somewhat less paranoid way. Clearly she was beginning to project less of her internal world onto the external world, and to acknowledge her miserable, hate-filled childhood, including her confusion, envy, rage, and guilt toward her mother, and in increasing amounts toward her father and toward me. Until recently, the sadism of her father was mitigated by the narcissistic gratifications of the incestuous relationship. Her hatred had been reserved for her abandoning mother. I came to think that Ms. B displaced her rage towards her abusing father onto her mother for having failed to protect her, in order to avoid a state of objectlessness (the experience of believing that neither parent could love her). There is at least hope in attacking a recalcitrant mother who might change, whereas to confront the known but repressed knowledge that the father is the conscious agent of so serious a violation, *in addition to* a sense of loss of the mother, might be considered equivalent to psychological death. Latterly, her outrage towards her father has at times seemed to equal or exceed any of her murderous fantasies against her mother and siblings.

The mood of the analysis gradually seemed to take on a depressed, grief-stricken quality compared with its previous, often histrionic disturbances and distortions. Although functioning better in certain respects, Ms. B had become consciously far more unhappy and confused. Her anorexia, a symptom since the age of 17, took on an increasingly emotional rather than physical form, in that she became preoccupied with calculating the degree to which she was permitted contact with others. She was eating better and maintaining a normal weight. In the past she had often confined her eating to occasional potatoes and milk, whereas she now ate a range of foods, all vegetarian. She remained anxious about desserts, which, she said, overstimulated her appetite. Her sessions became characterized by expressions of bitterness, regret, and despair as she faced the many losses in her life. Hatred of her father and of me was accompanied by sexualization of needs and affects, sometimes to the point of demanding that I molest her when she was extremely angry with me. The overall direction of the analysis seemed to move into a long, painful struggle in which her mutilated, infantile, female self attempted to resume her arrested development. She committed herself to this task and has since begun to acquire a certain capacity to think and to reflect. Although attacks of paranoia are less frequent, she remains vulnerable to them and to states of depressive collapse, particularly around holidays. An extract from a Thursday session a few months ago illustrates an improved capacity to tolerate her affects, and something of a shift from paranoid to more symbolic thinking and depressive concern:

P: I did something stupid yesterday. I went to the hospital where Dr. X [*her psychiatrist*] works and parked my car near to hers. I kept thinking of just sitting next to her. We wouldn't be saying anything special, just chatting. I wanted to go in but I was afraid she wouldn't have the time to see me. I know she's busy. I went home. [*Cries*]

A: Perhaps knowing that she would find it difficult to see you without an appointment spared you from feeling that you were being too demanding.

P: I knew I probably couldn't see her. You see, as a child I was always told to be good, to never ask for anything, never cry. I wanted to sit with her, that's all. I like her. She's been good to me. I can't make demands on anybody. The only thing that ever counted at home was being well behaved. [*Angry*]

A: I think you have been made to feel that to be demanding here will disturb me, but I think the truth is that you do feel demanding and angry when I don't meet your needs.

P: Yes I do. You are a rotten analyst, you know. I don't think you care. You don't give me enough time. I want more time, I want to read your books, ask you things, but you don't let me ... I'm sorry [*cries, pause*] ... I remember there was a boy in primary school who complained and he got to play in the sand pit. I never said anything. I was good and got nothing. [*Angry*] My mother was always smiling. Even at the doctor's once when he found something wrong with her, she just kept on smiling. It's ridiculous. I do nothing and all I have is the empty. I can't stand the empty. I miss you so much sometimes. I feel so lonely. Oh, fuck off!

A: Fuck off?

P: The Director's telling me to fuck off. He wants me to be quiet, stop complaining. He doesn't want me to speak to you. It's difficult for me, you know. Don't take me literally ... I don't mean it. I do mean it but ... [*Pause*]

A: Perhaps you do mean what you say. You are upset and angry with me because of the way you feel I neglect you. The Director warns you against complaining because he says I can't take it or everything will be over. But I think you want me to listen to you when you want to tell me to fuck off.

P: I'm afraid you'll throw me out. I want to be demanding ... do what other people do. I see them outside you know; they just do simple things like talk to each other or have a cup of coffee. I want to know how to do that, I want to have a life instead of always having to be good and be on my own. I want to know what a psychotic is. There's a book on your shelf which says psychotic. What does it mean? [*Pause*] Is it a psychopath? [*Pause*]

A: You're not sure?

P: [*Pause*]: No ... no, I'm not sure, really. [*Cries*]

A: Perhaps you can see how much you need to find out why things have gone wrong, and why you have been unwell for so long.

DISCUSSION

Ms. B's early identification with her mother clearly miscarried, leading to vulnerability to psychosis. She experienced her mother as incapable of loving her, and this gave rise to extreme feelings of exclusion, hatred, envy, and jealousy. Her stated grievance consistently centered around food. A fixation in her development occurred based on a double-identification. After the birth of Anthony when she was 5, Ms. B seems to have felt rejected forever by her mother and turned in desperation to her father. She appears to have been encouraged in this by her mother, a frequent precursor to incest noted in a number of studies (Eisnitz, 1984; Herman & Schatzow, 1987; Price, 1993). Up until this point we can understand how, under normal circumstances, the father might have helped Ms. B with the difficult task of separating from her mother. Yet it is here that Ms. B's development underwent lasting further trauma. Her attempt to establish an alternative object relationship was vitiated by the incestuous tie, leaving her with no viable object relationship of either gender. The father came to represent, in Ms. B's mind, a breast in the form of a penis, which was to be masturbated and fellated. Father was a "penis-breast mother" ejaculating "semen-milk." This combined "penis-breast-mother-father" figure made actual relationships with father and mother, and the construction of good inner objects, impossible. Another way of describing the father is as a perverse transitional object, perceived as comforting but also exciting in a terrifying way. The relationship created absolute confusion of objects. Ms. B actively built up a daydream life around her confused identifications, involving contact with sexually exciting, occasionally dangerous males. Her later work in military security was based on her unsuccessful attempt to identify with her father. She became a "heroic man" fighting for and protecting the motherland. Ultimately, her identifications were neither male nor female, but rather a part-object confusion of both.

The clinical material reported earlier lends support to the view that Ms. B established a double-identification early in her development, with fateful consequences. A manifestation of this is that in a dependent situation she feels herself to be a dangerous baby who endangers her mother, and who is in turn endangered by the mother. Her anorexia denotes a wish to regress to a pre-oral state in order to avoid destroying the mother by eating. Dreams and sessions consistently referred to food. One dream showed a baby bird starving in a nest and nobody came. Another had her being forced to suck her analyst's penis, which had shit on it that she must eat. In the violent food store dream tins of food were embedded in people's faces. Could an image like this be an unconscious reference to what it might feel like for a child to feed from an ejaculating penis? The search for food via the penis makes her later compulsion to masturbate schoolboys seem not unlike the hand-milking of cows. Ms. B's deepest anxieties, however, concerned her mother's body and the siblings that emerged from it. Her anorexic-cannibalistic crisis arose from terrifying feelings of starvation, rage, and envy towards her mother's body and towards her siblings. The dream of the baby in the country lane whom Ms. B cannot save from the truck may well be an expression of thoughts about a newborn sibling she wished to murder in order to gain access to her mother, aside from other meanings it might have. She also dreamed of being surrounded by cut-up fetuses. Fantasies of invasion of the mother lay behind her fears of burglary, stealing, and occupation of "maternal spaces" such as rooms, cupboards, houses, and bodies. When Anthony was born, Ms. B retreated into a cupboard under the stairs. Perhaps this makes most sense as a regression into the mother's womb, taking the place of Anthony. It was at this point that her anorexic-bulimic pathology came into being: With no object in sight to provide reliable nourishment, her never to be satisfied hunger was joined by a deep fear of destructiveness if she ate. Feeling herself to be a biting baby who endangers her mother and her siblings placed her, by projection, on the receiving end of this violence. She could destroy by eating or be destroyed by being eaten. The anorexic's fear of taking in the analyst's food for thought is similar: either the analyst will be devoured by the patient's greed, engendering guilt, or the patient will be consumed and destroyed. In later life, after menstruation and when pregnancy is possible, the sexual act may become confused with oral wishes so that the anorexic fears that the inside of her body will be taken over and destroyed by a penis containing her own projected, avaricious desires. Rey (1994) has noted such confusions in anorexia, especially the unconscious conviction that mothers have babies by eating them, and that birth takes place via a bowel movement.

The Director, the patient's psychotic advisor usually seen as a caretaker, appropriated the task of protecting her from these terrible fears. His comments led to her becoming catatonic or not eating or going to the lavatory—paranoid-schizoid solutions to the projective problem of "the woman next door" seeing or hearing her. Eating and shitting were felt to be highly dangerous to her mother, analyst, and neighbor. The hallucination of bulging walls, which a woman with a pregnant belly is trying to break through, is a graphic example of claustrophilia in which Ms. B located envious, murderous, little-girl wishes about her mother and siblings in the mother-neighbor. These wishes threatened to return and break through her defenses ("She is coming through the wall to kill you," the Director would advise), which would then lead to a state of psychotic claustrophobia. It has been by persistent interpretation of her severe paranoia *in the transference* that Ms. B has been able to begin to withdraw some of her projections towards her mother, her mother's body, her siblings, and me. To achieve this I needed to understand that her psychotic and nonpsychotic personalities were distinct, functionally and organizationally, and for some considerable time transference work took this into full account. This led to more conscious depression and grief in Ms. B. Her grief has been of a magnitude as to be tolerable only fleetingly. Nevertheless, after years of upheaval, she has become able to take an interest in and responsibility for her attitudes, including her anxiety and guilt at wishes to consume and destroy her objects.

It has become clear to me that, in view of her damaged identifications, Ms. B's search for an identification with a mother amounted to a descent into unbearable confusion and losses. She has been required to address her psychotic anxieties knowing she did not possess the psychological equipment to think or imagine them, only to enact them (cf. Jackson & Williams, 1994). Survival of the failure of her relationship with her mother was sustained through the use of borderline defenses. The incest, however, consolidated her confusion between fantasy, memory, and fact, leaving her gravely vulnerable to a psychotic process that very nearly destroyed her.

Obviously, not all patients who form a double-identification or who are sexually abused suffer the type or degree of psychopathology shown by Ms. B. However, these two developmental crises—serious failure in early identification with the mother, and a turning to the father, often with incestuous consequences—are reported by clinicians with increasing regularity, usually in the context of accompanying anorexic pathology. It is my view that, taken together, these obstacles may usefully be thought of as a single syndrome, and that the psychotic anxieties that accompany them can affect the entire lives of afflicted individuals as a result of their being prevented from forming object relationships with members of either sex.

REFERENCES

Bion, W. R. (1967). Differentiation of the psychotic and non-psychotic personalities. In *Second thoughts* (pp. 43–64). London: Maresfield.

Eisnitz, A. J. (1984). Father-daughter incest. *International Journal of Psychoanalytic Psychotherapy*, *10*, 495–503.

Grand, S., & Alpert, J. L. (1993). The core trauma of incest: An object relations view. *Professional Psychology: Research and Practice*, *24*(3), 330–334.

Herman, J. L., & Schatzow, E. (1987). Recovery and verification of memories of childhood sexual trauma. *Psychoanalytic Psychology*, *14*(1), 1–14.

Jackson, M., & Williams, P. (1994). *Unimaginable storms: A search for meaning in psychosis*. London: Karnac Books.

Price, M. (1993). The impact of incest on identity formation in women. *Journal of the American Academy of Psychoanalysis*, *21*(2), 213–228.

Rey, H. (1994). *Universals of psychoanalysis*. London: Free Association Books.

Rosenfeld, H. (1964/1965). On the psychopathology of narcissism. In *Psychotic states* (pp. 169–179). London: Hogarth Press.

Rosenfeld, H. (1971). A clinical approach to the psychoanalytic theory of the life and death instincts: An investigation into the destructive aspects of narcissism. *International Journal of Psychoanalysis*, *52*, 169–178.

Rosenfeld, H. (1987). Projective identification in clinical practice. In *Impasse and interpretation*. London & New York: Tavistock.

Winnicott, D. W. (1960). Ego distortion in terms of true and false self. In *The maturational processes and the facilitating environment* (pp. 140–152). London: Karnac, 1965.

Chapter 4

Making time, killing time*

Since the beginning, mankind has been submerged in a sea of
time.

—Hall (1984)

We have become aware of the time-sea in which we live only very slowly.
The first recorded awareness of time came late in evolutionary terms, 35,000
years ago when early modern man began burying the dead. Denoting the
phases of the moon and the migration of birds, animals, and fish has
always involved a temporal dimension. Recording the movements of the
sun, moon, and planets and the passage of time became a basic human
activity. Stonehenge and, later, clocks were employed to keep a record of
time. Clocks emerged in the 13th century as a response to the monasteries'
need for accurately kept services, the nocturnal office of matins being the
catalyst. Time as an external phenomenon—chronological time—is often
contrasted theoretically with psychological or subjective time; behind this
is the idea that there exist two or more different types of time. What if,
instead, there are no different forms of time? What if time is a unitary,
unifying phenomenon and a familiar dimension of our experienced sur-
roundings that is in itself distinct from the processes which occur in time
(Gell, 1992, p. 315)? Like its offspring, history, time is everywhere and
is mediated by cultural conditions and personal, psychological factors. In
other words, might the world be a big clock, albeit one that different people
read very differently (p. 96)?† Or are there truly different forms of time? In
this paper I discuss different experiences of time and give three examples
of time from patients in psychoanalysis, each experience reflecting a differ-

---

* This chapter originally appeared as a papr in R. J. Perelberg, *Time and Memory* (pp.
47–64). © 2007 Karnac Books. Reprinted with permission.
† Americo-Indians, African tribesmen, and other third-world groups can treat time with
exceptional patience compared to, for example, westerners. All concur that time exists, but
its salience in our affairs is strikingly different.

ent psychic state, and which point to a clear distinction between time, the subjective experience of it, and its organizing role in psychic structures.

Philosophers and writers have stressed the contrasting experiences of inner and outer time and their impact. There is no space here to review these contributions, but it can be seen that there are many contrasting positions that tend to be starkly differentiated. Plato, we know, appears to have refuted the passage of time, whereas in the work of the philosopher Bergson, by contrast, there is an attempt to try to conquer the dominance of the passage of time. Similarly, Whitehead and Nietzsche held radically opposed perspectives, the former seeing time as destroying permanence, whereas Nietzsche viewed permanence as an atrophying, destructive influence. Overcoming the very notion of permanence and surrendering to time was Nietzsche's key to advancement personally, politically, and socially. Wherever one turns in literature—in Proust, Kafka, Mann, Huxley, Rilke, Woolf, Beckett, and many others—one encounters a personal preoccupation with time and the need to understand and control its influence. Most vivid perhaps is Proust's conflation of time and memory as an indissoluble unity. This union of memory with time reaches its imagistic peak in the widely used literary device of life flashing before one's eyes. Time and memory here are compressed into a single unit denoting an overwhelming experience of the impact and rapid conflation of time and subjective experience. We recognize a milder version of this experience as we grow older: Time accelerates as the goals of the future become less important and the present becomes more important. The culmination of such a position leads to a perception of time as a feature of psychic reality.

Temporality is a basic aspect of experience and of consciousness in that our lives are shaped and can only be understood in the context of duration and how we grasp the parameters of ongoing experience. We have no actual sense organ with which to measure duration, and consciousness is notoriously unreliable in assessing it, especially in infancy and as we grow old, so when we speak about perceptions of time we are already speaking metaphorically (Gell, 1992, p. 93). Our grasp of time is therefore an interpretative act of the ego. To extend this view leads to a psychoanalytic perspective held by many analysts that time may be conceived of as an experience derived from a static or stable point, ultimately the self (Hartocollis, 1983). In this view, the self exists in relation to other selves or objects in a spatiotemporal framework. This is not, of course, the only psychoanalytic view, but it is a widely held one. A link to this view lies in the earliest experience of temporality, which may be the sensation of a heart beating—our mother's, our own, or both. This sequence may subsequently be detectable in clock time, in breathing, in walking, in musical composition, and even in ceremonial ritual. Underlying these expressive forms of duration lies the need to feel joined up in going-on-being as a consequence of being connected up to other people, internally and externally. The opposite experience, of being disjointed when separated from objects, is understood clinically to soon have implications for the understanding and experience of time. The origins of this problem are not difficult to detect: For the baby, feelings of displeasure, the inability to resolve such feelings, and their eventual relief through containment create the experience of an object that exists for the baby both inside and outside the nascent self. Separation in time or space from the object, internally or externally, initiates a primitive temporal perspective. These flows of experience come to structure the mind from the point of view of personal history and eventually will constitute memory (Resnik, 1987). Pleasant and unpleasant experiences of duration are often projected onto the world, and this process of externalization can affect our perceptions of reality. The experience of time as duration also implies a capacity to wait and to remember. Memory and fantasy may be seen as mediating elements in our handling the experience of duration, separation, and absence. Memory and fantasy structure the shape of psychic narratives generated to symbolize these experiences. Affects born of waiting and the ego's and superego's responses profoundly influence our experience of time. The superego's forewarning tendencies institute awareness of what may or may not happen, with all its impending consequences; whereas the need to manage normatively, repress, or, if necessary, even disavow affects gives rise to a past which can be sensed as irretrievable. Anxiety, as we know, invokes the idea that something bad may be about to happen to us; depression, by contrast, produces an experience of something bad having already happened to us. Development research into infant life has confirmed that the baby's anticipation of fulfillment involves the deployment of a hallucinated memory that protects the ego from anxieties that could lead to the break-up of the temporal sense caused by affects born of frustration and separation from the object. If the baby's capacity to hallucinate in this way fails, anxiety, fear, and anger may initiate regression to an undifferentiated "bad" self-object state in which the experience of temporality is undermined (contact with objects no longer being properly assessed), and ego activity can succumb to more primitive, pretemporal, *spatial* coordinates (Rey, 1994). From the beginning, the infant must deal with the temporal impact of separation and loss. A narrative constructed to symbolize these experiences must be generated and, if it is to be viable, must also presuppose mourning (Varvin, 1997).

FREUD'S TIME

Freud (1915) demonstrated how the unconscious has no temporal perspective yet plays a fundamental role in the experience of time. Its processes remain unaltered by the passage of time, and wishful impulses that have been repressed appear eternal, behaving throughout life as though they had just occurred. Freud's formulation of the origins of time perception involves the system *Pcpt.-Cs* (perceptual consciousness), which is sent out to experience the external world like an antenna, returning after having sampled its offerings. This discontinuous process gives rise to a conception of time (Freud, 1925). In his second theory of anxiety, Freud stated that anxiety reflected adaptive efforts to deal with mental disequilibrium (Freud, 1926). The ego, perceiving the self to be in danger (having cognized internal changes) mobilizes certain affects—a mental act involving consciousness. Freud was unsure about the existence of unconscious affects that exist independently and are not adaptive. The unconscious comprises *ideas* that may or may not become affectively conscious. These are cathexes, ultimately of memory traces, whereas affects are psychophysiological processes of discharge that express themselves as feelings. This is why anxiety can be experienced as such a powerful, conscious affect, but disappears when we are no longer afraid. Freud believed that it sank into the unconscious as a latent idea. Unconscious ideas, fantasies, and feelings regarding internal objects create a template for awareness of the passage of time; a disturbed sense of time indicates a crisis in the ego's relations to objects.

Time disturbances in neurotic disorders have been widely documented. Freud's observations on obsessive patients revealed their dislike of clocks because of the certainty they imply. To remain obsessive you need to hold on to an ability to doubt everything, except your doubts. The obsessive's rituals and compulsive thoughts are like individual time capsules, each warding off ideas of death and destruction. Fenichel (1945) noted how anal disturbances affect attitudes toward time, as well as money, expressed as excessive precision or unreliability. Extreme punctuality and greed were linked with feces by Jones and are motivated, he suggested, by anal erotism (Jones, 1918). Conversely, chronic neglect in infancy and the destruction of links with objects can give rise to a merging of temporal experiences into a "repeated eternity" that denudes time of all significance. Phobias, depersonalization experiences, chronic boredom, and other symptoms reveal a disturbance in the apprehension of the experience of time rooted in anxiety about internal objects. Klein's (1940) formulation of the depressive position is contingent upon a sense of time past and the impending fate of internal objects.

EXPERIENCES OF TIME

A typical example of neurotic disturbance linked to a sense of time employed defensively is illustrated by a mildly agoraphobic patient in her 30s who is consistently late for sessions. This is followed by apologies and relief at finding me waiting. The patient complains about not having enough time. She has a fantasy that her mother and I wish to leave her. She believes I find seeing her a duty that I abhor. By keeping me waiting and finding me here, she experiences some reassuring feelings that I do not intend to leave her. The idea that her mother's life and mine are independent of hers is disavowed, as is acknowledgment of her own rejecting feelings. I wonder whether she is also being protected from experiencing desires to be separate and perhaps sexual wishes that could signify an independent life. Censure and repression of feelings—desire, envy, humiliation, anger, and others—have disrupted her ego's mindfulness of its objects and her temporal judgment. At times, when object relations and temporality were felt to be seriously compromised, for example, in moments of personal crisis, some reversion to spatial reckoning was evident in her tendency to experience, when under stress, agoraphobic anxieties.

In severe disturbances, particularly borderline conditions, the capacity to wait and endure time passing has not evolved as an ego function and relations with time are therefore more deeply disordered. Temporal problems can come to take on an enveloping significance in the life of the subject, reflecting ways in which the original defect in ego integration of positive and negative experiences of objects has become an organized splitting defense against generalized anxiety (this gives rise to the "stable instability" evident in borderline thinking which, on examination, overlays a potential for disorganization, including temporal; see Kernberg, 1975). The borderline personality could be said to live in a *quasi*-present tense, so omnipresent are anxieties concerning negativity and the fate of objects, internal and external. The past and the future are rendered redundant as their reality demands on the ego are felt to be unmanageable. In their place is instituted a demand for immediate fulfillment as part of the chronic struggle to mitigate and avert crisis. If gratification is not forthcoming, characteristic rage may erupt, giving way in its aftermath to feelings of emptiness, despair, and in some cases the wish to self-harm or commit suicide. Rage at not being given immediate gratification is a defense against, among other things, experiencing feelings about the past, or future, or both. Intense, labile affects, especially aggression, denote the loss of an object who is now expected to provide instant satisfaction. This loss is usually internal—a psychic fact—as much as it is external, and is relived via the repetition compulsion as though the original fixation had just occurred. Alongside the intense affects involved may be the capacity to disperse affects producing boredom, detachment, and disgust.

An extract follows from a session with a businessman in his 20s who was brought up in well-to-do but emotionally impoverished circumstances. His preoccupation with time is very evident, particularly the present, and is centered on the accompanying threat posed by the emergence of certain feelings that arise in him as a consequence of the impact of time on internal objects. The following statement came at the start of a Friday session several months after starting analysis:

I felt panic again coming here, coming into the room. It seems to take me over and I think it will go on forever. The thing it makes me think of is sex. It takes me about two minutes to calm down. I have to make myself think of nothing, go blank and still, look at something like a plant or the door so that I know where I am. I listened to Gounod's *Solemn Mass* probably nine times I think between yesterday and today. I was feeling melancholic, lonely. It put me in touch with something. I felt better after a while. ... I heard from Janet [*his sister*] last night that she'd failed her law exams, I think for the fourth or fifth time. I'm worried about her. How long will they let her go on re-taking her exams? ... I had a row at work this morning. It's a rats' nest there these days. I'd put forward some ideas about Vancouver [*a proposed business deal*] but the people with the most to lose, the ones who can't stand anything new [*names several names*] started to try to water them down. I tried to complain but nobody took my side. It's always the same. It makes me feel hopeless and then I wonder what I'm doing there. Why don't I just leave and set up on my own? I feel I'm going on and on now and you're getting bored. I think what's worrying me most of all is Marie [*his wife*] going away for two weeks. I think she'll forget me, but I don't even know if I'll miss her.

The intensity of his anxieties; the rapid, shallow movement from one subject to the next; the transference implications regarding sexual feelings, depression at separation, the imminent weekend break—all stand out in their significance. However, I would like to focus on this man's extreme sensitivity to time. He is aware, emotionally, that the weekend has arrived and he feels loss. This is disguised by the movement from topic to topic so that the separation and feelings about it cannot be properly thought out. He feels panic which he says will go on forever, yet it takes only 2 minutes to halt it through the production of a "timeless" state. The playing of the same music induces a similar timelessness. His wife's absence for 2 weeks means she will forget about him entirely, which disturbs him, although he knows it isn't true. For his part he can't say whether he will notice she is gone. He is both anxious about and indifferent towards his objects, a contradiction reflected in his attitude to time.

One difference between this and the previous, female patient is the degree of splitting employed. This is apparent when my male patient shows concern about his sister and her exams (which I took to be a reference also to himself and to me). He is required to abandon the subject and speak about a row at work in which is ideas are opposed by a force that is reactionary. This force, represented by conservative, resistant work colleagues, refers to an aspect of the patient which is averse to wishes in him to have his needs met. Such opposition to his need for objects is evidence of severe splitting and, in this patient and many others, of a defensive structure that "organizes" the patient's retreat from object relationships (Rosenfeld, 1971; Steiner, 1993). After a further year of analysis the patient developed anxieties about being alone, driving, dealing with work colleagues, and a belief that his wife might die. To his disturbed sense of time were added problems of orientation and direction:

P: I was anxious driving here. Marie couldn't accompany me and I felt alone, as though nobody knew me and I was invisible. It's horrible, I want to curl up and hide. I felt shaky turning off the main road. I don't know why, it's not the driving, more the amount of oncoming traffic. It's a major junction and I don't know if I can rely on anyone letting me across, so I get anxious that I'll be stuck. The driving is getting worse. I get confused about which gear to use, especially going up the hill to our place. I used to do it in fourth, then third, but now I find myself putting the car in second, but this makes it rev too much so I go slower and worry about the traffic building up behind me. ... It was Marie's birthday on Saturday and we went to a restaurant. I found the food too rich and couldn't sleep later but I'm sure it was because I spent most of the evening worrying how I'd get back up the hill and what gear I should be in. It sounds ridiculous. What is strange as well is that although I want Marie with me I hate going into London with her in case we get separated. If I lose sight of her I start to feel like a speck in the crowd and I know I wouldn't be able to find my way home. I also get worried that she might get knocked down and I won't be able to do anything.

A: I think that when you leave here at the end of your sessions, you can feel that you have been abandoned by me, and that I no longer know or care about you. You feel you can't complain to me, even though the situation feels outrageous, and then I think you feel stuck. You struggle on, trying different strategies to cope, but I think the whole thing is feeling more and more difficult for you, as all the time I think you're afraid that I will find out you feel I am responsible.

For this man, to make time for himself or someone else, in order to reflect on the past or the future, exposes him to intense, primitive feelings. To accept the passage of time means being aware of, needing, and feeling concerned for others. Making time is a depressive-position activity, necessitating acknowledgment of the other's separateness and significance to oneself and of one's role in the well-being of the other person. To make time is, ultimately, an act of love. Even a solitary hobby benefits the object—in this case the self, in identification with the giver and the receiver. To be unaware of time—to kill time—is to renounce the need for the other, and the other in oneself. The borderline personality kills time to keep apart from his objects. His narcissism spares him the pains of needing, loving, and hating, even if the price may be lifelong suffering. There are expressions of killing time which are not necessarily symptoms of borderline states, but which also signify disavowal of object need. Compulsive daydreaming, dependency on alcohol or drugs, perversions, promiscuity, or living it up in the belief that this brings happiness—all these abolish a sense of time and dependency on others. One example of this is the father who, on being complimented on the beauty of his daughter at a party, boasted, "That's nothing. Wait until you see the photographs I had taken of her" (Schiffer, 1978). Living out of time, this father holds his objects at one remove, idealizing lifelessness. There are other, less obvious ways in which time has a powerful impact on the ego's organizing functions. Why are detective tales so popular, for example? One reason is that they create the illusion of suspended time. We passively enact fantasies filled with fear and curiosity, until all is revealed. Similarly, Sleeping Beauty magically takes control of time, as do Cinderella and Peter Pan. And, of course, we all feel sorry for Dracula if he doesn't make it into his coffin by dawn to achieve his macabre victory over time. Positive connotations of time include states of timelessness in which creative contemplation may be involved. Learning to do nothing constructively, for example, can be closely related to the concept of negative capability, to the practices of certain Eastern religions, and to a mother's capacity for reverie, which depends upon secure contact with internal objects. I recall a workaholic patient who reacted with horror and fascination to my comment that perhaps he longed to be able to have a session in which he could waste time—a session in which nothing "important" was achieved, but in which he could simply be however *he* felt. A kindred state to doing nothing, and one which is common throughout normal life, is *reculer pour mieux sauter*—a pause or retreat into oneself to gather strength, with the help of good internal objects, in order at some point to reenter life. These examples of experiences of apparent timelessness can be said to be appreciations of the immediacy of time and of the impact of the present tense in a life that is lived fully.

The most radical reaction *against* time occurs in psychosis. The psychotic patient, as Freud observed, detaches himself from external, temporal reality and lives in an internal, timeless reality. I recall a patient from an inpatient unit who demonstrated this clearly. This socially isolated female patient, who was prone to suicidal ideas, had been brought up by a psychotic mother. The patient's soul had, in my view, been murdered, in the sense Shengold (1978) describes. She related compliantly, convinced at a profound level that she was responsible for others' survival. While on the ward she maintained a delusion that she was healthy, married (sometimes with children), and that she was capable of predicting the future. She sometimes knew this delusion of plenitude to be false but believed it to be true. Delusional controls over the past, present, and future provided a psychotic alternative to life based on an appreciation of time.

Primary splitting in psychosis jeopardizes personality development through the dissolution of higher psychic functions (Hughlings-Jackson, 1950). The mental activity of such patients is often reduced to a waking equivalent of dreaming: Primary process ideas and shifting identifications or part-object identifications may be taken as objects, wreaking havoc with thoughts and affects and driving the subject to feel mad. Fantasy figures can come to dominate the ego while actual objects are renounced and go unrecognized for who and what they are. In the onset of schizophrenia, particularly of the paranoid type, objects and a sense of time may be present. As time goes by the schizophrenic's mind succumbs increasingly to psychotic mentation, and contact with objects and a sense of time diminishes leaving the patient clinging without awareness to the present. A sense of time dissolves into space-centered thinking, which can lead to memories being experienced as actual perceptions. Interobject space, necessary for the use of fantasy as trial action and experimental thought, is extinguished. The psychotic person becomes vigilant while seemingly caring about nothing. This is nowhere more apparent than in the intense, brittle precocity of the psychotic transference. The threat of immediate engulfment coexists with apparent unconcern. Time has vanished, yet each moment is treated as though it were the patient's last. The present is controlled in order to predict the future; killing time permits survival to the next second, the next hour. The patient's terror and vigilance engender an insane, glossolalic world of the future.

Here is an extract from a psychotic patient's analysis in which a particular confusion regarding time is evident. This 50-year-old woman had been diagnosed psychiatrically as suffering paranoid schizophrenia. Fantasy objects controlled her mental life and gave her psychosis expression, often through command hallucinations via a psychotic superego. In childhood, the patient seems to have had a poor relationship with her mother, who ignored her, and she complained of having been sexually abused by her father and brother. She developed anorexia in her teens and sought relief from her difficulties by engaging in sexual relationships, usually with younger boys. She lived a withdrawn and secretive life until her late thirties when she decompensated after experiencing a fleeting wish to have children. After hospitalization she began analysis but did not behave in the way one might have expected an analytic patient to behave until many years had passed, with acting out dominating the treatment. In the following Friday session from which I quote (from the first year of the analysis) she had brought into the room with her a Polaroid picture of a bed, a matchbox to put spiders in (apparently for their safety), a pack of razor blades, and sunglasses:

P: I just saw you on the station on the way here. Like in Westminster yesterday. You smiled at me. You looked pale so I went into a shop and bought Lem-Sip ... I was hoping you'd be leaning on a lamppost but when I came out you'd gone away ... Do you know that people who wear hats want to get inside me? I must be a good girl, you see. I must look after the animals. I have to look after the animals. You mustn't touch barn owls, just look ... Uncle Bill took me to the Albert Hall last night. It was my tenth birthday. I got a balloon. He said I'm a good girl. [*Sings "I'm a good girl, I'm a good girl."*] If I pull the string I feel it on the other end. Would you like me to do it for you?

A: I think you know it's Friday today and you feel upset about the fact that I am going to be leaving you until we meet again on Monday, but I think you're being told to think of sexual things instead of thinking about what *you* feel. Everything's fine, let's have a party, let's have sex. But somebody is not well. I think you realize that it's you but you feel afraid of talking about it with me.

P: He says cutting off my breasts and vagina makes things all right [*He being a psychotic figure who influences her thinking.*] You won't hit me, will you? ... Dead flowers can kill me, you see. You can't do that to animals. He says you're tricking me ... My tissues are broken, can I have one of yours?

A: I think you're feeling so frightened to tell me about how upset and jealous you feel because one or both of us will fall apart, you fear. You feel that everything will be a disaster if you tell me the truth, that I won't be able to stand it, but the truth is you are upset, and I think that inside you want me to know about it.

The patient is out of touch with the day, the year, and my whereabouts. Her need to voice her anxieties and dependency feelings is countered by sexualized and threatening psychotic ideas. Splitting and projection on a massive scale have virtually dissolved the ego's perceptual capacity. Internal experiences are expelled with violence and are felt to take place outside her. Inside, she feels disconnected, boundary-less, timeless, and engulfed—she is persecuted by her projections. Her awareness of time seems to have collapsed. The struggle to symbolize without the resources to do so gives rise to unusual, poetic phrases such as "broken tissues." Spatial orientation, a developmentally earlier "container" for infantile object representations than the time-sense, is reverted to, replacing lost higher functions. Many such patients inaugurate structural conditions of relating aimed primarily at defeating psychic dissolution as much as defending against psychic pain, as I think this patient is doing. Within such a desperate imperative time and separation have no psychological authorization.

The need to communicate psychic truth is what brings all patients into analysis, including the psychotic. This presupposes a life with internal as well as external objects, in time, in the real psychological world, with the pains and desires this inevitably brings. Appraisal of time passing is inaugurated in the ego's negotiations with its internal objects. This is implied in the developmental notion of "linear time," although this term fails to convey the many levels, digressions, and reversals that are a precondition of a concerned, depressive-position appreciation of the evolution of time. The philosopher Husserl defines linear time as "a network of evolving intentionalities," a definition that better reflects the complex irreversibility of time. Schafer (1976) draws psychoanalytic attention to the tragic dimension of such a view. He regards awareness of time passing as an accomplishment in the ego's system in that it demands a deep acceptance of separateness, mortality, and the fact that every passing moment is different and, once past, is lost forever. Nevertheless we try to make something of the time we have. T. S. Eliot famously echoes this human task in "Burnt Norton."[*]

> Time present and time past
> Are both perhaps in time future
> And time future contained in time past
> Time past and time future
> What might have been and what has been
> Point to one end, which is always present.
> And the end and the beginning were always there
> Before the beginning and after the end,
> And all is always now ...

In clinical work the repetition-compulsion gives emotional life a static quality based on fixation, repression, and the illusional security of suffering. The analysand enacts the same ritual at the same point in time, with the same people and consequences as at the time of fixation. The existence of the repetition-compulsion implies that the past may be redone, if not undone, and this is the work of psychoanalysis. As Balint (1952) stated, there exists the possibility of a "new beginning." The following simple, everyday poem indicates the sense of loss that may usher in temporal awareness of the kind often seen in everyday psychoanalytic work. The sense of the meaning of time contained in the poem, albeit amusing, is contingent upon mourning both for objects and for the lost opportunities development brings.

"Time"[†]

> We have twelve clocks in our house
> Still, there's never enough time
> You go into the kitchen
> get chocolate milk for your spindly son

---

[*] © 1944 Faber & Faber. Reprinted with permission.
[†] © 1995 Benny Andersen. Reprinted with permission.

but when you return
he has grown too old for chocolate milk,
demands beer, girls, revolution
You must make the most of your time while you have it
Your daughter comes home from school
goes out to play hopscotch
comes in a little later
and asks if you will mind the baby
while she and her husband go to the theatre
and while they are at the theatre
the child, with some difficulty,
is promoted to the 10th grade
You must make the most of your time while you have it
You photograph your hitherto young wife
with full-blooded gypsy headscarf
an opulent fountain in the background
but the picture is hardly developed
before she announces that it is soon
her turn to collect old age pension
softly the widow awakes in her
You would like to make the most of your time
but it gets lost, all the time,
where has it gone
was it ever there at all
have you spent too much time
drawing time out
You must make the most of time, in time,
roam around for a time without time and place
and when it's time
call home and hear
"You have called 95 94 93 92?
That number is no longer available."
Click.

Time is omnipresent and is a central human preoccupation. Varying definitions of time arise as a consequence of cultural and psychological influences reflecting subjective and social perspectives. Nowhere is variation in
awareness of the sense of time more apparent than in psychoanalytic treatment where the varied conditions of subjectivity are manifest. Differences in
the experience of temporality are related to intrapsychic relations between
the ego and its internal objects, in particular the capacity of the ego to tolerate and mourn separation and loss as durational phenomena—an essential
aspect of development. The three clinical examples given above illustrate
increasing disorientation regarding time in parallel with levels of disruption

to internal object relationships. Defensive, processual, and structural levels of disturbance reveal a progressive inability to mourn, and this is reflected in disturbances of time perception. However, the implacable presence of time that bears down on these patients insists upon an orienting response from all of us, and the examples given from poetry reflect this human imperative.

REFERENCES

Andersen, B. (1995). *Cosmopolitan in Denmark, and other poems about the Danes.* Copenhagen: Borg.

Arieti, S. (1994). *Interpretations of schizophrenia.* Northvale, NJ: Jason Aronson.

Balint, M. (1952/1965). On love and hate. In *Primary love and psychoanalytic technique* (pp. 141–156). London: Tavistock.

Eliot, T. S. (1944). Burnt Norton. In *Four Quartets.* London: Faber & Faber.

Fenichel, O. (1945). *The psychoanalytic theory of neurosis.* New York: Norton.

Freud, S. (1915). The unconscious. In J. Strachey (Ed. & Trans.), *The standard edition of the complete psychological works of Sigmund Freud* (Vol. 14, pp. 159–215). London: Hogarth Press.

Freud, S. (1925). A note upon the "mystic writing pad." In J. Strachey (Ed. & Trans.), *The standard edition of the complete psychological works of Sigmund Freud* (Vol. 19, pp. 227–232). London: Hogarth Press.

Freud, S. (1926). Inhibitions, symptoms and anxiety. In J. Strachey (Ed. & Trans.), *The standard edition of the complete psychological works of Sigmund Freud* (Vol. 20, pp. 77–172). London: Hogarth Press.

Gell, A. (1992). *The anthropology of time.* Oxford: Berg.

Hall, E. T. (1984). *The dance of life: The other dimension of time.* New York: Anchor Press/Doubleday.

Hartocollis, P. (1983). *Time and timelessness.* New York: International Universities Press.

Hughlings-Jackson, J. (1950). Factors of the insanities. In *The selected writings of John Hughlings-Jackson.* London: The Staples Press.

Jones, E. (1918/1950). Anal-erotic character traits. In *Papers on psycho-analysis.* London: Bailliere, Tindal & Cox.

Kernberg, O. (1975). *Borderline conditions and pathological narcissism.* Northvale, NJ: Jason Aronson.

Klein, M. (1940). Mourning and its relation to manic-depressive states. *International Journal of Psychoanalysis, 21,* 125–153.

Matte-Blanco, I. (1975). *The unconscious as infinite sets: An essay in bi-logic.* London: Duckworth.

Rayner, E. (1995). *Unconscious logic: An introduction to Matte-Blanco's bi-logic and its uses.* London: Routledge.

Rey, H. (1999). *Universals of Psychoanalysis in the Treatment of Psychotic and Borderline States.* London: Free Association Books.

Resnik, S. (1987). *The theatre of the dream.* London: Tavistock.

Rosenfeld, H. (1971). A clinical approach to the psychoanalytic theory of the life and death instincts: An investigation into the aggressive aspects of narcissism. *International Journal of Psychoanalysis*, *52*, 169–178.

Schafer, R. (1976). *A new language for psychoanalysis*. New Haven, CT: Yale University Press.

Schiffer, I. (1978). *The trauma of time*. New York: International Universities Press.

Shengold, L. (1978). Assault on a child's individuality: A kind of soul murder. *Psychoanalytic Quarterly*, *47*(3), 419–424.

Steiner, J. (1993). *Psychic retreats*. London: Tavistock.

Varvin, S. (1997). Time, space and causality. *The Scandinavian Psychoanalytic Review*, *20*, 89–96.

Chapter 5

The psychoanalytic therapy of "Cluster A" personality disorders

Paranoid, schizoid, and schizotypal*

"Cluster A" personality disorders comprise paranoid personality disorder (PPD), schizoid personality disorder (SPD), and schizotypal personality disorder (StPD). Patients who fall within these diagnostic categories are the least likely to present for individual psychoanalytic therapy because of the inflexibility and severity of the conditions, the comparatively poor response to treatment and, not infrequently, inaccurate diagnosis. However, the growth in public expectation from the talking therapies and the slow but steady progress made by researchers into the origins and prevalence of these disorders has led more Cluster A patients to seek out psychotherapeutic help than was the case in the past, although the number remains small relative to the treatment of borderline personality disorder. Demographically, Cluster A disorders affect 0.5%–2.5% (PPD), slightly less than 1% (SPD), and approximately 3% (StPD) of the U.S. population (with comparable rates in Europe), and the consequences for individuals affected can be highly disabling (Elkin, 1999). The incidence of each category appears to be higher in men than in women, and in describing this cluster of conditions emphasis has tended to be placed on odd, eccentric, or "cold" behavior. These characteristics are most evident in SDP and StPD. It is thought that a biological relationship may exist between the disorders and the schizophrenias, although of the three, StPD can be more demonstrably linked to schizophrenia phenomenologically and genetically (McGlashan, 1986). SPD and StPD are sometimes grouped as part of a continuum, given the similarity of certain symptoms. There remains no distinctive set of psychotherapeutic theories applicable to these conditions. More research is required into the developmental and psychic structural aspects of the illnesses before generally accepted psychological theories for the conditions can be established. There is, in fact, strikingly little research into Cluster A disorders compared with other personality disorders (notably borderlines), and more is

---

* An earlier version of this chapter appeared in J. Clarkin, G. Gabbard, & P. Fonagy, *Psychodynamic Psychotherapy of Personality Disorders: A Clinical Handbook.* © 2010 American Psychiatric Press.

needed if the conditions are to become better understood. Psychodynamic researchers have noted the stability of diagnosis and treatment outcomes (e.g., McGlashan, 1986; Sandell, et al., 1997; Stone, 1985, 1993). Clinical investigation into Cluster A–type personalities tends to study the nature of internal object relationships, defenses, psychotic anxieties, and transference-countertransference phenomena.* Attention to psychotic anxieties is of particular importance to those who study and treat Cluster A disorders. Psychotic elements occur in severe neuroses, psychosomatic disorders, sexual perversions, and personality disorders *alongside* neurotic constellations, and this is particularly the case with Cluster A. Such patients are not psychotic *per se*, but are vulnerable to psychotic thinking and compromised ego functioning that create confusion between internal and external realities.

In undertaking the treatment of Cluster A patients, analysts are faced with a series of theoretical, clinical, and technical challenges that will draw upon their resources to the full. The prevalence of psychotic anxieties in parallel to neurotic anxieties has led these individuals to fall out of the orbit of normal human relations. They display defenses that are sometimes seen in psychosis and will not respond to an analyst who does not take seriously their loss of faith in people. This lost capacity leaves a profound imprint on their internal world: Failed internalization of trusting relationships generates chronic mistrust and anxiety. Difficulty in the management of affects is one area, among many, that causes particular problems. They tend to "globalize" their affective experience due to chronic splitting, swinging from one set of powerful feelings to another with little capacity to integrate gradations of feeling or different and contradictory experiences. This in turn can be linked in some cases to the violent, coercive activity of an overdeveloped superego whose task it is to control affect storms and strong instinctual impulses with extreme rigidity. The guilt, shame, and despair in this seemingly irresolvable psychic conflict have been well documented (for a recent review of these conflicts in serious disturbance, see Wurmser, 2008). These affective crises tend to be more obviously and openly expressed in Cluster B personality disorders, and are more muted and internally directed in Cluster A (Gunderson, 2008). However, they are no less powerful for this and demand the steady attentiveness of the clinician if opaque internal crises are not to ferment into eruptions of acting out that may threaten the treatment.

Once in treatment, a capacity in the analyst for flexibility and careful attention to fluctuating countertransference experiences will improve

---

* Authors who have reported on these phenomena include Gabbard (2000), Grotstein (1995), Jackson and Williams (1994), Jackson (2000), Lucas (1992), Meissner (1986), Rey (1994), Robbins (2002), Rosenfeld (1964, 1969), Segal (1978), Sohn (1997), and Target and Fonagy (1996a, 1996b).

treatment prospects. Research into the role of countertransference factors has confirmed the centrality of the analyst's responsiveness (particularly to the patient's psychotic anxieties) for effective treatment, as well as the hazards of inattention to countertransference phenomena (Lieberz & Porsch, 1997; Hinshelwood, 1994). This is not to say that attending to these phenomena is undemanding. The inchoate configuration of the internal part-object world and fragmented ego results in unacceptable and incompatible feelings and fantasies being externalized, often with violence. As a result, the analyst who is open to understanding the patient will be impinged upon, even assaulted, by the projection of a wide range of feelings which may be difficult, if not impossible, to understand at first. One of the most unnerving of countertransference experiences is the unpredictability with which these baffling and powerful communications can arrive, leading to confusion, doubts about the progress of the work, and pressures to retaliate or act in order to diffuse their impact. It can be helpful to be aware that dealing with this intense projective activity is an integral part of the work with these patients. Furthermore, losing one's footing, becoming confused, experiencing doubts about oneself, and other feelings of crisis in the treatment are not only to be expected, but are necessary if a genuine understanding of the patient is to unfold. What matters is less the derailments themselves than the analyst's capacity to bear them, and the manner in which the analyst becomes able to recover a foothold in order to use the experiences on behalf of the analytic couple and the therapy. I do not think it an exaggeration to say that the analysis of the most severely disturbed personality disorders stands or falls on the capacity to work productively in the countertransference. For this reason, it may be prudent to consult with a trusted colleague(s) from time to time, not least in order to illuminate the complexities of the countertransference.

Potential transference difficulties may be obvious or may only be hinted at by the patient, sometimes evolving inaudibly. This may require the analyst to use occasional unobtrusive questions or to proffer provisional ideas based on countertransferential indicators that serve as much to illuminate the penumbra of object relations difficulties that beset the patient as they do to infer psychic reality. Many analysts find it important to obtain psychiatric backup during therapy to act as a support for both patient and analyst, often in times of extreme transference intensity when psychotic anxieties may threaten to overwhelm the patient's beleaguered ego.* Despite their cold, hostile, or bizarre behavior, Cluster A patients suffer painful, highly confusing experiences deriving from major problems of self-esteem linked to a fragmented personality structure and reliance upon primitive self-representations. Therapeutic gains in these areas, although sometimes limited

---

* For guidelines regarding the psychiatric treatment of Cluster A, a useful summary can be found in the *Australian and New Zealand Journal of Psychiatry*, 24(3), 1990, 339–350.

and usually the outcome of painstaking effort on both sides, can make a significant difference to the quality of their lives.

PARANOID PERSONALITY DISORDER

The main characteristic of PPD is distrust and suspiciousness. The motives of other people are construed as hostile and exploitative. The PPD patient's thoughts and feeling are preoccupied by conflicts and threats *felt to emanate from the outside*. Such individuals suffer doubts about the loyalty of others and anticipate betrayal as a "given" consequence of human engagement. As a result of their preoccupation with external threats, they are vigilant and seek to keep a safe distance from others. Relationships, where these are allowed to occur, may be conducted on an apparently polite, formal, and controlling basis in order to sustain disconnection from disturbing affects, ultimately of a hostile nature. Negative stereotyping may be a feature of relations with others and this may lead to a search for security through contact with people who share the patient's paranoid beliefs. Individuals can express PPD through hostility, sarcasm, stubbornness, or a cynical worldview. However, the beleaguered, self-righteous attitude characteristic of PPD conceals a deep sensitivity to the ordinary struggles of life (especially setbacks), an unwillingness to forgive, inflation of subjective judgment, and great difficulty in accepting another's viewpoint. An example of this negativity is conveyed in the following, typical type of exchange in the psychoanalytic therapy of a PPD patient. The vignette is taken from the twice-weekly therapy of an isolated man in his 30s, who entered therapy (with a male analyst) as a result of fears regarding self-harming and suicidal thoughts. In this session he had been complaining at length, not for the first time and without appropriate affect, about his boss's overbearing behavior:

P: ... that guy in the office behaves as though he knows everything. He's got a problem. Nobody gets on with him. Only last week he told one of the clerks that unless he got his act together she'd be out—in front of everyone! Somebody should blow the whistle on that sort of behavior ... it's offensive. ... [*Pause*]
A: It sounds like you are very angry today with your boss because of the crass, insensitive way you feel he deals with people and that you are struggling to control these feelings ... I am wondering whether a similar struggle takes place here when you sometimes feel talked down to as a result of the things we discuss, which are often difficult and painful.
P: What's that got to do with it? Why say that? It has nothing to do with you. Are you accusing me of blaming him when it's all in me? He *is*

offensive … you've got a professional job to do … you aren't allowed to behave like that … and anyway, I'd tell you if you did.

Here, the patient succeeds in communicating his anger (via splitting and projective identification) while denying its felt reality and a connection in the transference to his analyst. This need to control affects and interpersonal contact is common in PPD. Such defenses serve to conceal feelings of inferiority based on low self-esteem. Humiliation, shame, and depressive feelings are the underlying characteristics of PPD and these persistently threaten the ego. Sensitivity by the analyst to these threats to the personality is a priority. So great is the power of projective processes in PPD that it may take years for the patient to establish sufficient trust in the motives of his analyst to be able to talk about himself openly. The pressures on the analyst's capacity to bear countertransference experiences of being misunderstood, misinterpreted, and devalued are high. In this instance, tolerance of being treated with contempt as interventions were violently refuted was repeatedly necessary. Over time, it became clearer how the humiliation being heaped on the analyst reflected the patient's shame-ridden experience of being devalued by his father throughout his childhood, a situation that was made worse by the mother's collusion with the father's derision.

Encounters with PPD, such as the one described above, may leave other people disoriented, offended, or even provoked into conflict, sometimes without any proper understanding of how conflict originated in the first place. To the layperson, the emotional atmosphere can quickly take on a charged, dangerous quality that arises seemingly over nothing, leading to fear, confusion, and wariness. Initial history-taking by the clinician may provide the context of chronicity within which these acute crises arise. Careful discussion with the patient may indicate a withdrawal from relationships in childhood and a long-standing preoccupation with ruminative, conflict-based fantasies. These fantasies permeate the psychic reality of the individual, influencing attitudes towards external as well as internal objects. PPD can be differentiated from formal psychotic illness by an absence of delusions or hallucinations, although the scale of the projective mechanisms used can sometimes resemble delusional thinking. Medication—usually neuroleptics or SSRI antidepressants—may be given, often in combination with psychoanalytic therapy; however, PPD patients struggle with any treatment regime due to their abiding distrust.

Freud (1911) saw paranoia as the consequence of projecting (predominantly sexual) ideas which are incompatible with the ego into the external world, and the subsequent delusional elaborations as representing a "patch over the ego," an attempt to recover meaning in a world that had become disintegrated and meaningless. Although paranoia is still regarded as deriving from defensive projective systems, and an unconscious fear of being drawn into a homosexual relationship may be discerned in PPD, Freud's focus on homosexuality as the central pathogenic factor in paranoia has given way to wider consideration of the role of primitive emotional conflicts and modes of thought (Bell, 2003). These developmental processes involve difficulties in the acquisition of a stable sense of self; the management of powerful, primitive affects, particularly aggression (whether of innate or of a psychosocial origin or both); and ways in which the personality negotiates psychosensory and enactive modes of function and the processes of separation, self-object discrimination, and individuation (Mahler, Pine, & Bergman, 1975). There is a widespread view today that the perceived threat of the consequences of aggression for the subject's ego gives rise to pervasive splitting and the chronic use of projective identification, probably beginning early in life. Rycroft (1960), in one of the few articles on the treatment of paranoia in the extensive PEP electronic archive, notes this and how Freud, given his concern at the time with establishing fixation points for psychopathology, omitted to mention the concept of denial in his considerations of paranoia, a defense which nowadays is commonly coupled with projection and projective identification and is seen as providing the basis of paranoid disorders (p. 68).

Many clinicians today pay particular attention to the object-relations crisis in PPD in which the individual feels unable to surrender or yield to the experience of dependence upon the primary object for fear of unmanageable conflict leading to destruction. Melanie Klein contributed significantly to this understanding, having located the paranoid phase within Abraham's first anal stage and subsequently conceiving of this state of mind as the earliest object relationship of the oral stage, from which she evolved her concept of the paranoid-schizoid position. This concept is useful in understanding all Cluster A disorders and, in particular, the functional role of paranoia. The initial object in Klein's view is partial (the earliest representation being the breast, followed by the mother) and is subject to splitting into "good" and "bad" aspects—idealized and denigrated, respectively. The ego attempts to rid itself of "bad" object experiences using projective mechanisms. Introjection of the "bad" part-object threatens the infant with a fear of destruction. Splitting, idealization, disavowal, and denial contribute to a defensive, omnipotent attempt to ward off the "bad" object, and the ensuing interplay of projective and introjective mechanisms is today accepted by many as pivotal in the understanding of paranoid conditions such as PPD. Kernberg (1975), Rosenfeld (1969), Stone (1993), and Gabbard (2000), among others, have also noted how the PPD patient persistently and violently splits the object, leading to separated "good" and "bad" aspects, and reflecting a developmental failure of mentalization in infancy (Target & Fonagy, 1996a, 1996b). Object constancy (the internalization of a reliably available, caring other) is not established. The PPD patient succumbs, probably early in life, to chronic expulsion of aggressive impulses by projection. Projective identification locates these impulses in mental representations of others as a means of controlling fears of annihilating the object and of being annihilated in turn. Beneath this defensive strategy lie feelings of helplessness, worthlessness, inadequacy, and depression (Meissner, 1986; Rosenfeld, 1969). Environmental failure to contain disturbing infantile feelings, above all aggression and hatred, plays a fundamental paranoiagenic role in paranoid thinking (cf. Balint, 1969; Kohut & Wolf, 1978; Winnicott, 1962).

The psychoanalytic therapy of PPD demands exceptional tact and patience on the part of the analyst, as premature interpretation of aggression or of underlying depression and feelings of rejection and humiliation can lead to negative therapeutic reactions, acting out, and even termination of treatment. Defensiveness on the part of the analyst can play a part in these enactments. At the same time, the patient's painful states of mind are precisely those that require psychotherapeutic attention. Judicious use of transference and countertransference understanding of part-object experiences can lead to a deepening appreciation of the subjugation and humiliation of the ego by the superego and the ensuing incarceration of the patient's sense of self. The scale of superego dominance of the ego, through extreme, harsh, and intransigent injunctions purporting to provide protective advice and safety, is a focus for many analysts. In this respect, the experience of being refuted, marginalized, dominated, and having one's mind closed down requires of the analyst a paradoxical "open-yet-not-porous" responsiveness, if the patient's relations of oppression and domination are to be understood. Openness is necessary in order to be able to feel the human dimension of countertransference communications, benign or malign. At the same time, the analyst needs to maintain some capacity for reflection on their origin, their trajectory, and their impact on the analyst's feelings, from which a grasp of their meaning and object relations configuration can emerge.

The compulsive, irrational, globalizing, but constricted activity of the overdeveloped superego may, with enough time and insight, come to be differentiated from the patient's genuine wishes to trust the analyst, leading to the acquisition of a "third" position from which both participants become able to reflect together on the patient's crippling intrapsychic conflicts (Ogden, 1999). The beginnings of emotional dependence on the analyst as a distinct, trustworthy object may be profoundly disconcerting for the patient, as this can be felt to be an unprecedented and threatening new experience. The separation anxieties, feelings of loss, and confusion that can accompany the development of a genuine object-relating stance testify to a state of deep regression that may have prevailed throughout the course of the patient's life. A vulnerability to suspiciousness about others may remain with the PPD patient even after therapy ends; however, many analysts consider that with sufficient "psychic disinvestment" in the values and activities of the overdeveloped superego, and increased investment in grasping the libidinal and aggressive vicissitudes that accompany relations with objects, the PPD patient can achieve an impressive level of stability.

SCHIZOID PERSONALITY DISORDER

SPD is characterized by emotional detachment from social and personal relationships. Expressions of feeling towards others are limited because emotional contact is both painful and felt to lack personal meaning. Compelling interpersonal experiences seem to pass the SPD individual by, but at the same time they impact on the person in ways that can seem outwardly muted but which are internally powerful. The schizoid person can feel isolated and in great pain if left alone for too long. Forced to seek out contact with others to relieve this pain, the person may in turn become oppressed and persecuted if the contact is felt to be too prolonged or too intimate. Close association with others can lead to feeling overwhelmed by anxiety and a fear of loss of personal identity (sense of self). Hostility is rare; passive resistance and withdrawal predominate. Poor social skills and limited emotional range compound the "mechanical" characteristics of SPD behavior. When under threat, SPD individuals detach themselves still further. Confrontational therapy techniques are inadvisable as these heighten already severe anxieties. The fantasy life of SPD individuals can be intense; the difficulty for the analyst lies in accessing it, but if this is achieved, SPD patients can do well.

Conceptualizing schizoid psychic reality

Psychoanalytic theory considers the schizoid to be essentially someone who craves love but who cannot love for fear that love (not only hate) will destroy the object (Fairbairn, 1952). Fairbairn was one of the first psychoanalysts to depict in detail the mental processes involved in this extreme condition. In a summary of his work, Khan (1960) noted the main observations made by Fairbairn:

1. Schizoid conditions constitute the most deep seated of all psychopathological states.
2. The therapeutic analysis of the schizoid provides an opportunity for the study of the widest range of psychopathological processes in a single individual, for in such cases it is usual for the final state to be reached only after all available methods of defending the personality have been exploited.
3. Contrary to common belief, schizoid individuals who have not regressed too far are capable of greater psychological insight than any other class of person, normal or abnormal.

4. Again, contrary to common belief, schizoid individuals "show them-selves capable of transference to a remarkable degree, and present unexpectedly favorable therapeutic possibilities." Fairbairn went on to show the presence and importance of depersonalization, derealization, and disturbances of reality-sense (e.g., feelings of artificiality, experi-ences such as the "plate-glass feeling," feelings of unfamiliarity with familiar persons or environmental settings, and feelings of familiarity with unfamiliar ones); déjà vu also features significantly in their expe-rience. In their social extension of behavior, such persons can become fanatics, agitators, criminals, revolutionaries, etc. Fairbairn singled out three prominent characteristics of individuals in the schizoid category: an attitude of omnipotence, an attitude of isolation and detachment, and a preoccupation with inner reality (p. 428).

For Fairbairn, the fundamental splits in the ego seen in the schizoid individual create a concomitant oral-incorporative libidinal attitude that accounts for their tendency to treat other people as persons with less than inherent value (p. 429). This regressive stance towards objects Fairbairn connected to an experience of the maternal object as either indifferent or possessive. The schizoid personality has little experience of spontaneous and genuine expressions of love and affection that convince them that they are lovable in their own right, and depersonalization and de-emotional-ization of relationships come to characterize contact with people (p. 430). Additionally, the fact that schizoid people cannot give emotionally means that they relate by playing a role and/or by employing exhibitionistic atti-tudes. "Giving" is replaced by "showing." This superior attitude derives from overvaluation of the person's own mental contents and personal capacities, the use of intellectualized defenses, and a narcissistic inflation of the ego arising out of secret possession of, and identification with, inter-nal libidinized objects. Fairbairn's view is that in early life such individu-als were afflicted by a sense of deprivation and inferiority and remained fixated upon their mothers. The libidinal cathexis of an already internal-ized "breast-mother" is intensified and extended to relationships with other objects resulting in, among other things, an overvaluation of the internal at the expense of the external world. Such people must neither love nor be loved and must keep their libidinal objects at a distance (p. 430).

The following clinical extract illustrates some of the qualities described above and the particular problems faced by the analyst in dealing with SPD. The patient, a middle-aged man in psychoanalytic therapy three times weekly, began his session by complaining that he had felt bad after the session the previous day. He said he had had to drive to an appointment at lunchtime to see an acquaintance but got to a certain point on the jour-ney and realized he could either branch off and go home or continue on the road to his meeting. He went to the meeting. He then said he had had thoughts in his mind about his analytic session and had wanted to stop and write them down but he was on a busy road so couldn't do that. He had now forgotten what the thoughts were. He got to his destination but felt too tired to go up to the house and ring the bell. He had no energy left and thought of turning back. He turned the car round, pulled into a lay-by, and went to sleep for about an hour. Then he went home. It was early, he realized, but he was still tired and, when he got in, he went to sleep for several hours—three hours, he thought.

A: You said you felt bad after our session yesterday.

P: Bad? ... bad ... [Silence] ... I thought I hadn't been eating properly. Physically I am not entirely well, I still have a cough, maybe I am not entirely well yet ... [Silence] Tiredness ... heaviness. I can feel it in my body ... [Silence]

A: You seemed a little surprised when I reminded you of what you said about feeling bad after the session yesterday.

P: I don't recall saying that. I am not saying I did not, but if I did I am surprised that I did ... [Silence] ... I don't remember what happened in the session. It feels a very long time ago ... as if it were a long time ago.

In this brief vignette, typical of the type of interaction this man sustains with others (and which is also characteristic of many schizoid individuals), it is possible to see how the patient is "at a crossroads" with regard to his internal and external worlds. He attempts to engage with the external world, with his friend, and with his analyst, but is pulled back by anxiety regressively into his internal world, away from objects and towards a world of infantile orality which he experiences as less painful and conflicted.

A sense of latent hostility towards objects is also evident in the transference in the patient's references to falling asleep for "an hour" and "three hours," although the patient has no conscious awareness of this. In the above example, the analyst's countertransference experience, so common in the treatment of schizoid patients, was of feeling pushed away, dehumanized, but also tantalized into believing that the patient *might* have genuinely understood what was being said.

Many analysts elect to use a "two-step" model of intervention and interpretation, to allow the SPD patient to better tolerate the impact of references to the transference. Transference interpretations always draw the patient sharply into the analytic relationship and this can prove traumatic for SPD patients. Below is a vignette from a session with a different patient that demonstrates how a supportive interpretation is followed by a more traditional interpretation of transference content. The patient, a woman in her 40s, finds that the separation anxiety evoked by gaps in the therapy (between sessions, during breaks, etc.) is so painful that it makes her want to quit. She finds it difficult to "hear" interpretations of her mental pain as being linked to the separations, so focused is she on the pain itself and the action of quitting in order to relieve it. In this session she had reiterated that her only option was to quit the therapy. The analyst was able to say:

> I understand your wish to stop your therapy and, of course, I have no power to stop you. To do what we are doing would be a difficult undertaking for anyone and I think that recently you have been finding it especially painful. [*Supportive intervention*]
>
> I think you feel frustrated and hurt by the comings and goings to and from our sessions and are often left having to cope with a great deal on your own. I think this makes you feel resentful and you feel like quitting to stop the upset and pain. It must be very hard to talk about these feelings. I suspect that you are worried that I might not be able to stand it if you talk about them. [*Interpretation of underlying anxieties*]

By working through the crisis along these lines, the patient, better contained, gained more insight into her fantasy of the destructiveness of her feelings that was behind her wish to quit and she became able to begin to use object-related thinking and speech more, as opposed to making plans for direct action, to deal with her distress.

Clinical complications in treating schizoid individuals psychodynamically include the fact that they tend to provoke or seduce the analyst into a tantalizing relation to their material (e.g., in past history or internal reality), giving rise to the danger of overinterpretation. There is self-engrossment in relation to which the analyst is a spectator. The pseudoenthusiasm of these patients masks a dread of their sense of inner emptiness being found out. Affects have a discharge urgency about them. The ego of the patient either inhibits or facilitates this discharge but is not related to it. These patients need new objects and new experiences to enable them to experience themselves personally. They lean on the hopefulness of others, which they mobilize, and around which they can integrate their ego-functioning for short periods. In the end they reduce this to futility and the persons involved feel defeated. They repeat this with compulsion in the analytic situation to test the analyst, and the burden this puts on the clinician's countertransference can be enormous and exhausting (Khan, 1960, p. 431). Schizoid patients tend to "act out" their past experiences and current tensions in the analytic situation. They are terrified of ego-regression and dependency needs, and require the clinician's readiness to cooperate in a controlled and limited involvement. They have, however, a deep need for help and seek to use the clinician to bear their affective crises in order for the ego to integrate very slowly through identification so that they can begin to experience themselves as persons.

Anxiety is the greatest obstacle to treatment in SPD. This creates impasses, as the analytic situation through its very nature mobilizes large quantities of affects and aims at their containment and assimilation. Two techniques are used by schizoid patients to combat their anxiety states: The first is the translation of anxiety into psychic pain as seen in the above vignette, and some patients can become almost addicted to such pain (Khan, 1960, p. 432). The second technique is the translation of anxiety into diffuse and excessive tension states. These tension states can become a source of opposition to the analytic process, because the patient's intellectual defenses are fed from this source. Genetically speaking, anxiety in these patients is not so much a reaction to strong and powerful libidinal impulses or to a primitive, sadistic superego, but is more a sense of acute threat to the intactness and survival of the ego from the inner experience of utter emptiness and desolation. Any means of producing and maintaining psychic tension reassures them against the threat of anxiety deriving from this sense of emptiness. Psychic pain and masochism are used regularly to ward off this primary inner predicament. Masochistic pain raises the threshold of cathexes and so sponsors a sense of self (p. 433).

Fairbairn, Khan, Balint, Klein, Rosenfeld, Kernberg, and others have noted that the principal internal strategies of defense employed by schizoid individuals are splitting, the devaluation of objects and emotional experiences, excessive projective identifications, and idealization (Khan, 1960, p. 434). Regarding idealization, Khan makes the point that schizoid patients often give the impression of being psychopathic or amoral, and one is tempted to relate this to either defective superego formation or to a primitively sadistic superego. Scrutiny of intrapsychic functioning often reveals a highly organized *ego-ideal* not built from introjection of idealized primary parental objects but assembled *in lieu of* adequate primary figures. This way of dealing with deprivation derives from magical thinking. The idealized, magically acquired internal object that resembles an ego-ideal is used to fend off hopelessness, emptiness, and futility. In the transference, the patient will idealize the analyst and the analytic process to offset disillusionment and hopelessness, which they feel certain will be the outcome in a real relationship (p. 435).

SPD can be differentiated from paranoid personality disorder by a reduced level of suspiciousness of others and greater, chronic withdrawal. SPD is distinguishable from StPD by its less odd, eccentric, or obviously disturbed presentation, withdrawal again being its hallmark. Similarities of presentation of SPD with autism or Asperger's syndrome can sometimes make diagnosis complicated. Psychotic illness or severe depression may occur within SPD but can in some cases be linked to an accompanying personality disorder (such as avoidant or paranoid). Despite their detachment, many SPD individuals become very concerned about the unfulfilled lives they lead. Many do not marry or form sexual relationships, and if they do, settle for nondemanding partners. Enough contact to offset loneliness may be found in the workplace or through limited socializing. There is no generally accepted treatment for SPD. Group psychoanalytic therapy may be used to help with socialization. Psychoanalytic psychotherapy (which is usually individual but may be a combination of group and individual), perhaps with some medication, is sometimes recommended, analysis less so. Pharmacological treatments alone seem to have little impact on these patients, as their problems lie fundamentally in establishing relationships. Psychoanalytic therapy, although a potentially painful and confusing undertaking for schizoid individuals, probably offers the best hope for change. If the patient can become able to engage affectively with the analyst, even to a modest degree, the prospect of acquisition of insight and the promise of growth of the personality is a genuine one.

As with PPD, the psychoanalytic therapy of SPD requires tact and patience on the part of the analyst. Perhaps the principal area of challenge in understanding SPD lies in the primitive translation of anxiety (often pervasive) into psychic and physiological pain, which acts as a deterrent to dependency and trust. Without adequate respect for this terror and the pain that expresses it, the patient will not trust the analyst. At the same time, this source of terror may be connected to the sympathy SPD patients can evoke in the analyst, despite the hostility of the patient's defenses. It is difficult to spend time with a patient with SPD without feeling for the enormity of their dilemma and the devastating impact it has on every aspect of their life. It is therefore of inestimable therapeutic and developmental value to the SPD patient if they can begin to grasp emotionally, cognitively, and relationally the "impossibility" of the dilemma of claustro-agoraphobic relating (cf. Rey, 1994) and how this contributes to their heightened anxiety, mental pain, and chronic isolation. By becoming aware of this "global" crisis and by beginning to address the terms of reference of the psychotically based anxieties that underlie it, many SPD patients become better able to see and manage their extreme "suffocation-isolation" preoccupations and, over time, reduce the levels of omniscience and idealization that sustain them. This permits growing reflection on the fundamental fear of loss of the object that drives the patient's anxiety and mistrust in relationships. Eventually, the acquisition of a modest but sincere reliance on the analyst and the analytic relationship can have the enduring effect of moderating extreme anxieties, as the patient begins to feel connected to the actual world and to others. Depressive anxieties may arise, bringing with them a new order of painful experiences such as acute fears of loss and grief in respect to the past. These anxieties are associated primarily with neurosis rather than psychosis.

SCHIZOTYPAL PERSONALITY DISORDER

StPD is characterized by a "pervasive pattern of social and interpersonal deficits marked by acute discomfort with, and reduced capacity for, close relationships as well as by cognitive or perceptual distortions and

eccentricities of behavior" (*DSM-IV-TR*; *ICD-10*). "Schizotypal personality" is a category that derives from the term *schizotype* first employed
by Rado in 1953 to bring together schizophrenic and genotype into one
category. "Schizotypal" refers to a disordered personality in which there
are constitutional defects similar to those underlying schizophrenia. Brief
psychotic episodes due to stress may arise in StPD but these are usually
transient. Some StPD individuals may go on to develop schizophrenia but
they are a small minority. The principal characteristics of StPD are distortions in cognition and perception, including a disturbed view of the
body, and the presence of odd, magical, or eccentric beliefs or ideas. StPD
(and SPD) individuals have considerable difficulty in experiencing pleasure
(anhedonia). They may show ideas of reference and superstitions and they
suffer chronic social anxiety. Close relationships are felt to be threatening
and social isolation is not uncommon. StPD individuals feel themselves to
be at odds with, not part of, the world. They feel excluded, that they do
not fit, and are resentful of feeling this way, often appearing agitated, frustrated, or disgruntled while being unable to specify their complaint or the
extent of their prevailing feelings. Withdrawal and avoidance are used to
counter confusion and conflict. Strong feelings evoke intense anxiety due
to a fear both of becoming engulfed by feelings and immersed in conflict,
and this can threaten the patient's hold on reality. The need to avoid strong
feelings leads to a tendency to overfocus on tangential issues (hence the
characteristic of eccentricity). The patient may not be aware of the oddness
of their beliefs and behavior and feel threatened if confronted. Their illusions and preoccupations defend against fragmented ego functioning and a
precarious sense of self. Social contacts, support from family and friends,
and engagement in therapeutic relationships are necessary to counter the
tendency to remain withdrawn and thus become increasingly susceptible
to psychotic thinking. The chaotic and eccentric thinking that is characteristic of StPD may at times be mixed with paranoid and manic ideation.
Ongoing assessment of the StPD patient's ego strength is therefore required.
Containing the patient's multifarious anxieties and interpreting the meaning of their fixed ideas (that sometimes resemble delusions) is a prerequisite
for effective psychoanalytic therapy.

Despite the genetic link with schizophrenia and the susceptibility to ego
fragmentation, StPD patients who enter psychoanalytic therapy may do better than SPD patients due to their greater affective availability. StPD patients
may reveal areas of reasonable ego strength. This, combined with less rigid
defenses than SPD patients, may enable them to respond more readily to
analytic interpretations and to tolerate depressive affects. Progress may be
slow and erratic and results rarely approximate to a normal life, but gradual
personality integration is possible and this can lead to a marked improvement in daily living. Treatment, especially in severe cases, may involve

low dosages of the kind of medications used in schizophrenia. SSRIs can improve obsessive, compulsive, and depressive symptoms in StPD.

Treating the StPD patient

What follows is a description, rather than a clinical extract, of the psychoanalytic therapy of a 55-year-old woman with StPD. Its purpose is to give an indication of the range of complexities that confront the analyst when treating StPD. This particular patient is the sixth of seven children and was brought up in affluent but dysfunctional circumstances. She saw more of her rather austere nanny than she did her mother when she was a child. Her authoritarian but available father assumed the status of "rescuer" in the patient's mind, and she has turned to him throughout her life when in difficulty, despite feeling intimidated and humiliated when she does so. She has been able to talk to men with more ease than to women. Intimacy of any kind leads her to feel agitation, fear of conflict, and incipient guilt and shame. She complains of feeling unlike other people, excluded, jealous of people who seem to have close relationships, while at the same time she can idealize her own background and upbringing. She blames herself for her feelings of ingratitude. Periodically she can feel depressed and hopeless and she takes a low dosage of antidepressant medication to ease these feelings. The patient displays the troubled and tangential thinking typical of the StPD patient when faced with dependent feelings. For example, she can move from one subject to a completely different subject in a disconnected way, with little or no awareness of the incongruity. Conversely, she can fall silent, becoming prey to ruminative and persecuting thoughts. Her superego is overactive, often cautioning her about the multitude of dangers she faces if she trusts her analyst or anyone else. This leads to recurrent confusion as she often experiences her intense need for her trustworthy analyst and her wish to violently reject her "dangerous," untrustworthy analyst simultaneously. When she can no longer bear this exhausting mental conflict, she sometimes takes to her bed and can remain there for days. When withdrawn in this way she can disconnect almost entirely from others—her immediate family reported one occasion when she did not speak for a week and ate almost nothing. During such crises, her analyst reports sessions in which the patient is completely silent. The silence often contains an agitated, internal pressure within the patient to "do" or feel something that remains obscure and unamenable to help, as though the patient is engaged in a private battle with oppressors.

Her three-times-weekly psychoanalytic therapy has had a containing and stabilizing effect and she has come to value her relationship with her analyst. At the same time, her growing dependency has aroused levels of psychotic anxiety that in the past she has kept at bay by remaining distant from others. The anxieties are terror filled and seem to center around being dropped and abandoned, although this is, of course, not simple as the patient regularly "drops" her analyst when she feels that her hopes for the future depend upon the relationship. The support of her family has been helpful in containing these many anxieties. The split and fragmented nature of her mental functioning, typical of StPD patients and reminiscent of schizophrenic thinking, presents the analyst with the challenge of helping the patient to integrate into an already fragile ego potentially overwhelming, disparate thoughts and feelings that seem disconnected from each other and which are felt by the patient to be incompatible. The patient's internal object relations world reflects parallel fractures, with objects being experienced partially and usually in conflict with each other. One important aspect of her anxiety is the confusion that assails her from these partial, inchoate experiences, leading her to often feel dread at what she might feel or experience next. Compelling aspects of objects regularly intrude into her mind, being made more threatening by the projective activity of the patient, which heightens the impact of part-objects (Williams, 2004). One clear feature in this patient is an underlying paranoid quality to her relationships, which is similar to the primitive persecution seen in paranoid schizophrenia. Her dread of disintegration seems to be connected to dissociated feelings of narcissistically derived rage, which threaten to emerge when her capacity for idealization and withdrawal feel threatened. At these times she can feel terror that she will be annihilated as a consequence of the violent return of her projections.

It has required considerable containing activity on the part of the analyst in order for the patient to begin to be able to talk about her feelings, as she was consumed for a long time by a delusional conviction that the analyst could not bear her, and that this was the reason why (customary) breaks in the therapy, such as holidays, occurred. Containment and elucidation of her feelings of rejection and the associated paranoid anxieties that contributed to them was the principal therapeutic task. When she did talk of her feelings, she was impeded by thought blocking, retching (inside and outside the sessions, although she did not vomit), and a tendency to refute what she had said moments earlier, often in an implausible, histrionic manner, as though panicking. She occasionally brought with her a utensil/container as a source of comfort, and sometimes when she experienced fear of dying or of committing suicide she suffered physical symptoms such as shaking and rocking. The analyst's countertransference experience was decisive in understanding the patient's confusing behavior and thoughts. A particular set of repeated countertransference feelings comprised anxiety that therapy was hopeless and the patient would quit or, worse, was at risk of imminent death, alongside frustration at her inability and unwillingness to speak openly about what clearly troubled her. These countertransference responses, among others, enabled the analyst to reflect upon likely feelings the patient might be holding at bay and to speculate as to why.

Eventually, by carefully introducing ideas derived from these countertransference feelings, the patient was able to speak, little by little, of a lifelong tendency to be compliant, tremendous frustration at feeling "different" and misunderstood, and an internal hatred and bitterness at feeling neglected that gave rise to fantasies of murder and dismemberment—thoughts that she felt were unforgivable and therefore inadmissible. This case, thought somewhat severe, is not atypical of an StPD patient's responses to psychoanalytic therapy and underscores the need in the analyst for patience, sensitivity, and a progressive understanding of complex axes of transference and countertransference phenomena that encompass conflict, deficit, compromised and failed developmental milestones and, in particular, the intrusion of psychotic thinking that fragments ego functioning.

Conceptualization of StPD stresses early fragmentation of the ego and damage to the sense of self of a type associated with schizophrenic states. As a consequence, low self-esteem accompanies and fuels difficulties in personal relationships. Psychological functioning reveals primitive, part-object relationships, impoverished mental representations, developmental deficits in terms of the capacity to mentalize, and a potential for psychotic thinking under stress. StPD patients' failure to internalize adequate representations of the object means that they remain fixated at the paranoid-schizoid level of development (Klein, 1946), and because trauma (externally and/or internally derived) is held to have occurred at the oral stage, StPD anxieties are viewed as extremely primitive, requiring thoroughgoing containment followed by interpretation at points when the ego is neither overwhelmed by anxiety nor paralyzed by defenses. Both StPD and SPD patients fit the "philobatic" profile described by Balint (1969). He proposed two internal solutions to the failure of the relationship between mother and baby. The "basic fault" in the infant's personality may be expressed as either the "ocnophilic" or the "philobatic" tendency in later life. The former is a response to a chronic "emptiness inside" and seeks to fill it by compulsively demanding more and more from others. The latter involves giving up on others and retreating into a world of fantasy. Bowlby's (1969, 1988) "avoidantly attached" category is a similar characterization of these individuals who are too afraid of aversive contact to seek out relationships.

KEY CLINICAL CONCEPTS IN CLUSTER A

- Cluster A personality disorders are characterized by a prevalence of psychotic anxieties in parallel to the patient's neurotic anxieties. The expressive forms of these different levels of anxiety vary according to the condition, but all have in common a need for the clinician to pay particular attention to the impact of psychotic thinking on the therapeutic alliance, the transference, and the patient's ego functioning.

Analysts need to be aware of how they are being experienced by the patient in object relations terms—part or whole ("Who or what am I currently representing for the patient, and in what way?"). Sufficient engagement with the Cluster A patient is only possible if this awareness is acquired. At one moment the analyst may be experienced positively, even as an idealized figure, but this can change dramatically into the analyst being seen as a persecuting critic or tyrant. This change can take place without the analyst saying anything controversial, and signifies the radical disjuncture in the patient's capacity for affective control and the severity of splitting of the ego and objects. A nondefensive, nonconfrontational approach and willingness on the part of the analyst to tolerate being a "bad" (i.e., inadequate) as well as "good object" is a prerequisite to establishing basic trust and a reduction in splitting.

• Countertransference monitoring of how the patient is making the analyst feel (e.g., "I am now experiencing strong feelings [these may be boredom, sexual, aggressive feelings, etc.]. To what extent do these feelings originate in me or is the patient inducing me to feel these?") is perhaps the most critical component in understanding the use of splitting, projective identification, and the part-object functioning that characterizes Cluster A mental representations. It is likely that the patient's core pathogenic relationships will become discernible first and foremost via the countertransference.

• All Cluster A patients have suffered significant damage to their self-esteem. An awareness in the analyst of the patient's propensity for deep feelings of shame and humiliation will help in the weathering of bouts of acting out and negative therapeutic reactions. The latter are stubborn resistances to improvement usually following some improvement (cf. Freud, 1923; Riviere, 1936; Steiner, 1994). They are to be expected, as is acting out by patients over money, timings, holidays, etc., and need to be responded to by reality-based, firm but supportive interventions, together with interpretation of the anxieties being defended against.

• Avoiding malignant regression is important. Regression is a defensive reversion, under stress, to earlier forms of thinking and object relating and is often inevitable in therapy. *Benign* regression signifies a healthy satisfying of certain infantile needs by working these through collaboratively in the therapy. *Malignant* regression denotes a situation is which the patient tries but fails to have these needs met and the situation yields a vicious cycle of demanding, addiction-like states. Analysts, if they are to achieve the trust of a Cluster A patient, must avoid reacting to the patient in an over-emotional way that fuels malignant regression but remain rooted in analytic work, keeping in mind the compromised ego of the infant in the patient (Carpy, 1989; Gabbard & Wilkinson, 1994; Heimann, 1950).

- Awareness of deficit as well as conflict models is useful in understanding the quality of patients' attachments, as these can be highly primitive and confused.

- Therapeutic goals require realistic assessment and regular monitoring. Progress may be slow and erratic with setbacks and perhaps ultimately limited eventual gains. These gains may translate into improvements in daily living that are of inestimable value.

REFERENCES

American Psychiatric Association. (1994). *Diagnostic and statistical manual of mental disorders* (4th Ed.). Washington, DC: Author.

Balint, M. (1969). *The basic fault: Therapeutic aspects of regression.* New York: Brunner Mazel.

Bell, D. (2003). *Paranoia.* London: Icon Books.

Bowlby, J. (1969). *Attachment and loss.* New York: Penguin.

Bowlby, J. (1988). *A secure base: Clinical applications of attachment theory.* London: Routledge.

Carpy, D. V. (1989). Tolerating the countertransference: A mutative process. *International Journal of Psychoanalysis, 70,* 287–294.

Elkin, D. G. (1999). *Introduction to clinical psychiatry.* New York: McGraw-Hill.

Fairbairn, W. R. D. (1952). *Psychoanalytic studies of the personality.* London: Tavistock.

Freud, S. (1911). Psychoanalytic notes on an autobiographical account of a case of paranoia (dementia paranoides). In J. Strachey (Ed. & Trans.), *The standard edition of the complete psychological works of Sigmund Freud* (Vol. 12, pp. 3–80). London: Hogarth Press.

Freud, S. (1923). The ego and the id. In J. Strachey (Ed. & Trans.), *The standard edition of the complete psychological works of Sigmund Freud* (Vol. 19, pp. 12–66). London: Hogarth Press.

Gabbard, G. (2000). *Psychodynamic psychiatry in clinical practice.* Washington, DC: American Psychiatric Press.

Gabbard, G., & Wilkinson, S. M. (1994). *Management of countertransference with borderline patients.* Washington, DC: American Psychiatric Press.

Grotstein, J. S. (1995). Object relations theory in the treatment of the psychoses. *Bulletin of the Menninger Clinic, 59,* 312–332.

Gunderson, J. (2008). *Borderline personality disorder: A clinical guide.* Washington, DC: American Psychiatric Press.

Heimann, P. (1950). On counter-transference. *International Journal of Psychoanalysis, 31,* 81–84.

Hinshelwood, R. D. (1994). *Clinical Klein: From theory to practice.* New York: HarperCollins.

Jackson, M. (2000). *Weathering the storms.* London: Karnac.

Jackson, M., & Williams, P. (1994). *Unimaginable storms: A search for meaning in psychosis*. London: Karnac.

Kernberg, O. (1975). *Borderline personality and pathological narcissism*. Northvale, NJ: Jason Aronson.

Khan, M. R. (1960). Clinical aspects of the schizoid personality: Affects and technique. *International Journal of Psychoanalysis, 41*, 430–436.

Klein, M. (1946). Notes on some schizoid mechanisms. *International Journal of Psychoanalysis, 27*, 99–110.

Kohut, H., & Wolf, E. S. (1978). The disorders of the self and their treatment: An outline. *International Journal of Psychoanalysis, 59*, 413–426.

Lieberz, K., & Porsch, U. (1997). Countertransference in schizoid disorders. *Psychotherapy, Psychosomatics, Medical Psychology, 47*(2), 46–51.

Lucas, R. N. (1992). The psychotic personality: A psycho-analytic theory and its application in clinical practice. *Psychoanalytic Psychotherapy, 6*, 73–79.

Mahler, M., Pine, F., & Bergman, A. (1975). *The psychological birth of the human infant*. London: Karnac.

McGlashan, T. (1986). The Chestnut Lodge follow-up study III: Long-term outcome of borderline personalities. *Archives of General Psychiatry, 43*, 20–30.

Meissner, W. W. (1986). *The paranoid process*. Northvale, NJ: Jason Aronson.

Ogden, T. (1999). *Reverie and interpretation: Sensing something human*. London: Karnac.

Quality Assurance Project. (1990). Treatment outlines for paranoid, schizotypal and schizoid personality disorders. *Australian and New Zealand Journal of Psychiatry, 24*(3), 339–350.

Rey, H. (1994). *Universals of psychoanalysis in the treatment of psychotic and borderline states*. London: Free Association Books.

Riviere, J. (1936). A contribution to the analysis of the negative therapeutic reaction. *International Journal of Psychoanalysis, 17*, 304–320.

Robbins, M. (2002). Speaking in tongues: Language and delusion in schizophrenia. *International Journal of Psychoanalysis, 83*(2), 383–405.

Rosenfeld, H. (1964). On the psychopathology of narcissism: A clinical approach. *International Journal of Psychoanalysis, 45*, 332–337.

Rosenfeld, H. (1969). On the treatment of psychotic states by psychoanalysis: An historical approach. *International Journal of Psychoanalysis, 50*, 615–631.

Rycroft, C. (1960). The analysis of a paranoid personality. *International Journal of Psychoanalysis, 41*, 59–69.

Sandell, R., Blomberg, J., Lazar, A., Carlsson, J., Schubert, J., & Broberg, J. (1997). Findings of the Stockholm Outcome of Psychotherapy and Psychoanalysis Project (STOPPP). Paper presented at the Annual Meeting of the Society for Psychotherapy Research, Geilo, Norway.

Segal, H. (1978). On symbolism. *International Journal of Psychoanalysis, 59*, 315–319.

Sohn, L. (1997). Unprovoked assaults: Making sense of apparently random violence. In D. Bell (Ed.), *Reason and passion: A celebration of the work of Hanna Segal* (pp. 57–74). London: Tavistock.

Steiner, J. (1994). *Psychic retreats*. London: Routledge.

Stone, M. (1985). Schizotypal personality: Psychotherapeutic aspects. *Schizophrenia Bulletin, 11*(4), 576–589.

Stone, M. (1993). Long-term outcome in personality disorders. *British Journal of Psychiatry*, *162*, 299–313.

Target, M., & Fonagy, P. (1996a). Playing with reality II: The development of psychic reality from a theoretical perspective. *International Journal of Psychoanalysis*, *77*, 459–479.

Target, M., & Fonagy, P. (1996b). *An outcome study of psychoanalytic therapy for patients with borderline personality disorder*. New York: International Universities Press.

Williams, P. (2004). Incorporation of an invasive object. *International Journal of Psychoanalysis*, *85*, 1–15.

Winnicott, D. W. (1962). The aims of psychoanalytic treatment. In *The maturational processes and the facilitating environment* (pp. 166–170). London: Hogarth Press.

World Health Organization. (1992). *International statistical classification of diseases and related health problems* (10th Ed.). Geneva, Switzerland: Author.

Wurmser, L. (2008). *Torment me but don't abandon me*. Northvale, NJ: Jason Aronson.

Chapter 6

The "beautiful mind" of John Nash

Notes toward a psychoanalytic reading*

The remarkable story of John Nash, recovered chronic schizophrenic and Nobel Laureate, has acquired worldwide publicity through the success of Sylvia Nasar's biography, *A Beautiful Mind* (1998), and the film of the same name derived from it (2001). At the age of 30 (1958), already recognized as a mathematician of genius, Nash suffered a schizophrenic breakdown from which he did not recover for over 25 years. Drawing on several sources of information, these notes will outline some of the salient features that lend themselves to a psychoanalytic perspective on the nature of his illness; the different factors that may have predisposed him to a psychotic breakdown, and precipitated and perpetuated it; and the psychodynamic pathways which may have led to his eventual recovery. Certain features of his case, not explored in the book and film, have important implications for both psychoanalytic and psychiatric approaches to the understanding and treatment of severe psychotic illness, and these will be reflected upon in this chapter. The aim of the essay is to illustrate how object-relations concepts of modern psychoanalytic thinking can contribute in an important and practical way to the contemporary approach of psychiatry to schizophrenic-type and other psychoses.

---

* The impetus and most of the work for this essay was undertaken by my friend and colleague Dr. Murray Jackson, with whom I have collaborated on a number of writing projects. I am grateful to him for providing the opportunity to study the remarkable, tormented inner world of John Nash. Both authors stress that observations in this essay derive from extant sources, not from Nash himself. What is written here is the product of informed conjecture yielded by the study of texts, not the mind or speech of a human being. The authors make no claim for the clinical utility of their observations in the case of John Nash today. Such is the wealth of information available on the suffering and recovery of John Nash that the authors deemed it reasonable to explore this and to reflect on it from a psychoanalytic point of view. The authors have taken particular care to address the subject matter of this paper with the respect it deserves, and have made extensive efforts to ensure that nothing in the text is inaccurate or misleading. The essay was sent to Professor Nash for his comments prior to publication. The authors have proceeded on the basis of having made the best effort possible to ensure that the person and reputation of Professor Nash have been protected.

PROLOGUE

Although antipsychotic medication frequently suppressed Nash's psychotic symptoms, he eventually decided to discontinue it because it interfered with his thinking in a way that he found unacceptable. This decision deprived him of the protective effect of the medication and exposed him to the force of the suppressed psychotic process within him. However, it also allowed him to gradually use his residual sane thinking effectively and thereby to oppose his psychotic thinking and hallucinatory voices, and eventually to recover from his illness without the aid of medication. He returned to a normal and creative life, a remarkable outcome that was hailed as a rare and near-miraculous event (Nasar, 1998, p. 21).* Nash subsequently claimed that his recovery was achieved by his own intellectual efforts, without the help of medication. He was awarded a Nobel Prize in economics in 1996 for work done prior to his breakdown.[†] He came to understand his illness as an essentially psychogenic one, a view that contrasts sharply with the reductionist "biomedical" orientation of the biography, and of much of contemporary psychiatry. Although the film script shows a certain acquaintance with psychoanalytic theory (appropriate to the background of the scriptwriter[‡]), for example with H. A. Rosenfeld's (1987) "destructive narcissism," the film draws the same conclusion as the biography and, apparently in the interests of opposing the social stigma attached to schizophrenia, promotes the seriously misleading message that schizophrenia is an organic illness like diabetes. Although a well-made and moving film, it suffers by promoting a shallow and sentimental idealization of Nash, and of schizophrenia.[§] In the introduction to her biography Sylvia Nasar reports the account of a colleague who questioned Nash soon after the acute onset of his psychosis during a period of rationality: "How could you, a mathematician, a man devoted to reason and logical proof, believe that extraterrestrials are sending you messages? How could you believe that you are being recruited by aliens from outer space to save the world?" Nash replied, "Because the ideas I had about supernatural beings came to me in the same way that my mathematical ideas did. So I took them seriously" (p. 11).

This response is relevant to the role of unconscious mental processes underlying both creative and psychotic phenomena and of the loss of the

---

* A misunderstanding vigorously refuted in the American National Press by Harding (2002).
† Charles (2003) considered that this acknowledgment played an important part in his recovery.
‡ Both parents of the scriptwriter, Akiva Goldsman, were psychotherapists devoted to work with psychotic patients.
§ The filmmakers defended themselves vigorously against such criticism, and it should be recognized that it would be impossible to deal with his past homosexuality and the extreme destructiveness of some of his past behavior in such a film.

capacity to distinguish between the two. It might suggest that Nash may have had an unusual ability to preserve the capacity for curiosity and intellectual exploration, a talent which may have served him well throughout his illness and contributed to his eventual recovery. It is also interesting to note that the biographer is of the firm view that he emerged from his psychosis as a transformed personality, more emotionally mature and free of his previous arrogance and other disagreeable narcissistic personality traits.

Sources of information

The chief sources of information employed in this essay are Sylvia Nasar's biography, *A Beautiful Mind* (1998); a vast amount of material available on the Internet (which includes contributions by Nash himself subsequent to his recovery); and his historical lecture of 1996 in Madrid. The film *A Beautiful Mind* (2001), although offering no additional information, is of interest. A later documentary, *A Brilliant Madness* (2003), made with Nash's more extensive cooperation, adds further significant material.* Although much of Sylvia Nasar's biography comes from second- or third-hand sources, the meticulous detail and consistency of Nasar's reporting confers an authenticity and reliability to these sources. Nash's personal disclosures during and after his illness are also extremely revealing.

WHY STUDY THE ILLNESS OF JOHN NASH?

All the psychological factors that are considered in this essay are familiar to modern-day psychoanalysts working with psychotic patients, and can be found in case reports in psychoanalytic publications. The question could be posed as to whether it might be better to present a typical clinical case, successfully treated by a psychoanalytically oriented approach, suitably anonymized and reported in adequate detail,[†] rather than using conjecture that has not been confirmed by the patient himself. The traditional case presentation approach offers evidence for the conclusions reached, free of the speculative quality that is inevitable where so much crucial information is unavailable and mostly second- or third-hand. Readers could then easily make up their own mind about the conclusions presented. However, although recovery after such a long schizophrenic illness is not unusual (Bleuler, 1978; Harding, Brooks,

---

* In particular a photograph of a card sent to a friend during a depressive state, in which the words pity, justice, and mercy could be made out. We are grateful to Michael Sinason for finding this film.
† See, for example, Jackson (1993, 2003), Jackson & Williams (1994), Lotterman (1996), Robbins (1993), and Williams (1998).

Ashikaga, Strauss & Brier, 1987), there are certain features that make Nash's case exceptionally interesting. For example,

- The worldwide publicity arising from the award-winning film and its partial misrepresentation of the nature of schizophrenia
- Nash's remarkable capacity for a high level of abstract thinking that led many of his peers to regard him as the greatest mathematician of the century
- The fact that apart from periods of acute disturbance he retained a capacity for nonpsychotic thinking, and on recovery was able to resume creative work of a high order
- His considered decision to reject the antipsychotic medication which had been effective in suppressing his symptoms, and his insistence that he recovered by his own efforts—a claim that goes against the biomedical perspective of the book and film
- The likelihood (implied in Nash's comments as well as in the extant information about his illness) that a significant benign transformation and improvement of the immature aspects of his personality occurred as a consequence of a degree of working through of pathogenic unconscious conflicts

BACKGROUND

For those who have not read Nasar's book it is necessary to offer a synopsis of the text. This cannot do justice to the richness and complexity of the original. Nash (born in 1928), a loved and wanted first child, with a 2-years-younger sister, showed signs of exceptional intelligence from an early age. Somewhat isolated socially, he had a marked disrespect for authority and a tendency to present himself as an unrivalled and superior thinker, a trait that became more pronounced in his early adult life when he was often regarded by his contemporaries as arrogant and eccentric. He sometimes obtained malicious pleasure by playing childish, cruel tricks on his peers, and denouncing the work of others in his field. He burst onto the mathematical scene at the age of 19, and over the next 10 years established himself as one of the most remarkable mathematicians of the century.

His groundbreaking work into the processes of human rivalry and his theory of rational conflict and cooperation are achievements that have sometimes been regarded in mathematical circles as having the stature and importance of those of Newton and Darwin. Nash worked for some years as a part-time consultant to the RAND Corporation, a privately funded think tank employed by the U.S. military during the Cold War period, a post that brought him into contact with the Central Intelligence Agency. This political period of concern about Soviet nuclear development had a markedly paranoid quality, which found its most direct expression in the anti-Communist activities of the McCarthy Era. Games theory was at that time being considered as crucial to Cold War politics, when a preemptive strike was being seriously contemplated (cf. Milnor, 1998). At about the age of 23 (in 1951) Nash began a close and intense relationship with his colleague, "Mr. Jacob B.," which lasted several years (Nasar, 1998, p. 180) and which he continued for some time alongside a relationship with a young attractive nurse who became his mistress. At the same time he was involved in an affair with his future wife. The subsequent break-up of the relationship with his male friend was to have profound consequences. Nash's contributions to RAND came to an abrupt and humiliating end in 1954, when he was arrested and charged with homosexual behavior in public, and immediately dismissed. Some time after this traumatic event his mistress became pregnant and gave birth to a son (in 1953). Nash acknowledged paternity but his feelings about the boy were ambivalent, completely ignoring him for long periods, and attempting reconciliation at others. At first he considered marrying his mistress, but eventually rejected her in favor of his future wife. When she discovered his continuing secret sexual affair with his mistress and the existence of the illegitimate son, Nash declared himself emotionally devastated, bemoaning the loss of his "perfect little world." He thereupon abandoned his mistress and declined to help her and his son, who consequently suffered from considerable financial hardship for a long time. Shocked by what he regarded as Nash's "callousness" towards his mistress, and finding the threesome relationship too intense, Mr. B. terminated his involvement with Nash, 2 years before Nash's breakdown (in 1956). This loss was to prove of profound significance for Nash, evoking lasting bitter and vengeful feelings. In that year his mistress told Nash's parents of the existence of their grandson. Some time after this revelation Nash's father unexpectedly died, a loss that led Nash's mother to blame the mistress for provoking it.

The biographer's views

Sylvia Nasar's book is an exemplar of careful research and skillful and indefatigable, albeit often intrusive, interviewing. Her biography was unauthorized, and because Nash declined to disclose any personal information that might cause embarrassment, the depth of her investigation was of necessity limited. Nonetheless, her conclusions about the nature of Nash's vulnerability and of the factors precipitating his breakdown are highly perceptive. She considers that his extraordinary sense of self-importance had its roots in early childhood as an understandable way of protecting himself from a sense of loneliness, isolation, and jealousy, and that this hid a craving for love and affection. She thinks that Nash's mother, who was of impressive intellectual stature, might be considered to have been excessively ambitious for him and thus may have been experienced by Nash as intrusive, and that his father, a somewhat reserved, highly intelligent, and scientifically minded man, might have been experienced as emotionally unavailable at important stages of his son's development. However, she concludes that they were both obviously devoted and loving parents of exceptional intellectual standing, who had recognized in their son prodigious intellectual qualities and an inquiring mind, and who had supported his development unreservedly. Nasar also searched the history of his parents and grandparents but could find no evidence of transgenerational pathological influence. She gives importance to the fact that in the year before his breakdown began Nash narrowly failed to win the Fields Medal, the most prestigious prize for mathematics, and one to which he felt he was entitled. He had been shocked to discover that a rival had resolved a crucial problem some months before him, and retrospectively said that he believed that this was the reason why the prize had eluded him. Nasar considered this setback as an Icarus-like fall which, combined with new responsibilities brought about by his marriage, the death of his father, and parenthood, were the likely causes of his breakdown (p. 221). This uncontroversial conclusion is as far as her exploration goes, leaving open such questions as the nature of Nash's premorbid vulnerability or the meaning of his psychotic experiences. This omission reflects the opinion of the primarily biomedically oriented psychiatrists to whom she refers in the book, well-known researchers who maintain that schizophrenia is (simply) a brain disease, albeit with psychological concomitants,* and that psychoanalysis has been discredited as a means of treating schizophrenia (Nasar, 1994).

The film†

It should be recognized that the material in Nasar's book has been interpreted in different ways by three different authors: the biographer, the writer of the film, and the present authors. All three interpretations are inevitably speculative to varying degrees, and in some instances with little that would generally be considered as evidence. However, many psychoanalytically oriented psychiatrists are highly familiar with such cases, and examining the case from a psychoanalytic perspective may illuminate matters that are not addressed in the film or the book and which are pertinent to the disease.

The film, to judge by press reviews and the deluge of correspondence that has appeared on the Internet, was acclaimed as a masterpiece of cinematic

---

* For example, considering psychotic logic as "outgrowths of what the brain is experiencing" (p. 324). However, a few more balanced comments such as "it's things that get to the soul and self-identity and expectations of oneself" (p. 188) go some way to redress the balance.
† Producer: Brian Gazer; director: Ron Howard; scriptwriter: Akiva Goldsman.

art and an entertaining and emotionally moving Hollywood epic. The film-makers set out to involve the audience in Nash's experience, inviting them to empathize with him and hoping in this way to contribute to the de-stigmatization of mental illness and public awareness of the often terrifying nature of this type of psychosis. They illustrate dramatically what it can be like to experience the invasion of the mind by alien forces,* and to lose the capacity to distinguish a waking dream from reality. The viewer also has the opportunity of experiencing a sample of Nash's confusion (Britton, 1998) and perplexity by means of the director's device (explained in detail in the accompanying DVD of the film) of offering many subtle clues that point to the fact that what is being seen is Nash's delusional reality.[†] As the director (Ron Howard) admits, the film is, like the book, an unauthorized biography (Whipp, 2001), omitting any reference to Nash's homosexual tendency or to any less-admirable features of his prepsychotic personality, which are treated in detail in the biography. In consequence, the viewer who turns to the book may suffer considerable disillusionment about such cinematic idealization, as did one indignant correspondent who described Nash as a "bisexual anti-Semitic adulterer who abandoned his wife and illegitimate son to poverty" (thereby repeating the commonplace confusion between "madness" and "badness"). The filmmakers seem to have antici-pated criticism of these omissions, and defended their position vigorously.[‡]

Despite these omissions, the filmmakers created an authentic presen-tation of important aspects of the inner life of many psychotic patients. Their imaginative elaboration of Nash's dreamlike psychotic experience is in some respects psychoanalytically sophisticated. They invented a halluci-natory Mafia-like controller/supervisor of the CIA (William) from whose powerful influence Nash eventually struggles to escape, and an imaginary companion (Charles) who at first gives him constructive encouragement, but eventually incites him with seductive power to assume grandiosity and omnipotent thinking, thereby undermining his growing sense of reality. Like a murderous Mafia leader, William eventually reveals his sadistic potential and threatens to kill Nash and his wife and child if he tries to break free of the grip of the CIA "gang." These themes are well-documented features of psychoanalytic studies of psychotic conditions (H. A. Rosenfeld, 1987; D. Rosenfeld, 1992; Steiner, 1993b; De Masi, 1997; Jackson, 2003; Williams, 1998). This type of delusional organization has been described in detail by Herbert Rosenfeld (1987), whose concept of narcissistic omnipotent object

---

* Portrayed in its most horrific form in the film *Alien* and in other guises in *Fight Club* (cf. Sinason, 2003) and *Being John Malkovich* (Gabbard, 2001).
† A technique used with great dramatic effect in *The Sixth Sense*.
‡ Russell Crowe (playing the part of Nash) has commented, "The book is a great read, a wonderful biography, but again, it's a singular opinion. It's not necessarily the absolute truth. Neither is the movie. But there's an emotional path I believe that we've found and I believe it to be authentic" (Whipp, 2001).

relations cast light on the dynamics of certain adult psychotic states of mind. He described a narcissistic character structure, arising in infancy as a defense against a sense of unbearable helplessness, and explored its possible pathogenic consequences:

> Once a firm narcissistic way of living has been established beyond infancy, relations to self and object will be controlled in order to try to maintain the delusional omnipotent belief. Any contact with reality or self-observation inevitably threatens this state of affairs and is felt as very dangerous ... this omnipotent way of existing is experienced and even personified as a good friend or guru who uses powerful suggestions and propaganda to maintain the status quo, a process which is generally silent and often creates confusion. Any object, particularly the analyst, who helps the patient to face the reality of his need and dependence is experienced as dangerous by this good friend, who is afraid of being exposed as a phantom. When the patient's capacity for self-observation improves ... and he tries to free himself from being controlled, the persuasive, seductive nature of the omnipotent structure changes: it becomes sadistic and threatens the patient with death. Only then does one become aware that hidden in the omnipotent structure there exists a very primitive superego which belittles and attacks the patient's capacities, observations, and particularly to accept his need for real objects. The most confusing element in this process is the successful disguise of the omnipotent structure of omnipotent relating and the envious destructive super-ego as benevolent figures; this disguise makes the patient feel guilty and ungrateful towards them when he tries to improve (p. 87).

The scriptwriter's psychoanalytically oriented interpretation of Nash's inner world of object relationships can be considered a reasonably accurate dramatization of Rosenfeld's work on borderline and psychotic destructive narcissism.* Other subtle features of the film impart a psychoanalytic orientation. The portrayal of the (oedipal) child Marcie as never growing older (orphaned by her father's drunken driving), attests to the timelessness of internal objects. An interesting interpolation is to be found at the point when Nash's wife enters his study and is shocked to discover the wall covered with press cuttings, showing that her husband, whom she thought to be well at the time, had been pursuing his paranoid preoccupations in secret. A slow replay of this scene reveals that most of the items on which the camera focuses refer specifically to the oedipal and pre-oedipal content

---

* Although this could be an accurate description of the nature of Nash's arguments with his voices, it should not be forgotten that this is Goldsman's speculative interpretation, based on his own knowledge of psychoanalytic theory, not on the very limited information about Nash's hallucinations available in the biography.

of his preoccupations, either directly such as the birth of the first test-tube baby, or symbolically such as that of a happily retired couple living on a $300 pension, the recurrence of the numbers 2 and 3, and other significant, near-subliminal artifacts.

The film shows the dramatic change that gradually took place in Nash's personality, transforming him from a narcissistic, isolated, and haughty young man, into a more normal human being, able to accept help and dependence with humility, and it conveys his capacity to survive his delusional experiences and his determination to recover a grasp on reality. In a convincing manner, the film depicts the psychotic confusion of a dream-like inner world with external reality, the devastating power of delusional beliefs (wishful and terrifying), and the persuasiveness of the psychotic elements in the mind that struggle to undermine the patient's sanity. It also exemplifies some of the catastrophic consequences of such confusion for the family of a psychotic patient, as when Nash endangers the life of his wife and son by behavior aimed at saving them from death. The decision to portray Nash's world of psychotic thinking in visual terms, which is uncommon in schizophrenia, rather than in the auditory hallucinatory mode in which he actually experienced them, is an artifice that compels the interest of the viewer in a way that a story about hallucinatory voices might not. The filmmakers created Goldsman's speculative version of what Nash's internal object relationships might have been like, based on Nash's account of his hallucinations given in the book, and he gradually succeeds in opposing "the delusionally influenced lines of political thinking which had been characteristic of my orientation" (2002a, 2002b). In view of this psychoanalytic orientation in the film, it is striking to note that the filmmakers omitted the important fact of Nash's renunciation of antipsychotic medication, attributing to him the comment, made to the Nobel emissary in 1994, that he was currently taking the "newer medications." This insertion explicitly contradicts Nash's own insistence that it was his own mental struggles and not medication that led to his recovery. One is left with considerable admiration for the film, but also with regret that Ron Howard and Russell Crowe, who consulted extensively with Nash during the making of the film, may have missed an opportunity to introduce the importance of the destructive and reparative aspects of the mind suffering psychosis, and to convey a more balanced view of medication and psychotherapy in psychotic illness than the largely reductionist biomedical one that they have extracted from the biography, despite the psychoanalytic orientation of the scriptwriting. Addressing the issue of destructive and reparative motivations, however difficult this might have been, could have avoided idealization of Nash, the thread of superficial sentimentality that runs through the film, and the essentially misleading presentation of the actual nature of psychotic illness.

EVOLUTION OF NASH'S PSYCHOSIS

In 1958, although enjoying great success and celebrated in the media as the mathematician of the century, Nash was showing a marked instability of mood, with excitement over yet more imminent triumphs being marred by increasing self-doubt and resentful rivalries—for example, at being defeated for the major award to which he had felt entitled. It was against this background of repeated traumatic events and of personal and professional conflicts that he married, early in 1958, a brilliant physicist and Costa Rican beauty who soon became pregnant.

In the autumn of that year his mood instability became more pronounced, and he had a sudden transient homosexual infatuation. However, his friends only began to worry when at a fancy dress party on New Year's Eve Nash arrived almost naked, carrying a baby's bottle of milk, clad in a diaper and sash proclaiming the arrival of the New Year (Nasar, 1998, p. 239). Although the astonished guests accepted this as a witty idea of his wife's, some found the charade bizarre and disturbing, particularly since Nash spent much of the evening sitting on his wife's lap sucking the bottle. In the following weeks, this prodromal symptom was followed by clear signs of psychosis. He became cold and remote towards his wife, apparently suspecting her of infidelity, and this led her to become afraid for her personal safety.

He became agitated and deluded in his thinking, preoccupied with writing letters to the Department of Defense, heads of state, foreign ambassadors, and the Pope (p. 249), warning them that the world was in imminent danger of destruction by Communist Russia, or by alien extraterrestrial forces, and he announced that he was forming an organization for promoting world peace. As the psychotic process progressed, periods of relative rationality and lucidity were increasingly interrupted by his delusional preoccupations. In his delusional existence he often fluctuated between pride at being selected by (good) extraterrestrial entities as the world's only hope of salvation, and terror at being in imminent danger, along with the rest of the world, of annihilation by Communist agents or (bad) extraterrestrials. His delusional thinking and bizarre behavior compelled his distraught wife to have him admitted under a compulsory order to McLean Hospital, well known for its psychoanalytic work. Medication, individual and group therapy, family involvement, and psychoanalytic psychotherapy led to some improvement, but after six weeks, deliberately concealing his still-active disturbance, he discharged himself (in May 1959, a week after the birth of his son), a decision he came later to regret. This abortive period of treatment engendered a dismissive attitude in his friends to the psychoanalytic approach, in which latent homosexuality and his wife's pregnancy ("fetus envy") were considered to be important factors in determining his breakdown.* Over the next few years his illness followed a course of remission and relapse. He was repeatedly admitted to mental hospitals where antipsychotic medication and eventually insulin coma therapy brought improvement and helped him to recover some stability, but sooner or later he relapsed.

However, in the Carrier Hospital where he had spent a short time, again under a compulsory order, he came under the care of a psychiatrist who saw him regularly for supportive psychotherapy and control of medication over the ensuing 2 years. He left the hospital after 6 months, well enough to resume work, and an appointment was found by his colleagues who regarded him as recovered. However, he remained troubled and before long, opposing the strong advice of his psychiatrist, he discontinued his medication and departed for Europe (regarding himself, as he subsequently explained, as a great religious leader).

Onset of auditory hallucinations and thought insertion

It was not until a brief visit to Rome, some 6 years after the onset of the psychosis, that he began to hear voices, in the form of telepathic phone calls inserted (he later explained) into his brain by a central machine. Some voices in the calls he considered to come from "mathematicians opposed to my ideas." He returned to Princeton, where his disturbance escalated, and he was readmitted to Carrier. He stayed for 4 months, under the care of his previous psychiatrist, until his psychiatrist was satisfied that he was in a stable state of remission. However, this period of relatively good functioning did not last and his disturbance returned. He became excited, talked incessantly, and made no sense. It seems that he may have once more given up his medication and that this exposed him to the force of his long-suppressed delusions and confusion. Once again he was the savior of the doomed world, preoccupied with the politics of great leaders, good and bad, with magical and dangerous numbers, and coded messages from the *New York Times*. He was also accumulating household garbage. He traveled to the West Coast in an elated state, contacting Mr. B., who found him almost incoherent, and visited RAND where old colleagues refused to see him. He visited his cousin who found his behavior to be pleasant and rational, but punctuated by moments of incoherent talk. Returning to Boston, he made contact with his mistress and son. Depressed and lonely, missing his (still separated) wife and son, he began to take an interest in his illegitimate son, whom he treated with fatherly kindness and support. Filled

---

* "As absurd as it now seems, Mr. Nash's psychiatrists thought that Mrs. Nash's pregnancy was part of the problem and hoped he would improve after the baby's birth" (Nasar, 1994, p. 259). We shall later consider the evidence for this comment/diagnosis.

with a deep sense of regret, he wrote a "poignant and introspective" letter to his sister, referring to the struggle between his "merciless superego" and his "old simple me" (Nasar, 1998, p. 317). He resumed teaching and a colleague later recorded that Nash was "pretty sane," and that he had undergone a transformation in personality. His arrogance and obvious pleasure in humiliating others had disappeared and he was "nice and gentle, lots of fun to talk to. This old ego stuff was gone."

Final relinquishing of medication and entry into "the inferno"

Nash's attitude to his medication seems to have been reflected in his view that his remissions, far from being happy returns to normality, were "enforced interludes of rationality" (Nasar, 1998, p. 295). Finally, after 8 years of illness he abandoned medication permanently, later explaining that not only did it produce unacceptable physical side effects, but that it extinguished his voices and reduced his capacity for thinking to a distressingly superficial level. He thereupon entered a long period of confusion marked by delusional thinking, auditory hallucinations, and recurrent terror, in which he felt he was inhabiting a life of heaven and hell, an "Inferno,"* a purgatory, or a polluted heaven, "a decayed rotting house infested by rats and termites and other vermin" (p. 324).† This phase gradually subsided over a period of several years, leaving him in a state of social isolation but with sufficient sanity to allow him to spend part of each day at the Mathematics Department of Princeton University. He became established as a familiar, eccentric, and bizarre figure (the "Phantom of Fine Hall," p. 332), totally preoccupied with apparently meaningless numerical calculations. This was the condition in which he passed the next 20 years.

"Self-cure" and return to sanity

Nash's capacity for rational thinking gradually returned during these decades. Still unprotected by medication, he resumed part-time teaching activities and was able to return to his research interests. He lived with

---

* Nash's creativeness and his claim for self-cure can be compared with that of August Strindberg whose story "The Inferno" is an essentially autobiographical account of his paranoid psychosis (Lidz, 1964; Cullberg, 2006). Other versions of Inferno or Hell such as those of Dante and Milton recount the descent into an underworld of unimaginable suffering, and return in a transformed state of greater maturity, the archetypal "Hero's Journey."
† This is a very clear description of Nash's unconscious fantasies of his anal (polluting) attacks on the split (idealized) mother-imago and of the rival siblings/vermin (containing the projections of his own biting-soiling wishes) who are invading the maternal space (see also Freud on "vermin" as children-rivals, and also Mitchell, 2003; Volkan & Ast, 1997).

his mother, then after her death (in Autumn 1969) his wife took him back into her care. She had by then divorced him because she could not bear the hatred he bore her for being responsible for the repeated, forced admissions to mental hospitals. He slowly recovered the capacity for normal social relationships, for restoring lost friendships, and for creative work of a high order. In 1994 he was awarded a Nobel Prize in economics (shared with two others) for his work on games theory undertaken before his break-down. The famous "Nash Equilibrium" demonstrated for the first time how noncooperating players—at individual, group, and national levels—could share benefits by empathetically reflecting on the motives of com-petitors, rather than pursuing the destructive "win-lose" of "zero-sum" games. At the time of publication of Nasar's book, Nash was functioning apparently normally and living with his wife, and had restored relations with his illegitimate son. He and his wife were occupied in caring for their son who, after an initially brilliant career as a young mathematician, had a psychotic breakdown somewhat similar to his father's. Since his recovery Nash has lectured widely about severe mental illness, pointing out the limi-tations of the exclusive use of medication in treatment, and campaigning for the importance of a psychotherapeutic approach in the treatment of psychosis. In 1996 he delivered a remarkable lecture at the World Congress of Psychiatry titled "Rational Thinking: Is It Easy or Hard?", and in inter-views he is reported to have said that if his life had been otherwise he might have become a leader in the field of psychotherapy, a remarkable, albeit controversial, claim.

Pathogenic conflicts

One of the most striking features of Nash's case is the way in which his psychosis was precipitated by his wife's pregnancy (the "fetus envy" recog-nized by the McLean psychiatrists), an event that revived guilt-laden con-flicts of his early life. His adoption of the role of the baby at the New Year's Eve party suggests that its unconscious significance for him was that of an earlier traumatic situation that was now repeating itself. Rendered at risk of psychosis, perhaps from the beginning of his life, he was subsequently exposed in infancy and childhood to "unimaginable" emotional storms that threatened to overwhelm him and required powerful defensive measures to allow him to continue to develop. His need to model himself on the emo-tionless hominid Mr. Spock (of *Star Trek* fame) attests to the magnitude of his dread of the emotions that life, intimacy, and dependency threatened to release. His insulation against the pain of human feelings of inferiority, loss, envy, jealousy, guilt, and shame must have been severely threatened by the humiliation of his dismissal by RAND, an event that did not appear to have upset him at the time.* Further setbacks and professional disappointments, despite his acknowledged eminence, continued the trauma.

It is interesting to note that it was the birth of the legitimate baby and not the illegitimate one, 5 years before his breakdown, that breached Nash's defensive capsule. The intrapsychic and social characteristics of the two pregnancies were quite different. The legitimate pregnancy, occurring soon after his marriage, was preceded by a series of major stresses, such as the discovery by his mistress that she had been rejected in favor of his future wife, the death of his father, and the demands of mature responsibilities. Nash was further insulated against the potentially traumatic impact of the first pregnancy by his conscious strategy of leading a double life. For several years he had kept the life with his mistress and illegitimate son almost completely secret, maintaining it together with a long-standing and emotionally powerful relationship with his male colleague (Mr. B.) as a "threesome" with her. This triangle was of great emotional importance to him and this homosexual relation may have been Nash's first, or at least most powerful, experience of finding the love that treacherous (pregnant) women (mothers) denied him. He felt intense jealousy when Mr. B. showed interest in another man, and finally suffered an overwhelming sense of rejection when Mr. B., shocked by Nash's ill-treatment of his mistress, became emotionally disturbed and withdrew from this now too-conflicted triangular relationship (Nasar, 1998, p. 182).

This loss was emotionally devastating to Nash, who some years later described this friend as the one person in his life who had caused him the greatest personal injury. He incorporated Mr. B. into his delusional world, considering him to be his supremely malevolent betrayer (Nasar, 1998, p. 326), calling him Satan and Jacob and accusing him of the theft of his birthright.† Nash felt traumatized by an abandoning male, an event which would confirm for him that men also betray and that intimacy with neither man nor woman was safe. A further consequence of the exposure of his double life and the destruction of his "perfect little world" (p. 201) was that his parents, shocked at his duplicity, at first pressed him to marry his mistress (p. 207). The sudden death of his father, 3 years before his breakdown, led his mother to blame Nash's

---

* In an essay on the famous case of Judge Daniel Schreber, Steiner (2004) has remarked on the profound humiliation that Schreber had experienced and that extreme shame may have found expression in his autobiographical narrative Memoirs of My Nervous Illness (1903). We will later argue that the RAND episode must surely have caused Nash a comparable severity of shame, but that, in the absence of evidence, we must conclude that he must have suppressed or concealed his reaction to this devastating experience. We must also recognize that we do not know whether he had the capacity for shame (Kinston, 1983), or if he did, whether it was this catastrophe that helped to motivate his desire to invent a "repenting-ness" oscilloscope (which we shall describe).

† As Esau, he had lost much more than an important friendship.

mistress for being the cause of his death, probably also imputing it to Nash himself (p. 209).

Thus a chain of events, beginning with the collapse of his double-life strategy, had the cumulative effect of generating an increasing burden of persecutory guilt and of creating a seriously unstable inner situation, in which the birth of his legitimate son was unconsciously perceived as betrayal and abandonment. This escalating and enormous series of stresses finally broke open his elaborate but disintegrating defensive capsule, releasing long-banished destructive feelings and the accompanying "organismic" panic of threatened disintegration. Emergency projective and introjective processes rapidly strengthened the new psychotic equilibrium and allowed him to create a delusional identity in which he, the agent, became a victim, at times switching into a manic defense in which he was the Messiah.* Clinging to his remaining sanity for the 2 months following the New Year's Eve incident, he then experienced profound humiliation when he found himself unable to think coherently during a presentation of his claim to have proved the Riemann hypothesis (pp. 229, 246).† Speaking after his recovery, Nash (1996) attributed the triggering of his mental illness to the "possibly overreaching and destabilizing effect" of his attempts to resolve the contradictions in quantum theory over the 2 previous years. When questioning certain inconsistencies in Einstein's work on quantum mechanics, Nash remarked to Robert Oppenheimer: "I want to find a different and more satisfying under-picture of a non-observable reality" (p. 221).

Although this was presumably an example of the "ultra-logical thinking" Nash regarded as necessary to explore the highly abstract world of mathematics, a psychoanalyst might reflect on whether his wish was also to some extent motivated by an unconscious search for a deeper

---

* There are several related models of the mind in psychoanalytic theory (Fonagy & Target, 2003). The Kleinian model gives great importance to the place of destructive envy in mental illness, and attempts to relate present psychotic pathology to early infantile experiences (see Hinshelwood, 1980). The view of a universal innate destructiveness ("death instinct") is often disputed, but Klein's accompanying emphasis on the power of wishes to protect and preserve threatened objects, and in the depressive position to repair these objects, has not always been recognized. The "manic defense" provided Nash with the identity of the Messiah, in which role he could believe that he had the power to repair his damaged objects and (as with Lazarus) restore them to life. This "manic reparation" (in the "paranoid-schizoid" position) actually repairs nothing, and may play a part in the development of manic-depressive psychosis and psychotic megalomania. It is only at the more mature and integrated mental states of the "depressive position" that vengefulness and persecutory guilt can give way to "depressive guilt," a mature and healthy sense of responsibility, and to concern and pity for the victim of destructiveness.

† His confusion in the lecture might be understandable, considering that in his psychotic mind he was already becoming the most important person in the world, whereas acceptance in that lecture of his proof of the hypothesis might have made him the most important person in the world of mathematics at that moment. An unconscious, delusional triumph made the possibility of a conscious, perhaps realistic, achievement impossible.

truth that would help explain more of his inner world of psychological reality. This view might help illuminate the nature of the demons
that escaped from the Pandora's box of his mind in the form of long-
encapsulated envious and jealous feelings underlying his arrogant attitude towards potential competitors; the murderous quality of his bitter
rage against the treacherously "abandoning" Jacob B. (a complex symbiotic figure in his inner world); the developmental failure underlying
his bisexuality; the attack on his parent's union, and the unsuccessful
attempts to reunite their confused and confusing representatives (Mao,
Hitler, Ghandi, and others); and finally, the emergence of the normal
and manageable guilt of the depressive position (sorrow, repentance,
forgiveness, pity).

Desymbolization: projection of unconscious elements into the external world

The concreteness of thinking characteristic of many psychotic states of
mind can be considered from a variety of perspectives. Concepts such as
"palaeological thinking" (Arieti, 1974) and "symmetrical thinking" (Matte-
Blanco, 1998) can help in the understanding of psychotic logic, while "symbolic equation" (Klein, 1930; Segal, 1972, 1981) addresses the underlying
failure to differentiate self from other. In this view it is the developmental
failure that helps to account for disturbances in the acquisition of the symbolic function on which abstract conceptual thinking depends. In the symbolic equation, signifier and signified are confused, and as a result symbol
use and normal sublimation become impossible.* Thus *apparently* normal
events or interests such as pacifism (as already mentioned), the A-bomb,†
the Communist threat, vegetarianism, and numbers came to serve for Nash
as containers for unwanted omnipotent and hostile feelings and (in the case
of prime numbers) of wishful self-importance. In creating projectively this
delusional world he may have felt that he saved his mother and his inner
world from catastrophe while at the same time denying her separateness by

---

* Nash's determination to convince the authorities that the only way to avoid the coming
destruction of the world was to create a world government devoted to universal brotherly
love could be thought of in itself to be a sane ambition. The methods he used to promote
this cause revealed that his likely unconscious concern was to save his inner world from the
catastrophe that would overtake it if his "brotherly hatred" escaped his control. The projection of unconscious elements of his inner world into this pacifist theme seems to have led
to the disablement of symbol use and the failure of sublimation. He was then condemned
to doing the right thing for the wrong reasons.
† One schizophrenic patient, repeatedly attempting to burn himself to death in closed spaces
(an unconscious enactment of unconscious attacks on the pregnant mother of his childhood), at the successful conclusion of psychoanalytic psychotherapy expressed a new
understanding of his delusional beliefs that the world was coming to an end as "my mother
was my whole world!" (Jackson & Williams, 1994).

asserting that he was her prime and only interest (at the cost of becoming the victim of forces from which he had alienated himself).

LIFE IN THE DELUSIONAL WORLD: CREATIVE AND PSYCHOTIC THINKING

Nash's brilliant former capacity to form new and meaningful links (see Charles, 2003) was impaired by the dominance of the exclusively personal associations of psychotic logic. Confused between two realities, Nash seems to have been at times perplexed, manically excited, triumphant, and gratified by his assumed self-importance, and anxious or terrified by the murderous attacks that he believed were being made on him. It was only when doubt began to undermine his certitude that he started to suffer the extremely painful realization that he had been deluded and confused for a long time. In his plenary lecture to the World Psychiatric Congress (1996) Nash put this succinctly. He suggested that in his creative work rationality often interfered with the "ultra-logical thinking" necessary for the abstract world of mathematics, but that the "return to rationality after being irrational, can be a source of great pain."

Auditory hallucinations

Auditory hallucination may develop along different dynamic pathways,[*] may have widely different content, and may serve different purposes at different times. Critical comments and threats, often the expression of unconscious persecutory guilt, are the most frequent type (Freeman, 1994). Although hearing voices is not necessarily a symptom of mental illness[†] (Romme, Honig, Noorthoorn, & Escher, 1992; Johns, Nazroo, Bebbington, & Kuipers, 2002), Nash's voices almost certainly were. They began some years after the onset of his illness, at first taking the form of "thought insertion" (one of the classic defining features of certain schizophrenic disorders), which he experienced as voices of mathematicians opposed to his ideas. Sometimes they were frightening,[‡] and when he began to improve they exerted powerful pressure to try to convince him that his delusional

---

[*] In the course of psychotherapy of psychotic patients one can often observe how, when an emotionally disturbing thought is touched upon, patients will suddenly switch their attention to some hallucinated element, perhaps in another part of the room, to rid themselves of mental pain.

[†] Encouraging psychotic patients to engage hallucinatory voices in a "Socratic" dialogue has met with some success both in psychodynamic and cognitive-behavioral practice.

[‡] Nasar (1998) quotes a letter to a colleague: "My head is as if a bloated windbag with Voices which dispute within" (p. 328), a metaphorical description of alarming experiences demonstrating that his loss of symbol capacity was confined to his delusional preoccupations.

"political" thinking was entirely sane and realistic (an experience personi-
fied particularly dramatically in the film).

Delusions

Although the chronological evolution of Nash's various delusions is
unclear, the first obvious manifestations of Nash's breakdown appear to
have emerged in the weeks following the New Year's Eve party of 1958,
outlined above. He began to undergo a "strange and horrible metamor-
phosis" (Nasar, 1998, p. 240), speaking about threats to world peace,
warning that powers from outer space were communicating with him by
encrypted messages in the newspapers,* and that he had a unique mission
to save the world from its impending destruction by foreign governments or
alien extraterrestrial entities. His confused preoccupation with the belief in
imminent apocalyptic catastrophe, alongside the megalomanic gratification
of his new Messianic-type identity,† soon led to his compulsory admission
to the McLean Hospital in March 1959. As the psychotic process evolved,
his experiences increasingly assumed the form of persecutory guilt of an
extreme order. Freud (1911) saw paranoia as the consequence of projecting
(predominantly sexual) ideas that are incompatible with the ego into the
external world, and the subsequent delusional elaborations as representing
a "patch over the ego," an attempt to recover meaning in a world that had
become disintegrated and meaningless.

Although paranoia is still generally regarded in psychoanalytic theory
as deriving from defensive projective systems, Freud's focus on homosexuality as the central pathogenic factor has given way to wider consideration of the role of primitive emotional conflicts and modes of thought
(Bell, 2003). These developmental processes concern the acquisition of a
stable sense of self; the management of powerful affects, particularly of
aggression, whether innate—as in Klein's concept of envy as the expression of the death instinct—or of a psychosocial origin; and the "mentalization" of psychosensory and enactive modes of function and the
processes of separation, self-object discrimination,‡ and individuation
(Mahler, Pine, & Bergman, 1975; Fonagy, Gergely, Elliot, & Target,
2002).

---

* In his 1996 plenary lecture in Madrid, Nash recollects the delusional mood of the approaching psychosis, characterized by a sense of exhaustion and depletion, recurring and increasingly pervasive images, and a growing sense of revelation regarding a secret world that
others were not privy to (p. 242).
† Nasar reports much detail of the content of the megalomanic experiences, in which he
believed, for example, that he was the left foot of God, even God himself; that he was the
Pope; that the Pope had stolen his identity; and that certain numbers had a special personal
significance.
‡ Gaddini (1992) has pointed out that Kohut's concept of "selfobject" can be usefully applied
to the understanding of psychosis, albeit in a general "umbrella" way.

The view of Nash's psychosis proposed in this essay focuses on unmanageable pre-oedipal forces (innate or otherwise), specifically envy, on its elaboration in the form of unconscious oedipal jealousy, and the need for defenses against both. Although Nash's jealous rivalry was obvious, it seems to have been the destructiveness of more envy-laden feelings that was even more seriously damaging, since the aim of the feelings appeared to be the eradication of the goodness of the object. This type of envy may be much less obvious and only accessible via a negative therapeutic transference (H. A. Rosenfeld, 1987).

Numerology

In Nash's psychotic states of mind, the numbers 1, 2, and 3 came to assume a new and personal significance for him, possibly as metaphors representing his thoughts about his own place in dyadic and triadic relationships. It is also possible that his fascinated preoccupation with the indivisibility of prime numbers came to share a similar personal significance, and may have played a part in determining his long preoccupation with them. It is also conceivable, as Nasar suggests, that he found a stability and security in these numbers, which may have been lacking in his childhood, and in this sense they may have served to dispel somewhat his underlying psychotic conflicts. When a photograph of Pope John 23rd appeared on the cover of *Life* magazine, Nash insisted that it was his own photo that had been disguised to look like the Pope. He offered the evidence (completely convincing to himself) that John was not the Pope's given name but was a name that the Pope had (in reality) chosen for himself, and that 23 was his own, favorite prime number. Insisting that the Pope was himself also implied that he was the Pope, as at other times he insisted that he was the left foot of God, and even God himself. He also became afraid of the date of May 29th, which, apart from whatever magical significance the integers might have had for him, might have further reminded him of the date of his self-discharge from the McLean Hospital a week after the birth of his son.

Anti-semitism: Mao and Brezhnev

Some critics have considered that Nash possessed anti-Semitic tendencies. Since it is unlikely that a man of liberal humanitarian views like Nash would consciously harbor such prejudices, or at least any more than is perhaps universal in gentiles (or perhaps unconsciously in many Jews), it is likely that whatever provoked the criticism may have been of a different order, such as the Jewishness of some of his most successful rivals (including Einstein and Mr. B.) or the good/bad confusion of values and objects in his delusional world. An example of this confusion is provided by the episode reported in which he chalked on a blackboard the apparently incomprehensible cryptic announcement that "Mao Tse-Tung's *bar mitzvah* was 13 years, 13 months and 13 days after Brezhnev's circumcision" (Nasar, 1998, p. 332). Another concerned an imaginary letter from Khrushchev to Moses in which very large numbers were factored into two large primes. In order to try to understand such communications it is necessary to accept as a fact that all schizophrenic communications have meaning, however difficult it may be to understand. If the enquirer is in contact with the nonpsychotic part of the patient's personality it is possible to ask the patient to explain what he or she means. This example might be considered as an attempt, albeit a failed one, to bring together two incompatible (part) objects and ideologies, ultimately linked to the symbolic representatives of the loved and hated parents of his inner world (for comparable examples see Jackson, 2003, pp. 243, 268).

Bizarre communications, bisexuality

Like many psychotic patients Nash's capacity to differentiate love from hate, good from bad, male from female, waking thinking from dream thinking, and persecution from depression was impaired. The attempts to sort out the confusion may have led to his bringing together undifferentiated elements which did not belong together, a futile task and one that would be bewildering to others (see "combined parents" in Hinshelwood, 1989). At other times Hitler, Arabs, and Jews were brought together in an equally incomprehensible manner. Such failure to differentiate part-objects, part-processes, and part-identifications might help explain what could otherwise be quickly dismissed as merely the expression of latent homosexuality or anti-Semitism. The bisexual state represents a difficulty in separating the necessary parental identifications in inner reality. Speaking of borderline individuals who are confused in their sexuality, Rey (1994) commented that "the schizoid is neither hetero- nor homosexual, because his identifications depend on internal objects that are not properly differentiated or assimilated" (p. 13).

The "repentingness oscilloscope": from persecutory guilt toward feelings of concern

Some 10 years after the onset of his psychosis, although still dominated by psychotic thinking, Nash developed ideas about the possibility of constructing an oscilloscope that could display a "repentingness function" (Nasar, 1998, p. 326). This, together with the development of a painful sense of loneliness and of missing people who loved him and those he had lost (male intimates, wife by enforced separation followed by divorce, his mistress by her disillusionment with him) and pining for them, suggests an increase in integration characteristic of the "threshold" of the depressive position

(Meltzer, 1967). It seems likely that regret, remorse, sorrow, a sense of personal responsibility, and the desire to make amends for past behavior may have begun to mitigate the harshness of his superego and replace the terrors of persecutory guilt (Rey, 1979, 1994; Steiner, 1993a).

Pandora's box: rejecting medication

Nash discontinued antipsychotic medication because it reduced his capacity to think and silenced his voices. It is not clear whether he valued the voices as companions in his isolation, or whether (or also) he believed that they had a point of view that he respected, but progressively opposed in a scientific manner as "delusional hypotheses." His decision to refuse medication perpetuated his illness but kept open his psychotic core, thereby allowing a degree of working (and living) through his conflicts leading to an increased level of ego strength and reality testing. When an individual succumbs to an acute schizophrenic regression, particularly in "first-onset" cases of psychosis, the new situation is comparable to a nightmare—a "Pandora's box" with a spark of hope at the bottom. The careers of many brilliant schizoid mathematicians have ended in psychosis, suicide, progressive impoverishment of personality, or in the drying up of the springs of creativity, a fate that Nash escaped. It was the opening up of his infantile psychotic capsule that precipitated him into the "Inferno" of confusion and persecution by mental demons, the complex derivatives of primordial feelings of love, loss, guilt, and hatred, wishes to love and be loved by his primary objects and at the same time to protect them from impulses that he feared would harm them.

HOPE, RELIEF, AND NEW BEGINNINGS

Many paranoid psychotic patients may reach a stable adjustment by recognizing that their behavior is socially unacceptable. By keeping their delusional state hidden they thus become able to function relatively normally. However, with the careful use of medication, the support of relatives and friends, and the skilled application of modern methods of psychosocial rehabilitation (Harding, 2002) a majority of schizophrenic patients can achieve varying degrees of remission sometimes amounting to permanent recovery. If a "need-adapted" approach is available (Alanen, 1997, 2002; Cullberg, 2006) it will be found that many "first-onset" cases will require little or no medication. In some cases remission may, from a psychoanalytic perspective, represent a "sealing-over" of psychopathology with more or less degrees of stabilization, although in others a "working-through" to a higher level of integration and maturity may occur, sometimes even spontaneously (Rey, 1994). It is quite possible that Nash negotiated the terrifying consequences of such exposure essentially on his own, as he has claimed.* By renouncing the symptom-relieving medication he may have deliberately confronted the worst of his psychotic experience, a move necessary to allow the core of his disturbance to be reached and for the eventual resumption of an arrested growth process. Whether or not this was the case, it was the loyalty and devotion of his wife and the tolerance of his professional colleagues that provided something of a therapeutic community for him during this time. A containing environment seems to have allowed him to pursue a pathway towards recovery.† As he continued to face the extreme pain that accompanied his increasing sanity, his ego-strength increased. Over a long period of time he gradually became able to understand and oppose the seductive and tyrannical intimidations of the hallucinated omnipotent elements in his mind (De Masi, 1997, 2000, 2003) and slowly regain his lost capacity for reality testing. He recovered a normal use of numerical symbols, the "ultra-logical thinking" necessary for functioning in the abstract world of mathematics (Nash, 1996). His search for total rationality, however, eventually failed him, and he described how his return to sanity had caused him the most extreme mental pain, an agonizing experience portrayed vividly in the film.

A psychotic episode may indeed, for some individuals, represent a "second chance" to recover what was lost and to resume arrested emotional development. Laing (1967) considered that for some exceptional individuals schizophrenia may be considered an enforced journey into the inner world, where inner and outer realities are confused, but which, if successfully negotiated, can ultimately be considered as a healing process. Rey (1994) expressed the recovery process in the case of the schizoid individual as follows:

> A frankly schizophrenic episode may be necessary to return to the point of bifurcation between normal and abnormal development—a regressive dissociation of parts that have become assembled in a faulty way. At this point, the growth of a paralyzed affectivity, previously enslaved and rigidly controlled, may be resumed, and the edifice reconstructed (p. 15).

Individuals who regress from depression have a better prognosis ("schizoaffective") than those of insidious onset, and this might have been true of Nash's regressive deterioration. But whether or not he actually followed the "second chance" pathway, he seems to have become a happier and more

---

* We cannot know whether the group and individual psychotherapy that he received played a part in whatever degree of resolution of his unconscious problems he achieved.

† Nasar (1998) makes the interesting suggestion that it was the experience of loving Mr. B. and having his love returned that altered Nash's perception of himself in a fundamental and benign way (p. 181).

mature person. If he did take this path, his "recovery" could be regarded as a "discovery" of new assets of personality, a regrowth of development that may have been arrested in his childhood. It is possible for this to occur despite the fact that he still sometimes heard his voices and had occasional paranoid thoughts (Nash, 1996). Reflecting on the meaning of "recovery" Nash observed: "Can a musician be said to have recovered if he cannot compose great works? I would not treat myself as recovered if I could not produce good things in my work." When asked his views about the evaluation of recovery from mental illness, Nash remarked that there was a tendency to accept rather low standards for recovery, and that generally accepted criteria for recovery may have an essentially economic basis:

> If the "case" becomes inexpensive for society and/or the family to manage then it is classed as a recovery even though any special abilities or talents of the individual may have been lost and the lifestyle of the person may have become transformed to a more limited form, for example like the pattern of life of a monk or a nun.

When creative imagination is replaced by psychotic grandiosity

Psychotic identifications can serve different purposes, and once the regression from object relations to identifications began, Nash seems to have lost his capacity for the symbolic thinking that was essential to his creativity in mathematics, and was instead plunged into a world of omnipotent fantasy in which he experienced his worst fears and greatest ambitions as actually taking place in the immediate present. His omnipotent unconscious belief that his aggressive impulses were limitlessly destructive brought the dread of destroying his "mother-world," and his psychotic identifications brought him both terror and, when in a megalomanic state of mind, temporary delusional relief (as the messianic Savior) and the gratification of being the unique "number one." While in the identity of the Prince of Peace he momentarily overcame his destructive feelings; as God's left foot he seems to have found a delusional solution to his fate as Esau, the betrayed and rejected sibling. In his psychotic imagination he created a symbolic image of the loved and dependent son of God the Father. Faced with the imminent disintegration of his inner world and sense of self, he constructed a new, delusional reality and a kaleidoscope of new identities, struggling to avoid the imminent inner catastrophe by projecting the whole apocalyptic drama into the environment (Segal, 1972). This unconscious emergency defensive enterprise established the content of much of his subsequent psychotic thinking and was a typical example of a psychotic defense against the terror of dissolution of his sense of self, an extreme form of anxiety variously termed "traumatic anxiety" or "organismic panic" (Pao, 1979; Volkan, 1995), and which can lead to the adoption of new delusional identities.

The search for sanctuary and the claustro-agoraphobic dilemma

Conventional treatment produced many remissions in Nash's symptoms but does not appear to have reached the core of his psychotic condition. It was not until he had been ill for 10 years (1970), and had renounced the use of antipsychotic drugs, which had suppressed his auditory hallucinations (voices) and had restored a temporary stability, that he began to follow a different pathway. In a tormented and confused state of mind his imagination took him all over the world seeking shelter in remote places where he might find refuge from murderous pursuers. In these contexts he seems to have lived for a time in foreign embassies, bomb shelters, prisons, and refugee camps, moving from one to another. This search for a "containing" space in which he might hope to feel safe was replaced at other times by feeling trapped in an "Inferno ... a purgatory or a polluted heaven ... a decayed rotting house infested by rats, termites and other vermin" (Nasar, 1998, p. 324). The former state could be regarded as "claustrophilia" and the latter as "claustrophobia." At other times, living in fear of annihilation, he was in a state of "agoraphobia" (see Rey, 1994).*

Throughout this "descent into the Inferno" he struggled to find a sane and stable identity, but seems to have been dominated by shifting identifications, variously reflecting his omnipotent grandiosity, his exposure to murderous deities, and his own murderous sense of rivalry (Nasar, 1998, pp. 324, 327). One way of understanding the extreme violence of the Communist and "bad extraterrestrial" persecutors would be to regard them as mental structures (internal part-objects) created by projection of infantile unconscious murderous jealousy, felt as omnipotently powerful in early life, thereby reversing the psychological reality. Using this perspective, the identity of the vermin might be considered to be unborn babies (Meltzer, 1992), rival siblings (Freud, 1900), or offspring containing the projection of unconscious invasive and polluting attacks on the maternal body of infancy (Jackson & Williams, 1994; Jackson,

---

* For a detailed consideration of the symbolic derivatives of unconscious fantasies about the mother's body, its spaces, and contents see Meltzer (1967) and Rey (1994). A practical application of this theory can be seen in a recent study of homeless people living on the streets of Edinburgh, which showed that a great proportion were unable to accept the accommodation freely provided for any length of time, returning to the streets before long, and then repeating the cycle of homelessness. The recognition of the claustro-agoraphobic nature of this sort of homelessness provided new understanding of this big social problem (Campbell, 2006).

2003; Willoughby, 2001), of whom the mothers of his two sons were the present representatives.*

DEPRESSION, REGRESSION, AND NEW BEGINNINGS

Nash's illness may well have been at first a depressive one,[†] provoked by disappointment and threats to his well-defended, precarious self-esteem. This may have threatened him with such unbearably painful emotions as loss, shame, anxiety, rage, and guilt that it precipitated a regression to a level of functioning where the relief offered by projective defenses led to feelings of persecution (delusional mood), and finally to paranoid persecutory delusions. The coincidence of his wife's pregnancy (desired by Nash's rational self) seems to have broken open the unresolved, "encapsulated" core of infantile feelings associated with a level of development in which the small child must face the painful recognition that mother is not his exclusive possession. By analogy with his mathematical thinking, he was forced to realize that he was not her prime "number one" and was obliged to confront a dyadic/rivalrous and triadic/oedipal world of painful and complex emotional relationships. The most terrifying consequence for Nash of his unconscious defensive struggle seems to have been that he, the unwitting agent of infantile murderous rage, became in his mind, by the reversal brought about by projective and introjective defensive processes, the victim of Communist assassins. At the same time, the infantile self who in his inner reality harbored fantasies of hatred towards a mother who conceived someone other than himself, found expression in aggressive behavior towards his pregnant mistress and his wife, both during their pregnancies and subsequently. This confusion was well illustrated in the film where he was portrayed as being desperate to save both women from the assassins while at the same time putting them at risk. Nash's ensuing delusions of self-importance, which in his most disturbed state of mind extended, as described, to the belief that he was the left foot of God, or even God himself, might be thought of as a manic defense against his depression in the form of a megalomanic belief based on an identification with an idealized

---

* In naming both his sons John, as in the three previous generations, Nash may have been making an unconscious statement that he was really their father, that they were his own flesh, and not the rival siblings of his unconscious fantasy. It may also have been the opposite, an expression of the wish to delete the first John from his life completely.

† Steiner (2004) has recently argued that Schreber's illness was primarily a depressive one from which he regressed into the paranoid state. This may well have been true of Nash's illness, but insufficient evidence is available to support this conjecture. This possibility, in the case of Schreber, emphasizes the influence of the extreme humiliation that he had suffered. Nash had a comparable experience in the RAND episode, but we do not know whether he had the capacity for shame (Kinston, 1983), or if he did, whether it was this catastrophe that helped to motivate his desire to invent a "repentingness" oscilloscope.

father. Nash's recovery seems to have depended on his engagement in a long period of testing of his delusional thinking against reality. This painful process led to increasing awareness of his emotional fragility and to the wish to make amends for past attitudes, with the consequential development of a sense of regret and repentance characteristic of depressive concern. This increased maturity led to the attenuation of his "merciless" superego and to a more normal sense of guilt and of tolerance of painful feelings of shame, humiliation, and impaired self-esteem, a conjecture to which we will return. A new capacity for concern for fellow sufferers emerged. This was a creative achievement that found expression in his subsequent commitment to promoting an improved, psychotherapeutically based treatment for fellow sufferers.

It is not unreasonable to speculate whether, at the early depressive stage of his illness, Nash might have been accessible to experienced psychoanalytic psychotherapy if it had been available. Had this been possible and successful it would have involved the working-through of his dangerous underlying pathogenic conflicts in the safe containment of a therapeutic transference, an undertaking that would have required skill and experience on the part of the psychotherapist. A less ideal outcome would be a less intensive psychotherapeutic involvement that might have led to a reduction in the severity of pathogenic psychopathology, modification of the persecutory superego that was causing him so much suffering, and increased ego strength. Such an outcome might have recaptured the opportunity that he subsequently regretted having lost at the McLean Hospital at the onset of his illness.

Looking at the illness from a psychoanalytic perspective allows Nash's case to be freed from the dubious implications of the diagnosis "schizophrenia" and for him to be understood as struggling with varying degrees of success and failure in the context of developmental conflicts associated with loss, love, hate, protectiveness, greed, guilt, envy, and jealousy—struggles which we all have to manage as best we can from infancy onward. A catastrophic revival of this "unfinished business" of early infancy can be considered as presenting a "second chance," an opportunity to resume arrested growth and to integrate earlier discarded elements of his mind, if a return to the point of bifurcation where integration failed is possible. It is of interest to note that an eminent colleague of Nash's considers Nash's work subsequent to the breakdown to be more creative, rich, and important than the earlier economic-political work, which he considers to be an ingenious, but not surprising, application of well-known methods (Milnor, 1998).

Recovery and after

When recovery from a psychotic illness is considered as a "remission," it raises the question of the psychosocial and psychodynamic pathways that have been involved, the nature and quality of the recovery, and the stability of the improvement. Rather than using the term "cure," a psychoanalytic perspective suggests that reduction of psychopathology of varying degrees is a more realistic criterion in evaluating outcome. This allows consideration as to what extent the recovery process has achieved a new and more integrated level of mental functioning, or is more a matter of restoration of the pre-illness level of functioning. In the latter case the patient is at risk of relapse and long-term psychiatric supervision of psychosocial functioning and of medication, where appropriate, will be necessary. Even where an improved level of function has been achieved in psychotherapy, the patient may be left with unresolved difficulties, in which case "relapse" may be approached as an opportunity for further working-through of conflicts. In a case such as Nash's where relapse would seem, from the available evidence, to be unlikely, remaining issues may take such forms as disturbing traumatic memories, impressive dreams, and incomplete resolutions of personality pathology or of conflicts in personal relationships that had been previously hidden either consciously or unconsciously. Nash's life appears to have become successful and creative, but it is not devoid of distress, in particular it seems, in relation to his close involvement with his psychotic son, who may, perhaps, like his father, not have had a skilled psychoanalytic assessment early in his illness. However, whatever human problems remain for him it seems fairly clear that Nash has emerged from his long ordeal with new insights and with a new stability. It is impressive to see how he has described the residue of his intrapsychic upheavals. He feels sure that he won't suffer a relapse, and of the profound changes in his mental processes he has said, "It's like a continuous process rather than just waking up from a dream … when I dream … it sometimes happens that I go back to the system of delusions that's typical of how I was … and then I wake, and then I'm rational again" (Nasar, 1998, p. 389).

The implication of this type of experience is that he has acquired a working channel of communication with previously unsymbolizable elements of his unconscious fantasy life, and what seems to be a new capacity to express his preoccupations in symbolic form in his dream life. Although Nasar's biography, and especially the subsequent film, may have helped many people to better understand the plight of the severely psychotic person and to diminish the fear that is often attached to the term "schizophrenia," the stigma of the condition will undoubtedly remain deeply entrenched in the public consciousness. Nash himself observed: "You cannot remove the stigma. To do that would be to remove the illness."

DIAGNOSIS OF THE ILLNESS AND/OR
UNDERSTANDING THE PERSON

Psychotic illness presents in so many different forms that many clinicians consider the term schizophrenia to be so misleading that it should finally be abandoned and replaced by the term psychosis, as a generic category of severely disturbed states of mind. Under this heading a range of schizophrenia-type conditions can be studied, and the frequent associations with manic and depressive features better understood. A psychodynamic approach can complement such descriptive diagnoses as "schizo-affective" and "bipolar," and object-relations theory can allow exploration of the inner world of the individual. Kleinian concepts of paranoid-schizoid and depressive positions and the use of splitting, projection, and introjection have demonstrated the interplay of destructive and reparative motivations, throwing light on individuals' progression and regression over the course of their illness. The work of Wilfred Bion has made possible unparalleled advances in recent times into the study of the interplay between psychotic and nonpsychotic forces of the personality and the containment and treatment needed for personality integration in the individual with psychosis.* In addition, concepts such as "the infantile psychotic self" (Volkan, 1995), "fixation points," and "regressive potential" can help the investigation of the nature of psychological factors in the early environment which may predispose to subsequent psychotic developments. Using Volkan's understanding of an innate disposition in some individuals to psychosis in infancy, for example, it is possible to conjecture (knowledge being impossible) as to whether John Nash's extreme sensitivities may have been linked to a constitutional vulnerability from the outset, possibly in the form of a defective "contact barrier," which may have rendered Nash-the-infant inadequately equipped to withstand the power and impact of his affective responses and unconscious fantasies. The more knowledge clinicians have of the psychogenic aspects of psychotic illness, and the more skill they acquire in listening in an informed way to the individual patient's psychotic and nonpsychotic statements, the better able they will be to judge the severity and prognosis of the illness and to consider an optimum treatment plan. Hospitalization, in emergency situations and for more formal assessment and initiation of treatment, should ideally be on a "need-adapted" basis and be "psychoanalytically informed" (Alanen, 2002; Jackson & Williams, 1994).

A common misunderstanding is that the use of such methods makes for expensive psychiatry. The reality, as demonstrated by Finnish researchers (Pylkkanen, 1989) is the opposite. In today's world, keeping patients in the hospital for extended periods or arranging many repeated admissions upon relapse is hugely costly to mental health services, not to mention the

---

* See Bion (1957, 1961, 1963, 1965, 1967, 1970, 1977, 1992).

emotional cost to patients, families, and hospital staff. Even a modicum of structural *internal* change in the psychotic individual, undertaken in the multidisciplinary context outlined above, can often be a harbinger of improvement that leads toward greater self-reliance and fewer hospital visits, and often to successful taxable employment. The relief it can be to individuals and their families to discover that the disturbance—"schizophrenia"—with all its fearful and stigmatizing connotations, is actually a well-known illness that is treatable along the lines described, cannot be overestimated. At a practical level, approaching patients and their social network of relatives and carers in this psychodynamically informed manner allows the clinician to make informed judgments regarding patients who might be well suited for a trial of psychotherapy from those who are likely to be more accessible to psychosocial and behavioral approaches.

PSYCHOANALYSIS AND PSYCHIATRY TODAY

Psychoanalytic theories of psychosis and treatment approaches have advanced greatly since the time of Freud's groundbreaking formulations, and psychoanalytically based psychotherapy for selected borderline, schizophrenic, and manic-depressive patients by the right therapist in the right situation has been shown to be effective (Oldham & Russakoff, 1987; Robbins, 1993; Lotterman, 1996; Jackson & Williams, 1994; Lucas, 2003; Pestalozzi, 2003). The severely regressed psychotic patient requires the availability of specialized psychoanalytically informed hospital resources or community-based psychiatric care in which psychological and biological factors and treatment requirements can be assessed (Holmes, 2000), and appropriate interventions rationally planned. Such specialized resources capable of providing psychotherapeutically skilled intensive care can usually be provided only by publicly funded mental health services. Their extreme rarity attests to a crucial deficiency in mental health provision.* Current socioeconomic and cultural pressures prioritizes methods of brief therapy, but evidence is emerging that suggests that psychoanalytically informed, "need-adapted" treatment strategies (incorporating an option of individual psychotherapy) may be more effective in the long term (Pylkkanen, 1989; Alanen, 1997; Martindale, Bateman, Crowe, & Margison, 2000; Cullberg, 2002, 2006). It is becoming clear that current views of schizophrenia and certain treatment strategies represent a social denial of the huge burden usually suffered by the families of the schizophrenic individual. More broadly, Robbins (1993) suggests that the fundamental social issue involved is not so much the need for provision of better resources, however urgent this may

---

* A deficiency that is currently vigorously pursued by the International Society for the Psychological Treatments of Schizophrenia and Related Psychoses (ISPS).

be, but of recognizing the failure by world governments to confront the seriousness of the problems involved in schizophrenic disorders. The exposure of the patient's psychotic core in the course of psychotherapy, which is necessary if the therapy is to succeed, may bring risks (as, of course, does psychoactive medication) and this is why the training and skill of the individual therapist and the quality of the psychiatric supporting network is so vital.* However, under appropriate conditions the risks can be managed and the consequences of working through pathogenic processes using analytic methods can bring great benefit.† Without this help, many patients capable of making good use of treatment will be denied the developmental opportunity they deserve and might be able to use.

CONCLUSION

We all live in two worlds at once by day and night, but usually only become aware of the power of this inner ("psychic") reality in dream life, slips of the tongue, and neurotic and psychotic symptoms. The exploration of Nash's mind (conscious and unconscious) that has been presented in this essay could be viewed as an unwarranted intrusion into the private life of a respected public figure. Although some less admirable aspects of his personality have been brought to public view by his biographer, this piece tries to probe more deeply into reported aspects of his life, both external and internal, a conjectural undertaking the authors feel to be worthwhile in the service of education in mental illness. John Nash is no different from everyone else in the sense that he has had to negotiate as best he could universal problems of integrating profound, contradictory impulses that operate from birth onwards, the negotiation of which is the basis for the acquisition of self-esteem and a firm sense of one's own personality. Although Nash's innate biology may have made him more vulnerable than many to developing a subsequent schizophrenic-type psychosis (as might be true in the case

---

* Whatever the biochemical basis of the symptom-suppressing effects of antipsychotic medication might eventually prove to be, they can be of great short- or longer-term benefit to many acute and chronic psychotic patients, and should not be regarded simply as an inferior substitute to psychotherapeutic working-through of conflicts. Nor should medication be regarded as an alternative to psychotherapy, but, at least in the first instance, as an aid to pursuing whatever level of verbal communication is possible at a particular time. On the other hand, many psychotic patients in experienced hands will need no medication; for them analytic psychotherapy is the treatment of choice (Karon & vanden Bos, 1981).

† The usefulness of less-intensive psychoanalytically based treatment for selected psychotic patients, sometimes as the treatment of choice (Karon, 2003) rather than a more readily-available resource, has yet to be properly recognized (cf. Jackson, 2003). It is also important to recognize that the earlier the illness can be detected, and the earlier a psychoanalytic approach can be brought to bear on the case, the more successful are psychotherapeutic interventions likely to be. Much of the pessimism conveyed by writings on schizophrenia stems from the fact that they so often concern patients who have drifted into chronicity.

of his son), it appears to be his psychology that has determined his fate and, with the help of medication at certain times, has led to his recovery. We all live with our personality difficulties and we usually strive to make the best of a bad job. Nash seems to have succeeded in working through his conflicts to a degree sufficient to qualify as a recovery, rather than as a potentially unstable remission. If further justification is required for writing this particular essay, it might be found in Nash's own passionate hopes that the future will see new research and more effective ways of understanding and helping his ill son. However much John Nash's real experience may diverge from the foregoing speculative pathways, his achievement of a major remission seems beyond doubt. At the same time, when this occurs as a result of increased mental integration, spontaneously or as the outcome of successful psychotherapy (rather than an unstable "sealing over"), the individual concerned may not necessarily be free from further difficulties. If, for example, a prepsychotic basic personality disorder has not been sufficiently worked through or if a residue of significant psychopathology persists, he may remain vulnerable and could experience a return of symptoms if he encounters sufficient specific stress in his inner or outer world.

In her epilogue, Nasar (1998) offers a vivid description of the transformation of Nash's personality, of his new warmth and humanity, of his remarriage to his long-divorced wife, of the recovery of lost relationships from the past (particularly with his illegitimate son), and of his closeness to his psychotic son,* and she records that he has come to appreciate how vital his wife's support has been to his recovery. Even if Nash has not fully understood or resolved the issues that his dreams may be presenting to him or sufficiently mourned his great losses, he seems, from all accounts, to have acquired a significant increase of ego strength, in particular of the capacity for reality-testing, and a major attenuation of his "merciless superego" (p. 232). He appears to have discovered reparative motivations and has sufficiently abandoned damaging projective and splitting activity† to allow a weakening of processes of paranoid-schizoid thinking and progress towards the depressive position, with the growth of a capacity for concern for others.‡ Although the extent and stability of his new level of mental integration and the precise way it has been achieved is unclear, this is an impressive outcome. Before his illness, Nash's "ultra-rational intelligence," his spirit of scientific enquiry, and his determination had led him to successful exploration of the secrets of the material world. It may be that this same quality helped him to take his delusional world seriously, to oppose the psychotic

---

* Speculations about the nature and dynamics of his son's illness would be intrusive and inappropriate in the context of this essay.
† To some extent reclaiming parts of his self and inner world lost by projection into various containers (Steiner, 1993a).
‡ A maturational achievement not to be confused with clinical depression.

logic of the "hypotheses" promoted by his hallucinated voices, and thereby to promote the intrapsychic changes that ultimately led to his recovery.

Many people with chronic schizophrenia argue ineffectively with their voices, but Nash's tenacious dedication to scientific enquiry, as well as to confrontation, helped him in the struggle to free himself from the deadly propaganda of the voices and to weather the storms of his long ordeal without permanent deterioration or suicide. Eventually he seems to have found a way of living with himself, which enabled him to achieve a sane, creative, and more emotionally mature life. Although a large part of his life may have been wasted (but hopefully mourned), it is possible that he may even regard the benefits of his improved personality to have been worth the enormous cost.

EPILOGUE: PITY, JUSTICE, MERCY—THE TAMING OF THE "MERCILESS" SUPEREGO

Although it is impossible to draw sound conclusions from the evidence of three words scrawled on a postcard, it is important to consider what they might possibly tell us about the mental state of the writer and about the dynamic processes that could have finally brought him relief from severe depression.

At the time when Nash was improving he wrote a letter to his sister, which Nasar records: "... he was seized by a terrible sense of regret that he poured into a poignant and introspective letter to Martha, full of references to the struggle between his 'merciless superego' and 'old simple me'" (p. 317). Conjecture presents two opposite possibilities. Addressing his plea for clemency to an inner figure in the words on the postcard might imply that he had made considerable progress in differentiating external from internal reality, but whether this represents a state of inner persecution, or progress towards the depressive position, depends on whether he was feeling himself to be the *victim* or the *agent* of such cruelty.

If it were the latter it would suggest that the "humanizing" of his superego was achieved by the unconscious withdrawal and "reclaiming" of projection of his own destructive behavior, first from his deluded perception of his imminent destruction, and now encountering them in his inner world. The question remains as to whether his state of mind was one of self-pity, or of a dawning regret about his past treatment of others, in internal and external reality. The words he has chosen connote universal issues of the suffering and the alleviation of guilt.

No one has expressed this theme better than Samuel Coleridge in his immortal poem, "The Rime of the Ancient Mariner." A psychoanalytic reading of this powerful poem suggests the following psychodynamic processes—after an act of wanton cruelty (the Albatross symbolizing, in

Kleinian terms, the beautiful "breast-mother"), the mariner enters into a state of psychotic depression alone in the company of his dead companions ("destroyed internal objects"). On the brink of death, and after a long period of terrible suffering in a "trance," during which he hallucinates angelic figures passing judgment on him, he observes the beauty of the little sea creatures swimming around in the dead and becalmed sea. Seized by a flood of new and benevolent emotions he begins to recover his capacity for love, concern, and pity, and his merciless superego begins to relent and he recovers his sanity.

> O happy living things! No tongue
> Their beauty might declare:
> A spring of love gushed from my heart,
> And I blessed them unaware:
> Sure my kind saint took pity on me,
> And I blessed them unaware.
> That self-same moment I could pray;
> And from my neck so free
> The Albatross fell off, and sank
> Like lead into the sea.

The companions who had formerly reproached him savagely undergo a ghostly reanimation and, having silently worked the ship in the newly sprung wind, disappeared one by one into the heavens in a state of blissful happiness, which the Mariner observes as an event of great beauty. Although his objects are now repaired (possibly expressing a manic idealization), his ordeal has not reached an entirely happy ending. His ghostly judges pronounce sentence on him:

> Quoth he, "The man hath penance done,
> And penance more will do."

The Mariner's sentence is to live the life of a wanderer on the earth, repetitively recounting his tale to those he chooses, to promote the realization of the fate that awaits thoughtless (unconscious) destructiveness. This "psychotherapeutic" activity might be considered to resemble a happy outcome of the tale of our fictional Nash, and as being one of psychotherapeutic intent and of reparative motivation. To seek an analogy in the case of the real John Forbes Nash, one could instance his spreading his hard-won insight in widespread lecturing about the importance of psychotherapy in the treatment of stigmatized psychotic patients who deserve pity, skilled understanding, and justice.

There are many other aspects of the story of the real John Nash that might be considered as being parallels between internal and external realities, raising such questions as whether Nash's inability to share helped to motivate his eventual creation of ways of creative sharing; his achievement of some degree of personal equilibrium foreshadowed by his Equilibrium theory; and his dedication to research in cosmology motivating his "scientific" approach to his experience of internal psychological reality. Whether these otherwise unrelated items are causally or analogically related is an interesting question.

No information is available which suggests that Nash may have suffered some obvious emotional disturbance in his early childhood, or any environmental event that might have constituted a psychogenetic predisposing factor. However, this does not exclude the possibility. The type of information that would qualify as suggestive evidence is usually readily accessible, commonly taking forms such as maternal puerperal depression, the death or illness of siblings, or major disturbance in feeding or sleeping. More subtle influences and elements may be difficult or impossible to identify or confirm,* and the possible influence of the unconscious fantasies of both mother and child are even more inaccessible. It is at this point that conjecture must cease. Although this essay could be viewed as a psychobiography, this would be a mistake. It was written to illustrate ways in which psychoanalysis can add depth and meaning to the conventional psychiatric thinking about psychotic illness. The aim was to avoid assertions, for which in any case there would be little or no evidence, and to stimulate interest in a psychoanalytic approach to psychotic mental states by illustrating certain mental mechanisms that may be involved in psychotic functioning. Before his psychosis, Nash's ideal was the emotionless hominid Mr. Spock. He wished that he could create a passionless "thinking" machine. During the course of his illness he wished that he could construct a "repentingness" machine. This evolution, the psychological importance of which cannot be overestimated, may have represented a developmental advance from solipsistic, paranoid-schizoid thinking to depressive anxieties and genuine concern for others. Whether or not the conclusions reached in this essay about this fictional Nash are relevant for the real individual John Forbes Nash, they are certainly relevant to many patients with illnesses precisely of the kind discussed here and who are encountered by psychiatrists and psychoanalytic therapists in their everyday work.

---

* Nash's gross disturbance of his sense of identity and impairment of symbol use during his psychosis and his delusions of world destruction certainly suggest the likelihood of such early psychobiological events, and the fact of his son's psychosis suggests (but does not prove) a genetic vulnerability.

REFERENCES

Alanen, Y. O. (1997). *Schizophrenia: Its origins and need-adapted treatment.* London: Karnac Books.

Alanen, Y. O. (2002). Vulnerability to schizophrenia: An integrated view. *Psychiatria Fennica, 33,* 11–30.

Arieti, S. (1974). *Interpretation of schizophrenia.* London: Basic Books.

Bell, D. (2003). *Paranoia: Ideas in psychoanalysis.* London: Icon.

Bion, W. R. (1957). Differentiation of the psychotic from the non-psychotic personalities. In *Second thoughts: Selected papers on psycho-analysis* (pp. 43–64). London: Heinemann.

Bion, W. R. (1961). *Experiences in groups and other papers.* London: Tavistock.

Bion, W. R. (1963). *Elements of psycho-analysis.* London: Heinemann.

Bion, W. R. (1965). *Transformations.* London: Heinemann.

Bion, W. R. (1967). *Second thoughts: Selected papers on psycho-analysis.* London: Heinemann.

Bion, W. R. (1970). *Attention and interpretation.* London: Tavistock.

Bion, W. R. (1977). *Learning from experience.* London: Heinemann.

Bion, W. R. (1992). *Cogitations* (F. Bion, Ed.). London: Karnac Books.

Bleuler, M. (1978). *The schizophrenic disorders: Long-term patient and family studies.* New Haven, CT: Yale University Press.

Britton, R. (1998). *Belief and imagination.* London: Routledge.

Campbell, J. (2006). Homelessness and containment: A psychotherapy project with homeless people and workers in the homeless field. *Psychoanalytic Psychotherapy, 20*(3), 157–174.

Charles, M. (2003). *A Beautiful Mind*—Review of the film. *American Journal of Psychoanalysis, 63,* 21–37.

Cullberg, J. (2002). One-year outcome in first episode psychosis patients in the Swedish Parachute project. *Acta Psychiatrica Scandinavica, 106,* 276–285.

Cullberg, J. (2006). *Psychosis: An integrative perspective.* Routledge: London.

De Masi, F. (1997). Intimidation at the helm: Superego and hallucinations in the analytic treatment of a psychosis. *International Journal of Psychoanalysis, 78,* 561–576.

De Masi, F. (2000). The unconscious and psychosis: Some considerations on the psychoanalytic theory of psychosis. *International Journal of Psychoanalysis, 81,* 1–20.

De Masi, F. (2003). On the nature of intuitive and delusional thought. *International Journal of Psychoanalysis, 84,* 1149–1169.

Fonagy, P., Gergely, J., Elliot, L., & Target, M. (2002). Affect regulation, mentalization, and the development of the self. In *Psychiatry.* London: Free Association Books.

Fonagy, P., Gergely, J., Elliot, L., & Target, M. (2003). *Psychoanalytic theories: Perspectives from development psychology.* London: Whurr.

Freeman, T. (1994). On some types of hallucinatory experience. *Psychoanalytic Psychotherapy, 89*(3), 273–281.

Freud, S. (1900). The interpretation of dreams. In J. Strachey (Ed. & Trans.), *The standard edition of the complete psychological works of Sigmund Freud* (Vol. 5). London: Hogarth Press.

Freud, S. (1911). Psycho-analytic notes on an autobiographical account of a case of paranoia. In J. Strachey (Ed. & Trans.), *The standard edition of the complete psychological works of Sigmund Freud* (Vol. 12). London: Hogarth Press.

Gabbard, G. (Ed.). (2001). Psychoanalysis and film. In *International Journal of Psychoanalysis Key Paper Series*. London: Karnac

Gaddini, E. (1992). *A psychoanalytic theory of infantile experience: Conceptual and clinical reflections*. London: Routledge.

Grotstein, J. S. (1997). The psychoanalytic concept of schizophrenia. *International Journal of Psychoanalysis*, *58*, 403–542.

Grotstein, J. S. (2000). *Who is the dreamer, who dreams the dream?* Hillsdale, NJ: The Analytic Press.

Grotstein, J. S., & Rinsley, D. B. (1994). *Fairbairn and the origins of object relations*. London: Free Associations Books.

Harding, C. (2002). Beautiful minds can be recovered. *New York Times*, March 10.

Harding, C., Brooks, G., Ashikaga, T., Strauss, J., & Brier, A. (1987). The Vermont longitudinal study of persons with severe mental illness. *American Journal of Psychiatry*, *14*(4), 727–735.

Hinshelwood, R. D. (1980). The seeds of Disaster, *International Journal of Therapeutic Communities* 1.

Hinshelwood, R. D. (1989). *A dictionary of Kleinian thought*. London: Free Association Books.

Hobson, P. (2002). *The cradle of thought*. London: Macmillan.

Holmes, J. (2000). Fitting the bio-psycho-social jigsaw together. *British Journal of Psychiatry*, *177*, 93–94.

Jackson, M. (1993). Manic-depressive psychosis: Psychopathology and individual psychotherapy within a psychodynamic milieu. *Psychoanalytic Psychotherapy*, *7*(2), 103–133.

Jackson, M. (2003). *Weathering the storms: Psychotherapy for psychosis*. London: Karnac Books.

Jackson, M., & Williams, P. (1994). *Unimaginable storms: A search for meaning in psychosis*. London: Karnac Books.

Johns, C., Nazroo, J. Y., Bebbington, P., & Kuipers, E. (2002). Occurrence of hallucinatory experiences in a community sample and ethnic variations. *British Journal of Psychiatry*, *180*, 174–178.

Johnson, S., & Ruszczynski, S. (1999). *Psychoanalytic psychotherapy in the independent tradition*. London: Karnac Books.

Karon, B. F. (2003). The tragedy of schizophrenia without psychotherapy. *The Journal of the American Academy of Psychoanalysis and Dynamic Psychiatry*, *31*(1), 89–118.

Karon, B. F., & vanden Bos, G. R. (1981). *Psychotherapy of schizophrenia: The treatment of choice*. New York: Jason Aronson.

Kinston, W. (1983). A theoretical context for shame. *International Journal of Psychoanalysis*, *64*, 213–226.

Klein, M (1930). The importance of symbol formation in the development of the ego. *International Journal of Psychoanalysis*, *11*, 24–39.

Laing, R. D. (1967). *The politics of experience and the bird of paradise*. London: Penguin Books.

Lidz, T. (1964). August Strindberg: A study of the relationship between his creativity and schizophrenia. *International Journal of Psychoanalysis, 45*, 399–406.

Lotterman, A. (1996). *Specific techniques for the psychotherapy of schizophrenic patients.* Madison, CT: International Universities Press.

Lucas, R. (2003). The relationship between psychoanalysis and schizophrenia. *International Journal of Psychoanalysis, 84*, 3–9.

Mahler, M. S., Pine, F., & Bergman, A. (1975). *The psychological birth of the human infant.* London: Karnac Books.

Martindale, B., Bateman, A., Crowe, M., & Margison, F. (Eds.). (2000). *Psychosis: Psychological approaches and their effectiveness.* London: Gaskell.

Matte-Blanco, I. (1998). *Thinking, feeling and being.* London: Routledge.

Meltzer, D. (1967). *The psychoanalytic process.* London: Heinemann.

Meltzer, D. (1992). *The claustrum: An investigation of claustrophobic phenomena.* London: The Clunie Press.

Michels, R. (2003). The relationship between psychoanalysis and schizophrenia by Richard Lucas: A commentary. *International Journal of Psychoanalysis, 84*, 9–12.

Milnor, J. (1998). John Nash and A Beautiful Mind. *Notices of the AMS, 45*(10).

Mitchell, J. (2000). *Mad men and medusas.* London: Penguin.

Mitchell, J. (2003). *Siblings.* London: Karnac Books.

Nasar, S. (1994). The lost years of a Nobel laureate. *New York Times News Service.*

Nasar, S. (1998). *A beautiful mind.* New York: Simon and Schuster.

Nash, J. (1996). Plenary lecture to the 10th Congress of Psychiatry, Madrid.

Nash, J. (2002a). Interview with John Nash: "How does recovery happen?" American Experience. Retrieved from http://www.pbs.org/wgbh/amex/nash/sfeatures/sf_nash_11.html.

Nash, J. (2002b). John F. Nash Jr.: Autobiography. Nobel e-Museum. Retrieved from http://www.nobel.se/economics/laureates/1994/nash-autobio.html.

Ogden, T. H. (1989). *The primitive edge of experience.* London: Jason Aronson.

Oldham, J. M., & Russakoff, M. R. (1987). *Dynamic therapy in brief hospitalization.* London: Jason Aronson.

Pao, P-N. (1979). *Schizophrenic disorders: Theory and treatment from a psychodynamic point of view.* New York: International Universities Press.

Pestalozzi, J. (2003). The symbolic and concrete: Psychotic adolescents in psychoanalytic psychotherapy. *International Journal of Psychoanalysis, 82*, 515–532.

Pylkkanen, K. (1989). A quality assurance program for schizophrenia. *Psychoanalytic Psychotherapy, 4*, 13–22.

Rey, J. H. (1979). Schizoid phenomena in the borderline. In *Advances in the psychotherapy of borderline states* (J. le Boit & A. Capponi, Eds.). New York: Jason Aronson.

Rey, J. H. (1994). *Universals of psychoanalysis in the treatment of psychotic and borderline states.* London: Free Association Books

Robbins, M. (1993). *Experiences of schizophrenia.* London: Guilford Press.

Romme, M., Honig, A., Noorthoorn, E. O., & Escher, S. (1992). Coping with hearing voices: An emancipatory approach. *British Journal of Psychiatry, 161*, 99–103.

Rosenfeld, D. (1992). *The psychotic: Aspects of the personality.* London: Karnac Books.

Rosenfeld, H. A. (1987). *Impasse and interpretation.* London: Tavistock Publications.

Schreber, D. P. (1903). *Memoirs of my nervous illness* (I. MacAlpine & R. A. Hunteer, Eds. & Trans.). London: Dawson.

Segal, H. A. (1972). A delusional system as a defense against the emergence of a catastrophic situation. *International Journal of Psychoanalysis*, *52*, 393–401.

Segal, H. A. (1981). Notes on symbol formation. In *The work of Hanna Segal*. New York: Jason Aronson.

Sinason, M. (2003). On film review essay: *Fight Club*. *International Journal of Psychoanalysis*, *83*(6), 1442–1444.

Steiner, J. (1993a). Commentary on "The analyst at work." *International Journal of Psychoanalysis*, *83*(5), 1012–1015.

Steiner, J. (1993b). *Psychic retreats*. London: Routledge.

Steiner, J. (2004). Gaze, dominance and humiliation in the Schreber case. *International Journal of Psychoanalysis*, *85*(2), 269–284.

Volkan, V. D. (1995). *The infantile psychotic self and its fates*. London: Jason Aronson.

Volkan, V. D., & Ast, G. (1997). *Siblings in the unconscious and psychopathology*. Madison, CT: International Universities Press.

Whipp, G. (2001). "Mind" games: Ron Howard, Russell Crowe aim for the truth, but missed facts. *Los Angeles Daily News*, 26 December.

Williams, P. (1998). Psychotic developments in a sexually abused borderline patient. *Psychoanalytic Dialogues*, *8*(3), 451–491.

Williams, P. (2004). Incorporation of an invasive object. *International Journal of Psychoanalysis*, *85*, 1333–1348.

Willoughby, R. (2001). "The dungeon of thyself": The claustrum as pathological container. *International Journal of Psychoanalysis*, *82*(5), 917–931.

Part II

Applied chapters

A friend suggested that I preface this section of the book with the following words: "Unless you are keenly interested in the application of psychoanalytic thinking to society and culture, why not skip this part of the book and do something you really like doing?"

Under such circumstances, he would do this. So, I have to say, would I.

I did not take the suggestion very seriously, believing it to be a lighthearted aside, until I realized that a fundamental, sober point was being made about human freedom. Unless we are free to do what we want, in accordance with our needs, character, and circumstances, we are oppressed. Oppression is understood clinically by psychoanalysts to be a predominantly internal phenomenon. A great deal—perhaps the greater part—of human misery could be said to derive from the capacity for self-deception and the impact of internal conflicts, leading to oppression. As psychoanalysts we set about understanding these self-defeating processes in order to assist individuals to free themselves from their inner oppression. However, it can escape no one that oppression is also an external phenomenon. Certain parents and families create a hotbed for oppression. It can occur in schools, the workplace, religious movements, academia, or anywhere people come together. Political groups risk redundancy without it, and nation-states risk all to defeat it. The capacity for human beings to oppress each other appears to know no bounds, and it has fallen to social anthropology and sociology to try to delineate the forms these conflicts take and to offer explanations for their origins. Psychoanalysis has contributed insights to this work, particularly in its attempts to clarify the role of the unconscious mental life of individuals as it applies to group behavior and social interaction. The early history of social anthropology made extensive use of analytic contributions and this tradition has not disappeared. Today, the nature of the "self" and its development and vicissitudes are discussed by scholars from both disciplines (cf. Molino, 2004). In the chapters that follow, a theme that recurs is the significance of the impact of unconscious mental life in the behavior of groups. Knowledge of unconscious mental life in individuals has grown considerably, but unfortunately knowledge of unconscious mental life in social contexts is accorded little attention by comparison, with the implicit risks of the repetition of history this implies.

Not all the chapters in this section have an anthropological bent. The discussion of Green's "central phobic position"—an important concept by Green that throws new light on borderline mental states—shows, among other things, how difficult it is for analysts to discuss in a nonsupervisory, collegial manner, new and different ideas. Perhaps the social interaction of psychoanalysts merits study from the point of view of unconscious motivation. I suspect that difficulty in achieving rational debate may be one of the most important threats to our discipline in this age of unfettered pluralism. The chapter on "The Rat Man" is designed to illustrate the prescience of Freud's thinking on obsessionality, particularly in the light of subsequent theoretical developments in psychoanalysis.

REFERENCES

Molino, A. (2004). Ed. *Culture, Subject, Psyche: Dialogues in Psychoanalysis and Anthropology*. Connecticut: Wesleyan University Press.

Chapter 7

Madness in society

Two disciplines are implied in this title, perhaps three. Madness refers to a mental state. Society is the domain of sociologists and social anthropologists. Implicit in any study of them together is history. I shall touch upon all three in this chapter. The critic Terry Kupers pointed out the recurrent problem that has faced many sociologists in trying to account for madness. Certain sociological theories argue that our current social arrangements cause emotional disorders, and they envisage a society that could be less alienating. If this is the case, why have socialist societies failed to ameliorate emotional distress? If we persist in blaming reified capitalist relations for the existence of schizophrenia, how do we test this theory if these are the social relations we are stuck with (Kupers, 1981, 1988)? The idea that the schizophrenic's utterances mirror the real truth of our social existence, which is masked by false consciousness, retains a powerful hold over many people, particularly in Western cultures. Normal citizens are socialized to ignore this truth, the theory argues. Isolated schizophrenics break down under the weight of their burden of harsh truths, and this plight is what led Laing and Cooper (1964) to glorify the lucid utterances of their psychotic patients. In France, Deleuze and Guattari (1977) wrote their compelling countercultural treatise, which linked the mechanical, deadening world of the schizophrenic to the machines and mindlessly repetitive, corrosive effects of late capitalist relations of production and their social *sequelae*.

These arguments fall into the category of grand theories—large-scale hypotheses designed to illuminate major elements of social history. Michel Foucault was perhaps the most influential recent grand theorist and his impact cannot be ignored (Foucault, 1965). I shall return to his ideas shortly. Most sociological and anthropological theorizing about the relationship between mental health and society looks at ways in which madness is defined, allocated, and managed. What are the premises that underpin definitions of madness; which groups have an investment in supporting and maintaining these definitions; and what are the social consequences of the dynamics that ensue? The reader might be forgiven for querying whether these pursuits are an intellectual distraction from the urgent work of dealing clinically with those afflicted by madness. However, it needs to be kept in mind that the treatment of insanity as a psychological or psychiatric condition is a relatively recent undertaking, originating in the early 19th century, and its emergence coincided with ways in which relations of order and power were administered in a newly industrializing world. These influences have had tremendous impact on the ways individuals are viewed and treated, and the consequences affect every individual today who is diagnosed as being, in one way or other, mad. They also underwrite the methods by which the mentally ill person is likely to be viewed, treated, and managed.

If we look further into the situation prior to industrialization, we see that as with the poor, the mad have always been with us, and although what has defined them and their management has altered over the centuries, a persistent theme recurs that has less to do with ideas of care or therapeutics and more with practices of social exclusion and control, with powerful consequences for different groups. Of course, this does not mean that there have not been movements devoted to pastoral care of the insane. Bedlam Hospital outside London, now the Royal Bethlem Hospital, is perhaps the most well known example, having taken in disturbed individuals since the thirteenth century. However, the proportion of the population in the United Kingdom designated insane has been far from predictable or consistent and has been closely linked to the particular organization of society at any given time. There seems little doubt that ideas about what defines madness are bound up with prevailing sociopolitical and cultural values. Attempts to separate these definitions and the treatments they give rise to from their sociopolitical contexts serve to obscure who defines whom as mad and why, and how the mad are perceived and treated. There is a significant body of literature dealing with these phenomena, upon which this is paper is based. Authors of importance are Thomas Szasz (1991, 1997), Joel Kovel (1988), Michel Foucault (1965), Roy Porter (1987), William Bynum (Porter, Bynum & Shepherd, 2003), and Terry Kupers (1981, 1988), all of whose ideas are implicit in the ensuing argument.

DEFINING MADNESS

In classical Greece, definitions of madness tended to be variations of a broader idea that illness was not a phenomenon that was contingent or the automatic outcome of fate, but was the consequence of imbalances that affronted the natural laws governing the body—and by implication, the mind. The mind was not seen to be phenomenologically distinct from the soma. Patients and healers shared, by and large, comparable systems of thought, and these collective ideas advocated a lifestyle that eschewed extremes but instead reflected a holistic attitude towards health. Although these ideas were widespread, they were put to therapeutic use by some more than others. Access to this type of balanced lifestyle was, inevitably, unequal, giving rise to what, with a little imagination, could conceivably be seen as the first free market system in healthcare. As Greek culture became gradually more assimilated and the West made the turbulent transition to values based on Christianity, so there arose far greater emphasis on a distinction between conceptions of good and evil and this was to have an important impact on how diseases came to be viewed. Diseases became in some respects much more analogous to sin—the consequence of a failure to adhere to precepts likely to preserve the individual in a state of grace and good health. In turn, health became more likened to the pursuit of elevated standards of moral rectitude through designated practices designed to "improve" the individual. Physiological explanations of illness came to be employed alongside and within certain theological frameworks, and this gave rise to a number of definitional problems in relation to insanity. Cultures based on values supported by a religious doctrine increasingly came to employ a physiological model of illness. At the same time descriptions and definitions of physical illnesses and aberrant states of mind became increasingly precise, and this led to forms of madness no longer being seen as synonymous with bodily illness. In other words, madness gained a particular set of characteristics of its own deriving from new methods of classification, and it eventually emerged as a domain of study in its own right.

At the same time, from a religious point of view, the mind came increasingly to be viewed as affiliated to the soul and its vicissitudes. The soul was an entity that was held to be immortal, rather than being a physiological organ, and as such it could not become diseased in any conventional sense. This gave rise to an obstacle in the explanation of the nature of madness and became a tension that affects perceptions of madness to this day. One commonplace manifestation of this tension today is the use of "evil" and "wicked" in tabloid headlines to explain insane acts, with schizophrenia being seen as synonymous with a violent or murderous disposition, according to popular opinion. In other words, a dualistic approach emerged during the early Middle Ages from this coexistence of models that continues to affect contemporary public perception of mental illness. The church evolved its own particular form of understanding and management of mental distress (assuaging the distress of tormented souls through prayer, confession, absolution, exorcism, etc.), while a more secular approach arose that employed precipitates of Greek medical practices along with ranges of medicines, aromatic plants, charms, remedies, and other novel therapeutic practices as a basis for an emergent physiological model. There are a number of ways in which the mad were characterized and treated as the Middle Ages unfolded, but perhaps the lesson this period teaches us is that despite repeated attempts to explain madness, it never yielded itself to a single or unitary concept or theory. In my view, this is because madness could not ultimately be separated from the social conditions under which it appeared. Attempts to produce unitary theories risked appropriating ideas on behalf of particular groups and disciplines, and this risk persists. For example, the recent postmodern "decade of the brain" has greatly influenced contemporary psychiatry. Its insistence that the schizophrenias are the consequence solely of genetic abnormality is an example of appropriation of biological ideas from their social and political context by groups with interests that are scientific, academic, political, and commercial. One outcome of this hegemonic orientation is that a generation of Western psychiatrists has been taught to greatly emphasize the biological over the psychological, to the inestimable cost of patients.

FOUCAULT

I shall illustrate some aspects of this problem of definition by looking at how one sociologist, Michel Foucault, approached the question of how the mad come to be defined. Foucault developed the question of why there have arisen methods of appropriation and control over ideas and groups of people designated insane through his monumental analysis of madness as a disease of civilization. Whatever one's view of the Foucault *oeuvre*, its impact on views of madness in contemporary society, as well as the way we run our psychiatric hospitals and prisons, has been widespread. Many of his predictions concerning the encroachment of Big Brother attitudes, the surveillance and monitoring of populations, and the control of deviance have shown themselves to have been prescient.

Prior to the appearance in the nineteenth century of the psychiatric subject, that is to say what we now call the psychiatric patient, insanity was accounted for by a range of approaches, as I have implied. These included Galen's humoral and pneumatic materialism, explanations reflecting Aristotelian and neo-Platonic thought, mysticism, and hermeticism. These prescientific responses were driven by a range of motives or qualities, including a relentless fear of insanity, sympathy for the afflicted, and academic interest in trying to understand the origin and nature of madness. It was only with the advent of modern science that there arose an explicitly institutional response to the mad. Foucault's preoccupation was the identification of the social and institutional factors implicated in the rise of this institutional response, which was represented by a new breed of doctors called psychiatrists. The overarching factors he identified were the emergence of the nation-state; the extensive, potent effects of the scientific revolution; and the discoveries of physiology and neurology, which gradually replaced earlier fears, prejudices, and interests. This constellation of institutional authority and emerging academic knowledge proved to be unassailable in its categorizing power and was what made the discipline of psychiatry successful.

Foucault's analysis of institutional psychiatry focuses on *authority* in its visible and invisible forms, and what he calls the construction of the psychiatric subject—the mentally ill patient. Identifying strategies of power and forms of resistance to these strategies enabled Foucault to formulate a set of oppositional frames of reference such as sanity/insanity, men/women, parents/children, legal/illegal, and so on, which he used as vertices for analysis. These antinomies do not merely reflect different kinds of struggles with authority; they constitute, he argued, profound, perennial conflicts over definitions of identity and the status of difference and are endemic to the human condition. The "government of individualization," as Foucault described it, is a form of social organization that emerged in the post-Enlightenment era and employs knowledge, expertise, and language as its operational levers. The power relations that these levers control acquired the capacity to transform individuals into subjects, and their submission to subjectivity today constitutes the source of the principal Western social antagonisms. The articulation of power through the use of *consent* is central to the government of individualization and therefore to facilitating institutional methods of managing the mentally ill. Consent, not consensus, is the lubrication of authority, and it appears nowhere more so than in the authority used to define and control madness.

Foucault's is a grand schema delineating personal and institutional processes that lead to the sanctioning of individualizing and totalizing power, and through which dominant values become integrated into the subject and the social fabric, by consent. He went so far as to argue that the growth in pastoral and therapeutic forms of authority that use *interpretation* in the construction and management of personal identity reflect what he viewed as perennial underlying processes of domination, only now expressed through consensual agreement in a contemporary humanistic guise.

At this point Foucault unaccountably fails to include an important additional factor: the role of the unconscious in mental functioning and, by extension, in social relations. Psychoanalysis has a great deal to say about tacit yielding to consent, false consciousness, and the meaning of autonomy in mental life, which Foucault marginalizes in his account. Indeed we find no account of human motivation in Foucault. For Foucault there is no resolution to the problem of domination of one sort or another. Terms like *ideology* become redundant because domination and resistance *are* the human condition. This does not mean that Foucault constructs a naïve juxtaposition of oppressed and oppressor, or idealizes the subject. He acknowledges that subjects are endowed with capacities. Although they are subjects of power, their own power is nevertheless realized in and through a diversity of bodily capacities and forms of subjectivity that stem from a resistance to domination. Foucault's analysis is analogous to Kant's belief in the possibility of human progress through faith in the capacity to transcend the limits of human powers. Conflicts between systems of authority and forms of resistance are the stuff of life and development, and consume the modern human race. Psychoanalysis also deals with conflictual systems and, in particular, the autonomy of unconscious mental life. Psychoanalysts view the unconscious as a phylogenetic endowment that marks the site of division within our primate selves, and between ourselves. The unconscious offers a form of accommodation for the crises Foucault identifies in a personalized form, which is compatible with analysis of the social forms of dominance and resistance he identifies. The role and fate of the unconscious in mental functioning is pivotal in the generation and outcome of personal and social conflict. Ignorance of unconscious mental life produces the fuel that sustains the relations of domination and submission Foucault deplores. Knowledge of unconscious mental life provides a means of freeing ourselves from domination within and beyond ourselves.

Foucault's study of social formations marked out the figure of the modern individual or subject. This is something many people have examined and is central to an understanding of how psychiatry and psychology perceive madness today. We know that the way we define and understand the role of the individual human being has altered significantly over time. Prior to the Enlightenment when the Western economy was agrarian, an individual was identified by his allegiance to and participation in his group and by his relationship to his god or gods. Notions of autonomy, individual agency, or personal responsibility were far less evident in the innumerable, non-stratified contexts in which people lived out their lives. It was through the emergence of science and forms of productive activity other than agriculture that the capacities of the individual came to be identified and accentuated. At the same time, this process was accelerated by systematic attempts by scientists, philosophers, and theologians to define rationality and irrationality as distinctive features of human behavior. Descartes and Hegel were fundamental to this development, but perhaps the most vocal ally of the modern, rational individual was Nietzsche. He, along with Dilthey, Schopenhauer, Heidegger, and others, strove to establish a sense of meaning for the newly individualized subject, whom they viewed as the product of unprecedented social change and secularization. Nietzsche's nihilism and his seizure of the void left by changes in the world that heralded, for him, the death of God, led him to call for a new and more authentic moral existence through self-validation. This appeal found its psychological echo in Freud's audacious decision to become his own patient. Nietzsche, Freud, Baudelaire, and other architects of modernism knew that a sense of identity could now only be found within the constraints of a secularized, modernizing society: The alienation of labor, as Marx put it, in place of real work; the linear unfolding of a seemingly endless potential in the form of the golden promise of the industrial revolution; and the disintegration of established forms of self-representation were the characteristics of bourgeois philosophy these modern thinkers attempted to overcome.

THE UNCONSCIOUS

One difficulty that arose in this new age of rationality was that, with the advent of modern science, there was theoretically nothing that could not now be known. Everything "out there" was quantifiable and amenable to objectification through reason. What was not known, which of course remained a great deal, had to be located to a growing extent *within* the subject, including within the subject's unconscious mental life. The concept of the unconscious needed to be formulated, in part, in order to ward off the realization that there existed an unknown or unconscious *out there*, in the external world, which could no longer be grasped or understood, modern ways of thinking notwithstanding. The idea of the unknown was anathema to bourgeois reasoning and so a home for this disavowed, feared reality—which had always existed within and outside the individual—came to be located within the psyche of man. The contemporary psyche came to represent that which could not be rationally or visually connected to bourgeois society. The unconscious assumed the burden of a dynamic that was deemed absent elsewhere. This backdrop acted as midwife to the birth of psychoanalysis, and to the exploration and codification of the self and of memory that came to underpin modernist inquiry in all its forms through the work of Freud, Klimt, Joyce, Thomas Mann, Beckett, Proust, Picasso, and others.

Contemporary forms of psychology, as Richards has argued, appropriate the modern human subject in the name of science, and at the same time they respond to the demand of the individual for the provision of a place in our modern, rationalized world, despite the insuperable difficulties in achieving this (Richards, 1989). It is the strategic management of this dual identity that is implicitly asked of those who work in the mental health services. Richards' argument is that the ambivalent creation and maintenance of the modern European welfare state, exemplified in the United Kingdom, represents an effort to meliorate the destructive effects of contemporary industrial market relations. He suggests that the welfare state represents a countervailing action by the state designed to regulate the limits of destructiveness of modern life. The emergence of psychological practices is, historically, coincident with the emergence of welfare capital, and the psychological therapies represent above all the scenes of contradiction and attempted resolution evoked by the social and personal crises contingent upon modernization.

Psychiatry and psychology—from behaviorism to psychoanalysis—see psychological illness as a maladaptive response to the environment. Social settings are decentered from these perspectives of the problem. The uniqueness and unity of the individual are established at the psychobiological level, which is deemed to be the highest level of organization of the individual. Mentation is the subjective dimension of this organization in which bodily processes and affects are "integrated." Why is the burden today located, maintained, and treated within the individual, when we clearly live in a world of maddening contradictions and illusions? Is it that psychology has become the place or site where we try to work through our confrontation with modernity in order to theorize what it means to be an individual, as Richards (1989) argues? Psychology exists to develop solutions to the problems of being an individual in the modern world. It attempts to reconcile efficiency with individuality. In this way the practices of psychiatry, psychoanalysis, psychotherapy, and counseling are forced to pay attention to the contradictions created within society, yet from a necessarily incomplete perspective.

Modern life has become increasingly inhospitable to a belief in the autonomy of the individual. As the possibilities for authentic experiences and relationships have been gradually eroded, the theme of "subjectivity" has taken center stage and the psychological sciences have burgeoned. Richards quotes Marcuse, who suggested that "the cult of subjectivity is a direct response to its eclipse." As we are made less individual, so the study of individuality intensifies. One consequence of this attention to subjectivity is that much therapeutic practice has failed to maintain a critical stance in respect of the actual contradictions individuals suffer, and has tried to soften the face of psychology through allegiance to a belief in the essential harmony of things. Reconciliation, harmonization, and integration are the languages of welfare state psychological practices (Richards, 1988). These mainstream psychological activities are concerned with synthesizing science and the person with the aim of reconciling the irreconcilable; they attempt to resolve harmoniously tensions between incompatible forces and principles. This venture may rest upon grandiosity and manic denial. Harmonious relations between and within people are evidently unachievable within our present society and are inconceivable in any future similar society. The very premise is a victory for hope over realism.

What are therapists to do if they want to treat their patients authentically? How are they to deal with those who go mad in ways that are more therapeutic than palliative? We need to attend to the actual as well as the internal contradictions by which we and our patients live and through which we are defined, so that they are acknowledged and faced, with honest as opposed to illusory strategies of reconciliation pursued. Perhaps the unconscious offers a compelling, accessible vehicle for understanding the eclipse of the autonomy of the individual. The role of the unconscious as a barometer of the subject's state of freedom or subjugation in this endeavor is peerless. Psychoanalysis does not balk at contradictions that fracture and confuse. The decentered nature of its focus (on that which is absent) could be said to be an exercise in the containment and understanding of what constitutes conflict, contradiction, and paradox. Integration and reconciliation are important aims, but they arise only if unencumbered by false hopes, undemanding conclusions, and acceding to received opinion. Psychoanalytic therapy does not set out to "cure," in the biomedical sense. This is one reason why healers are prolific and effective psychotherapists are hard to find. Psychotherapists who know their work understand that integrative movement within the subject and between the analytic couple is possible only though immersion in, not control of, uncertainty, contradiction, and paradox. Attempting to make friends with unacceptable parts of ourselves is, as Joseph Sandler put it, the condition of psychic change. This type of change is not only personal; it affects all social interaction engaged in by the subject.

We face problems with who we are, not only because of the social conditions touched upon, but because of what we are. In addition to the oppressive and emancipatory qualities of the civilized world, each infant confronts an inheritance of powerful, contradictory capacities. Our instincts, strength, and intelligence exceed our capacity for judgment, which is why we require the most prolonged period of maturation of any primate. The acquisition of a psychic apparatus came about only recently in the evolutionary scheme of things, in order to accommodate the social evolution of the higher primates—the chimpanzees and humans. Emotion is our most basic sensory response to one another, and the development of emotional and social intelligence reflected our need to infer intentionality and to envisage responses. This was the first theory of mind. Our brain evolved in parts, and only became more of a "whole" in anatomically modern humans, that is, a few minutes ago on the evolutionary time clock. Some psychoanalysts like Henri Rey (1994) argue that this has a bearing on our capacity to move from part to whole object representations and back again. Our higher psychic functions are vulnerable to reversal or dissolution, an idea that goes back from Freud to John Hughlings-Jackson. Vulnerability to regression and the risk of dissolution is the price we pay for having evolved so successfully so rapidly. Being alive makes for complex sets of demands. In addition to the impact of the modernization of society and its insatiable need to control every aspect of individuals' lives, the personal endowment of sexuality is, as Christopher Bollas points out, traumatic for each child and hence for each adult. We struggle with the psychic consequences of aggression, and the vicissitudes of narcissism underscore the obstacle-strewn path of contemporary individuation. It is striking how humans have managed to sustain themselves for so long under such circumstances and begs the question of how long the species can continue to flourish under the weight of the fractures of postindustrial life and the intended and unintended consequences it yields.

In contemporary psychoanalysis, definitions of mental health focus on relationships with objects (the unhappy psychoanalytic term for people), by which is meant internal and external relationships to significant others. Object-relating structures are the principal dynamic agents of psychological change. They are also organizers of interpersonal behavior. Psychic change is the function of a shift of emphasis between different mental models of object relationships. This can take place because object-relating structures are not static; they are dynamic and evolve or devolve. Work at the psychic structural level, with the unconscious, is the vehicle for ameliorating relations of oppression, domination, subjugation, resistance, and inequality. Perhaps this area of potential in modern human subjects constitutes a lifeline in the face of the eclipses of individual and social freedom carefully enumerated by Foucault. The amount of work that is required in psychoanalysis to help the individual change habits of a lifetime is considerable. A relationship in the unconsciously determined transference reshapes the neurotic patient's object-relating structures to provide a different view of how life and relationships might be lived. The individual with psychosis suffers both fracture and dissolution of higher psychic functions resulting in primitive ways of thinking in which dependence on human relations is abolished in favor of relationships with pathological object-relating structures and fantasy objects and systems that keep the patient preoccupied, isolated, and ill. Treatment of psychosis or madness is difficult when the patient's allegiance to human dependence has been forfeited. Only under specific conditions can the therapeutic task be implemented. Is it any wonder that our caring agencies behave defensively when faced with this enormous crisis that replicates the effacement of the subject in the modern world? The unacknowledged reality is that patients with psychosis are admitted to hospitals as part of a collusion between the family and doctors that conceals the fact that the behavior of the patient cannot be tolerated any longer by the family. Hospitals and mental health staff implicitly take responsibility for a psychiatric, familial, social, and political problem that is beyond their capacity to resolve. Why is this situation allowed to persist as though normal and reasonable? Elliott Jacques was one of the first to note that social phenomena show a striking correspondence with psychotic processes in individuals; that institutions are used by their individual members to reinforce individual mechanisms of defense against anxiety; and that the mechanisms of projective and introjective identification operate in linking individual and social behavior (Jacques, 1995a, b). He argued that the primary cohesive elements binding individuals into institutionalized human association is that of defense against psychotic anxiety. Projective and introjective processes are basic to even the most complex social processes and they are at the bottom of our dealings with one another. We have the potential to suffer the anxieties psychotic patients suffer, and anything that arouses these anxieties in us we will do almost anything to stop. People who work with psychosis feel at times that they are being driven mad, because projections of psychotic states activate their potential for psychotic thinking. Similarly, it is not difficult to identify psychotic mechanisms at work in any large group or institution as a consequence of the intersubjective stimulation of psychotic anxiety that arises whenever groups of human beings gather together.

Perhaps it is clearer why social change seems so difficult to achieve, and why many social problems are considered intractable. Change in social relationships and cultural practices call for a restructuring of relationships at the fantasy level—at the unconscious, object relations level—and this places a demand on individuals and groups to face up to their defenses against psychotic anxiety. This is a considerable demand to place upon every institution. The psychiatric setting arouses the very psychotic anxieties we repudiate, and in well-run settings these are specifically addressed. As Isobel Menzies Lyth (1988) argues, the situation confronting the psychiatric nurse resembles fantasy situations that exist in every individual in the deepest and most primitive levels of the mind. The intensity and complexity of the nurse's anxieties are to be attributed to the peculiar capacity of her work to stimulate afresh those early situations and accompanying emotions. In most hospitals there have evolved socially structured defense mechanisms that employ routines and division of tasks that preclude the nurse relating as a whole person to the patient as a whole person. The aim of these devices is the depersonalization or elimination of individual distinctiveness in both nurse and patient. Unfortunately these defenses can turn the caring, therapeutic principle of nursing on its head, by objectifying the patient who is redefined as a problem, even an enemy, to be resisted. If an institution defensively resists paying attention to its vulnerability to the anxieties generated by its patients and/or its staff, a destructive cycle of denial and increasing persecution is bound to follow.

The madness that exists in society is externally and internally generated. We live in a complex, confusing, contradictory, and frequently destabilizing world. From a psychoanalytic standpoint, madness can be generated and exacerbated by our disavowed responses to madness evoked and projected into us and others, and by our own responses to the exigencies of being alive. Repudiation and disavowal by returning these projections, usually with interest, creates mistrust and leads to the persecuted and suspicious atmospheres so often found in social and institutional settings. The problems of mental health services in the West are not only brought about by patients and their impact on staff. The demands placed on mental health workers are often quite unrealistic and this is another external fact that is denied. The outcome can be a culture of illusory goals and aims that can appear to be delusional, as is the case with the workload of much of current Western psychiatry. Paying attention to areas of inherent personal and social contradiction is difficult, confusing, and painful, but is the basis of reality testing and of truly authentic therapeutic relationships. Without attention to these fractures and the capacities of individuals and groups to work with them, little serious improvement in our understanding and treatment of madness at the social or personal levels can take place.

REFERENCES

Deleuze, G., & Guattari, F. (1977). Anti Oedipus: From psychoanalysis to schizopolitics. *Semiotexte, 2*(3).
Foucault, M. (1965). *Madness and civilization: A history of insanity in the age of reason* (R. Howard, Trans.). New York: Pantheon.
Jacques, E. (1953). On the dynamics of social structure: A contribution to the psychoanalytical study of social phenomena. *Human Relations, 6*, 3–2.
Jacques, E. (1995a). Why psychoanalytical knowledge helps us to understand organizations: A discussion with Elliott Jaques. *Human Relations, 48*(4), 359–365.
Jacques, E. (1995b). Why the psychoanalytical approach to understanding organizations is dysfunctional. *Human Relations, 48*(4), 343–349.
Kovel, J. (1988). *The radical spirit: Essays on psychoanalysis and society.* Free Association Books: London.
Kupers, T. (1981). *Public therapy: The practice of psychotherapy in the public mental health clinic.* New York: Free Press.
Kupers, T. (1988). *Ending therapy: The meaning of termination.* New York: New York University Press.
Laing, R., & Cooper, D. (1964). *Reason and violence: A decade of Sartre's philosophy.* London: Tavistock.
Menzies Lyth, I. (1988). *Containing anxiety in institutions: Selected essays.* London: Free Association Books.
Porter, R. (1987). *A social history of madness: Stories of the insane.* London: Weidenfeld & Nicolson.
Porter, R., Bynum, W., & Shepherd, M. (2003). *Essays in the history of psychology.* London: Routledge.
Rey, H. (1994). *Universals of Psychoanalysis,* London: Free Association Books.
Richards, B. (1989). *Crises of the self: Further essays on psychoanalysis and politics.* London: Free Association Books.
Richards, B., & Figlio, K. (2001). Psychoanalysis and the public sphere: Some recent British developments. In R. Hinshelwood & M. Chiesa (Eds.), *Organizations, anxiety and defense: Towards a psychoanalytic social psychology* (pp. 183–203). London: Whurr.
Szasz, T. (1991). *Ideology and insanity: Essays on the psychiatric dehumanization of man.* Garden City, NY: Doubleday Anchor.
Szasz, T. (1997). *Insanity: The idea and its consequences.* New York: John Wiley.

Chapter 8

The worm that flies
in the night*

In addition to psychoanalysis, I shall refer in this chapter to anthropology, poetry, and art to give indications of how creative thought might emerge, and how it can be destroyed, not least by psychosis.† As psychosis is inherent in all of us, in the sense that we all experience anxieties of a psychotic nature (Jackson & Williams, 1994; Williams, 1998), I shall not confine myself to a psychiatric diagnosis of psychosis. The aim of this article is to stimulate thinking rather than seek out answers. The reader is implicated in this paper more than usual: As you follow the words and images on these pages, it is hoped that something of the *experience* of how creative thought arises may become apparent.

* This chapter, originally given as a spoken presentation with slides, was delivered as the 2006 Lionel Monteith Memorial Lecture at St Thomas' Hospital, London, and as part of a day seminar on severe disturbance at the Psychoanalytic Center of California, Los Angeles. It was subsequently published in the *British Journal of Psychotherapy*, 23(3), 2007, 343–364. Reprinted with permission.
† This paper presents a number of difficulties for the reader. It was originally written not for publication, but as a talk to psychoanalysts, and a particular kind of talk. The aim was to share with those people present examples and experiences of ways in which creative thought is generated using examples from psychoanalysis, anthropology, poetry, art, and ordinary life. These included some moving images of film *in utero* of a 12-week-old fetus stepping and leaping rhythmically, something that is impossible to convey in print. The fact that this talk now exists on the printed page deprives the reader of much of the felt experience of the images and poetry discussed. However, the paper is included here in the hope that at least something of the beauty of these images, and the profound effort required to generate them, will interest the reader.

The capacity to remain open to the influence of the unconscious and preconscious, and to be able to mentally represent these areas of mental life, is a prerequisite for the generation of creative thought, which is contrasted in this paper with reflexive thinking and mimesis. The conditions for generative, dialectical mental activity are discussed. Through a clinical example of a psychoanalytic treatment of a disturbed young man, processes of destruction of generative thought by psychosis are also discussed, as well as the conditions required for this destructive activity to diminish and even be reversed. Paramount among the analyst's forms of engagement with patients is the employment of intuition as a means of identifying unconscious reality within the patient and the analyst, and of creating a basis for a "third" analytic experience, without which the growth of mind is not possible.

IN SEARCH OF SYMBOLS: A CLINICAL VIGNETTE

What follows is an extract from a session with an intelligent 32-year-old man, whom I shall call James, whose analysis is in its 10th year.* When James first came to see me he was in a psychotic state, close to collapse. He is the second child of highly disturbed parents, whose first son died at the age of 5 months in doubtful circumstances, probably of neglect. James was born 10 months later—a replacement child, he told me—but over time I came to doubt this idea. He revealed, in his analysis, a sense of never having had another person, or a self, he could rely on. He did not recognize a sense of self that was his own, or any meaningful sense of agency. This was, he said, something that went back as far as he could recall and stemmed from a belief that everything he did as a child was wrong:

P: Nothing I did was right. It wasn't about making mistakes or getting things wrong. It was like I got everything wrong—as a matter of principle ... when I was small I thought I could please her. I tried but by the time I went to school I felt hopeless. Nothing worked ... she couldn't bear to look at me ... not disapproval, although there was a lot of that ... more that I was some burden she'd had forced on her. It was very difficult ... there were moments when she would seem OK but then fly into a rage. I knew it would happen but never when; I would forget and suddenly get screamed at. It took years to realize that the whole thing was impossible. By the time I was 7 or 8 I thought I'd be better off dead. I would feel relieved when I went to bed that I'd got through another day and pray I wouldn't wake up. For years I went to bed to blot everything out.

A: You feel that you died as a child.

P: I do [cries] ... everything went wrong ... I have been stuck with it all my life. I think my childhood was ruined ... it wasn't a childhood ... now I feel like her and I ruin it myself. My life isn't my life. I exist because of what I am for others.

Uncontained, projected into, and deprived of potential space, James lived a sham life of servitude—his words. Despite intelligence and a warm personality, his capacity for symbolization had been crippled for 3 decades. A core belief of his in analysis was, "There is nothing to say." By this I came to realize that he meant that his words, his thoughts, and even his existence were of no significance to me, or anyone. He felt himself to be a "non-person" or else a fabrication. James told me that he felt close to no one in his life, except his dead brother. Over time I came to appreciate that James

---

* For a discussion of this case and its implications for an analytic understanding of violent projections into the infant, see Williams (2004).

had, early in life, been required to dispose of any signs of a developing personality. Behind a seamless second skin that afforded him a spurious sense of integration laid a void, the consequence of never having been adequately contained in his feelings, nor recognized for himself. Here is a statement made at a time when he experienced me as an invasive, psychotic person bent on preventing him from thinking his own thoughts: "Something in me wants to smash and smash you and shut you up so I don't have to listen to you anymore." James wailed as he shouted. After some time he settled and said, "As I'm saying this it reminds me of my mother and how I couldn't stand the shouting … I couldn't do anything about it."

To surrender to intimacy was, for James, to submit to deadly assault. He equated love with being narcissistically savaged. When James's true, alive self did stir, he could experience a sense of alarm that he was betraying his reality, and this led to confusion and suicidal thoughts. For James, mourning had been unattainable. Thanatos, in the form of a cruel, moralizing God, had taken pitiless hold of his life. After some years of analytic work, James said to me: "I feel I have to pay attention every day to that child I was. It's like visiting someone in hospital or a grave. If I don't think of him or hold his hand, I feel lost. I will never let him go again."

I shall return to James in a moment, but first consider the masks in Figures 8.1 to 8.5.* These are not war masks: They are not meant to terrify. Pay particular attention to your immediate response to them. Are you shocked? Surprised? Amused, maybe? Perhaps you are moved by their solemn playfulness. Mask-wearing like this serves many functions, but one of them is to shake us up. They betoken an otherness in each of us. Masks occupy a liminal domain of experience. Liminal space, an anthropological term for in-between states, denotes thresholds or spaces that allow for differentiating experiences or which permit passage from one context or level to another (Turner, 1969). Masks also invite us to go behind them— perhaps to take a step closer to reality. They could be said to prefigure symbolization; in other words, they startle or otherwise stimulate a particular symbolizing activity from the tumult within us. At the same time, they do not set out to symbolize reality or eternity. Icons typically represent reality, whereas idols substitute for it; masks sit uneasily somewhere between the two, somewhere between sensation and meaning. Analogously, Winnicott regarded interpretation as most effective when the patient is on the verge of grasping unconsciously what is happening—"half way between gesture and thought" (Winnicott, 1971). Masks, viewed from a psychoanalytic perspective, inaugurate a space for a similar psychic transition from action

---

* The low hut in Figure 8.1 is, in some cultures, referred to as the "House of Words." It is used to bring warring factions into dialogue. As you can see, no one would be able to stand upright once inside. All mask images appear with the kind permission of Professor Gerhard Kubik.

Figure 8.1 Tribal masks. With kind permission of Prof. Gerhard Kubik.

to symbolization. The common link here is the establishment of *space*, a core activity of psychoanalytic work. Masks create mental and imaginative space and they also help us to think about what it means to be authentic. For example, some masks may be used to pay homage to a dead twin or to a sacred, sacrificed placenta that gave life to the newborn child. Others may denote ancestors who are the revered, true owners of the land, or permit the worship of spirits, and so on. Like a compass, masks create a bearing (a psychic trajectory) for a course towards the internal world. In order to grasp the impact of masks it is necessary to identify the principal characteristic of primitive mental life. By "primitive mental life" I refer to basic mental processes in all people. I believe that the main characteristic is improvisation—a continuous, do-it-yourself grappling with unconscious ideas and bodily-generated emotions, the affective derivatives of which we fear ultimately have the capacity to overwhelm us. In healthy children this is done in connection and identification with the mind of another, and the developing capacity for improvisation is the embarkation point for the acquisition of a capacity to play. In psychosis, improvisation does not presage play—it is employed in a quite different manner as a deterrent against the threat of psychic collapse.

Figure 8.2 Tribal mask. With kind permission of Prof. Gerhard Kubik.

Masks artfully stimulate improvisation towards forms of symbolization. We commonly associate this kind of symbolizing activity as one that occurs within the individual, which it does. However, in many non-Western societies, a sense of collective solidarity through ritual or other cultural activity may stand as the expressive form of symbolizing activity for both the group and the individual. In these social formations, an experience of personal coherence is reproduced through the symbolic partitioning and sharing of communal identity. We might extrapolate a particular common link between these collective symbolic forms and that which occurs within the individual, namely, that there is the creation of a space for a third position that permits the individual and the group to better share a capacity to withstand the unknown, the dread of the past, and death. It is no secret, of course, that psychoanalysis addresses primitive mental life in a ritualized, prescribed setting. We, too, aim to open up a third psychological position to safely ignite

Figure 8.3 Tribal mask. With kind permission of Prof. Gerhard Kubik.

and sustain the subject's capacity for symbolization and play. Improvisation, space, and the emergence of a third position are characteristics, it seems to me, of both collective and the individual symbolizing processes.

Improvisation in primitive mental life cannot properly be discussed without reference to Lévi-Strauss's (1966) famous spiritual tinker, the *bricoleur*, or shaman, seen in Figure 8.6 marking out, in a trance or waking dream, a space within which everyday bric-a-brac is employed to reorder perceptions of *rites-de-passage*, illness, loss, and death. The *bricoleur* is a practitioner who acts as mediator in the symbolizing process (Lévi-Strauss, 1966, 1982). Integration that yields depressive position thinking of the psychoanalytic kind is neither sought nor attained. The *bricoleur* is a hybrid who identifies unconscious themes in liminal space and who uses a mythical narrative to invoke an alternative psychological perspective. Like the jungle that weaves

Figure 8.4 Tribal mask. With kind permission of Prof. Gerhard Kubik.

patterns around an abandoned, ruined temple, he proceeds seemingly haphazardly but, on closer examination, employs improvisation to generate a space within which it becomes possible to think differently about calamity, dread, and the threat of change. His work should not be thought of as inferior to Western psychiatry or religion, as its context is quite different, as are its criteria for efficacy. If proof were needed, indigenous treatments of psychosis have been undertaken outside institutions by *bricoleurs*, sometimes without recidivism, demonstrating the power of social representational forms to contain and reorder states of mind. A question arises, one that is beyond the scope of this present chapter to pursue, concerning differences between cultures where liminality or transitionality is evident—that is, cultures that foster the use of potential and transitional space in contrast to cultures that are based on identification and identity. The former, it seems

Figure 8.5 Tribal mask. With kind permission of Prof. Gerhard Kubik.

to me, tend to be characterized by alive objects, whereas the latter tend to be characterized by dead objects.

In light of the above comments on mental space, I would like to return to James. He had fared no better than many African or other Third World children, and probably worse. Unlike African children who live in symbolizing cultures, James was betrayed by a family that was such in name only, by a harshly individualizing and impoverishing working-class consumer culture, and by himself. He slipped through almost every safety net in childhood and almost killed himself in serious road accidents as a teenager. For a time in adulthood he came close to drug addiction and alcoholism. A yearning for something better for himself (what occurred in infancy to facilitate this hope is a crucial, unanswered question) turned him into a successful entrepreneur who, with newfound security, became depressed and suicidal. He coped with severe depressive episodes by spending long periods lying on a hardwood floor in order to "avoid falling further." James

Figure 8.6 Shaman. With kind permission of Mary Lou Walbergh.

told me how, from as early as he could remember, his parents brawled. The fights seemed to take a repetitive, ritualized form involving an exchange of insults that escalated into climactic screaming, followed by withdrawal and mutual detestation until the next encounter. James came to understand these battles as a brutal method his parents employed to deal not only with their hatred of each other but also to manage their fears of intimacy. For years, James lived in fear that his parents might kill each other and spent countless hours thinking of ways to stop them. His accounts of these scenes contained little suggestion of excitement or curiosity, but rather fear that accumulated to become a terror with which he lived throughout childhood. James's father, an addict, relied increasingly on drugs during James's childhood, eventually dying in his 40s after virtually no contact with his son. After leaving home at age 16, James saw his mother again only once, many years later, dying in a hospital. He did not feel malice toward her but was relieved when she died and mourned only what might have been.

James's late brother had died before James's birth; the death was never discussed with James. It appears that neither parent mourned the death. James's view was that both his parents were psychotic and had conformed to a superficial, stereotypical fantasy of marriage without thought to its implications, demands, or responsibilities. The reality of living together was unmanageable. While James's father's dependence on drugs deepened along with his neglect of his family, his mother, who seems to have led a bizarre life characterized by hypomanic moods and erratic behavior, embarked on trips away from home that made her more and more independent of her husband and children, finding poorly paid employment in different places and staying away from the family home for very long periods. It became clearer, as the analysis proceeded, that James's mother, who craved freedom, had projected into James a hatred of her own and his dependency needs, against which she defended using manic activity. In addition, there appears to have been a projection into James of a primitive, residual hope, perhaps for herself, which she could not sustain in her own mind. It is possible that the mysterious source of James's hope for himself may have lain in his mother's unconscious projections that could not be used by her due to an inability to mourn her many losses. This hope may have been transmitted to James in a way unconsciously designed to keep a last vestige of hope safe so that mourning that had been unattainable might one day become possible in another generation. This, of course, is speculation. For the main part James, unable to experience a third mental position let alone mourn, functioned by identification and a compulsive rescuing of people, a skill he later found useful in business. Notwithstanding his external successes in adulthood, the diffuse hope that helped him to survive was eventually overwhelmed by hopelessness and a profound wish to be dead, which led him to seek analysis.

GENERATIVE THOUGHT

Improvisation, whether of James's traumatized variety or of the African liminal type, cannot be said to be synonymous with creative activity. For something original and authentic to arise, not only is space required but also the functioning of another mind with which generative dialogue, external and internal, can take place. The principles underlying the conditions for generative thought include, importantly, the deployment of intuition. Intuition is related to projective identification, as both involve a yielding up of oneself to the other through which subjectivity is reformed. Intuition permits contact with unconscious emotion, the most elemental form of human communication. As analysts we intuit, initially through faith, at a sensory level, in abstinence—without memory or desire, presupposition, or other curiosity-ridden form of security. We tolerate frustration, eschew closure, and try to remain open to coincidences. Unconscious emotions in the analytic relationship regularly coincide and occasionally, within the matrices of meanings these potentially hold, a widened sense of truth may emerge, albeit fleetingly. This form of communication is akin to revelation and the experience of mystical thought. Whether we like it or not, psychoanalysis has certain epistemological affinities with the practice of mystics regarding the apprehension of metaphysical phenomena. Genuine analytic work heals, I suggest, in proportion to the depth of truthful communication. We need to create a new object—not a different object, but a new object—and in so doing we seek out space (potential space) as the condition for establishing a third position using the mind of another, and hence truthful, imaginative experience toward the object. If access to potential space is precluded, including because the object's mind cannot engage, the ensuing absence may herald the attendance of creativity's inconsolable dead twin, mimesis—imitation. This is notably apparent in false-self or "as-if" personalities. When transitional experience founders, a mimetic life may be adopted. Mimesis, a dead twin within, and Thanatos then come together in commemoration of this developmental catastrophe.

I would like to make it clear that I am not at ease with the terms "creative" or "creativity." I face a void when trying to think about them. The *ex nihilo* inference of "creativity"—the idea of creation of something out of nothing—seems, to me, to imply godlike powers associated with, among other things, individuals suffering psychosis. As far as I can grasp, creativity is a modest undertaking, unlike the work of gods. Our capacity to create enables us to escape our fate by reshaping what exists in ways that are unpredictable and which increase the number of islands in the visible ocean of the unknown. These islands go on to form archipelagos that eventually constitute our various cultures (Arieti, 1976). The impulse toward creative thought begins with infant and mother who intuitively find each other's gaze, evoking an archetypal representation of holding, potential space, and generative thought which has great impact, including on anyone who is a witness (see Figure 8.7).

Might this process begin earlier? How does the fetus accommodate to the mother's internal organs and somatic rhythms, and vice versa? The ultrasound image in Figure 8.8 seems to denote a mutual, primary accommodation of this kind, with its conflicts, struggles, and adjustments. Does this activity embody a future potential for relatedness, possibly even for adoration?

For those interested in advances in uterine research, the remarkable ultrasound images in Figures 8.9 and 8.10* are stills taken from a video recording produced by Professor Stuart Campbell of Kings College London, and they show in unprecedented live action detail and real time the remarkable agility and range of strenuous movements of a 12-week-old fetus.

---

* These images appear with permission of Professor Stuart Campbell, Create Health Clinic, London.

Figure 8.7 Mother and child.

It is, of course, important not to invent psychological states to accompany such early developmental activity. But what we can say with a certain amount of confidence is that here is a space containing a fetus, within which an array of activities linked to the necessity of mutual accommodation is being undertaken. Finally, what do we make of the patient who risks embarking upon an analysis and breaking down, notwithstanding the horrors of a psychotic regression, in a last-ditch belief that finding an authentic self might still be possible? The courage and dignity involved may, to us, be unsurpassed. My question is: What makes such a painful undertaking thinkable? What makes such faith possible?

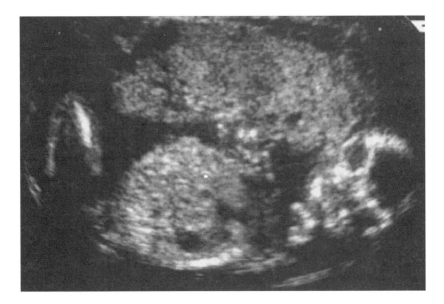

Figure 8.8 Ultrasound, 16 weeks.

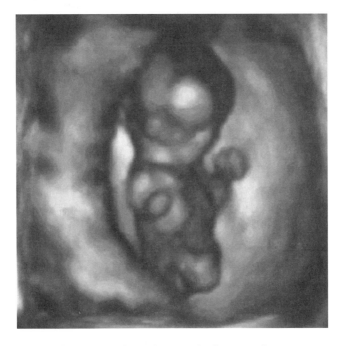

Figure 8.9 "Stepping." Still image from ultrasound video recording.

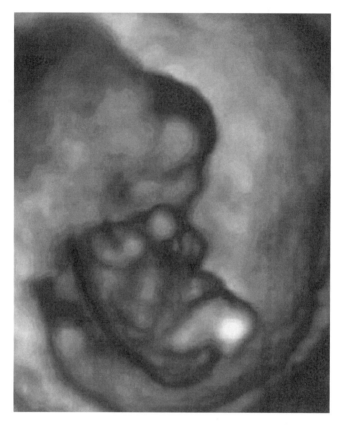

Figure 8.10 "Leaping." Still image from ultrasound video recording.

GENERATIVE THOUGHT IN CULTURE

> Oh Rose, thou art sick!
> The invisible worm
> That flies in the night,
> In the howling storm,
> Has found out thy bed
> Of crimson joy,
> And his dark secret love
> Does thy life destroy.

> —Blake, "The Sick Rose"

In Blake's famous poem "The Sick Rose," we see metaphor, displacement, recognition of similarity in the dissimilar, and allusions to sexuality, beauty, destructiveness, and illness. But what precisely makes this poem so powerful? Arieti (1976) suggests that we recognize the woman *in* the rose, her beautiful life destroyed by illness, and we sense the connection between illness, destructive sexuality, and looming death. My associations, on reading this poem, went to James and his mother who got pregnant not once but twice. Why did she do so? Did James become the worm that flew in the night, and thus became a dangerous attractor for Thanatos? The power of Blake's poem derives, I suggest, from a particular process of symbolic construction at work. Primary and secondary processes oscillate, *but neither is allowed to prevail.* Both processes are held in tension—in a space, if you like—to produce a *tertiary* level of experience, a third quality that embodies both but is more (cf. Arieti, 1976). We experience a confluence of conscious and unconscious emotions, intuitive and rational thoughts, all at the same time. We are aware of individuality and particularity and yet feel the need to synthesize and generalize, as with much poetry. The outcome is an expansive, third level of experience. I believe that the aesthetic prescience and the sublimeness of poetry derive from metaphors selected for their capacity to concatenate at this tertiary level. Perhaps this type of process takes place in a lower register in all generative thought, no matter how ordinary. In great poetry, however, it is as though the underlying dynamic is thrown into astounding relief. The schizophrenic patient who recognizes only the manifest content of the poem would equate the rose *with* the woman, and in so doing divest the poem of meaning. For Blake, recognition and a heightening of similarities in the dissimilar (conscious and unconscious) become the basis for generation of new tertiary categories of meaning (unlike in *identity* where meaning is stillborn). Poetry may at times employ concrete imagery that might in other contexts emerge in psychosis, but the use to which it is put is quite different as in, for example, verses like these:

> Carrying home
> her baby sister—
> a sermon walking.

> —Mike Garofalo, "Above the Fog"

> When you hear your inner voice,
> forget it.

> —Hyoen Sahn

Here, primary process collides with secondary process producing a saturation that, disturbingly, overloads cognition. We are forced back onto prior sensations in order to try to grasp the meaning of the condensed imagery. An interesting psychoanalytic question arises from the generation of a third position and a new object in poetry and other forms of art: Does this tertiary level of experience signify a new internal object? If so, what kind of object? A woman? A baby?

WORKS OF ART

No matter how enigmatic, works of art must not diverge too far from ordinary thinking. Originality, though crucial, is not enough, which is why dreams are not in and of themselves creative, although they are always original. Imagination is impaired if overexposed to the unrealities of the unconscious or to the rigidifying tendencies of consciousness (Arieti, 1976). Generative thought germinates in primary process and establishes a relationship with cognition via the preconscious. Artists must tolerate perturbations across these levels of mental functioning, and this severely taxes the ego. A mentally ill person might succumb to such pressure, confounding primary process thinking *with* reality under the sway of the pleasure principle. The artist, by contrast, exploits the space between primary and secondary processes, and internal and external reality, through a commitment to psychic truth—the opposite of omnipotent wish fulfillment. The image, visual or auditory, is so important in generative thought because it not only represents what is real, but it also sanctions the construction of the unreal. The image is an innovation, a state of becoming that does not and must not faithfully reproduce reality. Its purpose is to absolve us of our passivity by shaping an alternative reality—that of the absent object; absent as in no longer there, or absent as in never having existed (Arieti, 1976). Whereas secondary process thinking is predicated upon Aristotelian concepts of logic, primary process imagery is interchangeable: the handbag as vagina or precious image of selfhood, the house as maternal body, and so on. Art originates in this *pars pro toto* area and in so doing reveals its kinship with insanity. Artists, in the incubation phase of their work, scrutinize and mine for coincidences and combinations, with only the most compelling metaphors surviving. The predatory, oral-sadistic dimension involved in this aspect of the production of art cannot be overestimated. A finished work of art may combine indistinct themes that converge in a distinct structure like a poem or a play, triggering explosions of the senses. Or, in contrast, reality-based, more concrete phenomena can dissolve into something more elemental, as in painting or musical composition. In music, there can be no content without form; manifest and latent content, form, and meaning are merged. It was Paul Klee who made the observation that best addresses the problem of human creativity, whether for artists or for anyone else. He wrote in 1908: "How shall I most freely cast a bridge between inside and outside?" (Brody, 2001). Freud's response to this problem was to draw a sharp distinction between fixation on infantile fantasies versus mature adjustment to the demands of reality. Acceptance of this disjunction became a goal of psychoanalytic therapy. Freud's is a stoically dour view of life that does not satisfactorily recognize that the interchange between inner and outer—subject and object—is a core propensity and vital human need. In 1988, Winnicott wrote:

> Between the mother who is physically holding the baby and the baby, there is a layer that we have to acknowledge which is an aspect of herself and at the same time an aspect of the baby. It is mad to hold this view, and yet the view must be maintained. (p. 167)

Winnicott identified, in the infant's hallucinatory wish fulfillments and use of transitional objects, the momentous significance of a space that is employed for symbolization of the object. This space allows for the *use* of an object and symbolizes the union of two now separate beings at the point in time and space of their separateness (see Deri, 1984). For Winnicott, the location of joy and love of reality lies in the gap between objects and mental states—an intermediate area in which fantasy and reality nourish each other precisely because they are not separate. This is the basis for libidinal investment in a sense of inside versus outside, first articulated through the skin boundary and the emotions. Communication across boundaries in mental space comes to be experienced as desirable, and symbolization is instituted through illusion and normal hallucination, initially of the breast. Here lies the generative experience of the symbolic "third" (Ogden, 1999). It follows that objects exist neither in the external world nor in wishful hallucinations, but paradoxically in both. Attempts to "solve" this paradox serve only to split the subject's self. Paradoxes like this cannot be solved, only resolved. James, my patient, embodied such a paradox long before he became able to symbolize it. For example, he was compelled to fire me as his analyst—as an unconscionably bad object—regularly, month after month, on one occasion to the point of psychotic enactment, while hauling himself punctually to each session to try to find out if he existed or not and, if so, in what form.

The kind of generative communication I have referred to between inner and outer, subject and object, dream and reality, can only emerge out of the provision of a potential space, the use of the object, and through this, the self-sculpting of personality (cf. Winnicott). No original state, ideal congruity, homology, or *a priori* certainty between subject and object exists to be found. We bring a demand for relatedness born of our need to represent—to recreate—what already exists. Similarly, we might say that transitional space does not lie between internal or dream reality and the external world; it is interwoven *with* external reality and dreams. It is typically reflected, for example, in the shoals of psychic life that swim beneath analytic dialogue in every session.

A Cartesian division between inside and outside can only be adapted to, never created, as James demonstrated. The infant deprived of transitional experience dies emotionally or, more accurately, is consigned to a state of limbo and a life of imposture as the only available means of commemorating a dead twin. Imitation or mimicry, a normal introjective activity prior to identification, can develop excessively and, instead of acting as a precursor to normal introjection as is the case in a good-enough childhood, installs itself instead as a substitute for introjection. Imitation—mimesis—may then be utilized to avoid all subsequent identificatory conflicts, crippling the child's personality through dissimulation rather than relation. Such patients do not know who they are and do not know they do not know.

The transitional field, by contrast, is sustained by spontaneity. It does not reject received wisdom but is predicated upon intuition and imagination. The emancipatory factor in psychoanalysis, in my view, lies in the emergence of the analytic third object, the origins of which, I have argued, lie in the use of intuition. What is the difference between intuitive experience and hallucination? "Intuitions without concepts are blind, and concepts without intuitions are empty" was Bion's response (Stitzman, 2004). This view suggests that in abandoning memory and desire—I would argue our own personality—intuition duly transformed approximates to wisdom more than it does to thought. The emergence of the analytic third reflects this. The convergence that unifies analysand and analyst, while at the same time retaining their difference, gives rise to a new creation that could not have emerged otherwise. We create this third object in order to be given back to ourselves by the other. The act of having oneself given back is not a returning of oneself to an original state, but a creation of oneself as a transformed subject always for the first time. We need this to escape from the solipsism and peripatetic nature of our internal object world. Projective identification could be seen as a variation of the analytic third from which reappropriation of the transformed subjectivity of the interdependent, separate participants takes place. Something larger and more generative arises which, when subsequently worked through in order to weave secondary with primary process, emancipates each party and enriches subjectivity. I shall give an example of this in relation to James shortly. What emotion accompanies and authorizes intuition? I suggest it is passion. Passion has been defined by Bion (1963) as "an emotion experienced with intensity and warmth without any suggestion of violence." It is not dependent upon the senses. For senses to be active only one mind is necessary. Passion is evidence that two minds are linked. Passion makes us known to each other directly and disturbingly, signifying our deepest needs and innermost vulnerabilities.

All these elements—emotion, faith, passion, intuition, and reverie—may come together through the dreamwork of a session to create an intuitive interpretation. When such an event occurs it encompasses subject, object, and their transitional union, and is identifiable by a *psychoanalytic aesthetic* similar, I believe, to the tertiary experience in poetry, art, and music. The impact of this psychoanalytic aesthetic—an expansion of our apprehension of reality—is humbling in its co-created origins. Overuse by the analyst of any component of inquiry, such as curiosity or cognition, can undermine the waking dreaming needed for its birth. The conditions for this generative phenomenon to occur require a space to yield ourselves to an object, internal and external, so as to permit the emergence of a hitherto unknown third experience. In art this is expressed as the outward recreation of the object based on an internal dialogue with it—an extraordinary feat for one person to achieve (in this sense it may seem unusual to think of Freud's self-analysis as a work of art, but similarities to the production of great art are apparent). In psychoanalysis we co-create the analytic third from which analyst and analysand emerge, re-found, as a new subject/object—not a different object but a renewed, richer object.

A GENERATIVE DREAM

James had a dream, one of a number, that seemed to reflect an internalization of a capacity to enter potential space and engage in transitional thought. The dream was, I believe, a co-creation of an analytic third object, as opposed to a bizarre object. He was walking at twilight down a leafy street, similar to where he attends his sessions, his mind ticking over in thought, when an iridescent green, chameleon-like iguana with a small shark's or dogfish's body slid alongside him. James was enchanted but unnerved. The iguana seemed friendly, had lost its way, and was beseeching James for help, but could not speak. Spontaneously it threw itself into James's arms, biting his wrist lightly, and as it did so James saw its smooth, white underside. He associated to the underside of an airliner taking off in sunlight. The iguana had the eyes of an owl and the face of a very young boy. James felt tender feelings towards this strange creature. This dream emerged in part out of work on James's incomprehension that he could occupy a place in my heart, as opposed to my mind. He held a conviction that my interest in him could only be clinical or professional. My attempts—to him often pointless—to analyze his fight to improvise a life, along with his experience of my acceptance of his shame and his love and hate of me, had over time communicated to him unconsciously something of what he meant to me. Slowly, he began to reveal a modest curiosity about life, alongside a deep grieving and hopelessness over the childhood he never had. Through the iguana dream, James and I re-found aspects of each other. For him, the dream was the expression of an acceptance of the complex figure he had created for himself in desperate circumstances before words were available. For my part, I was changed by a deepening of my respect for James. The analysis, so often difficult, had begun at moments to feel effortless, until I grasped what might have made me experience this. James's repeated decisions to trust me, or at least to not give up on me, were acts that went against his every instinct. Persisting with the analysis required him to make emancipatory leaps of faith into spaces that must at times have felt like imminent catastrophe or even psychological death. In doing this, James helped me to appreciate how the worm can fly in the night in the howling storm in search of health, not solely of destruction.

CONCLUDING COMMENTS

Figure 8.11 shows the last piece by Paul Klee, left standing on his easel in 1940. It is considered by many to be the most monumental work of his career. The painting unites familiar objects of Klee's studio (the glass

Figure 8.11 "Still Life" 1940 by Paul Klee. Reprinted by permission of Art Resources, New York.

muller, the coffee pot), images from his career (the strewn flowers, sometimes in the shape of P, also the coffee pot), objects that signify the void and death (notably the angel of death portrayed humorously), and crosses reminiscent of earlier work at the time of his mother's death (see Brody, 2001). Klee, in poor health, had been occupied by concerns about death for many years. Here, he demonstrates his remarkable capacity for utilizing potential space and transitional thinking, expressed through the simultaneous freedom of composition and unity of structure. He creates a symbolic bridge that unites his past and present artistic life and world and his impending death (Brody, 2001). Primary, secondary, and tertiary levels are held in tension to a pitch that cannot fail to move. Paintings by schizophrenic patients (see Figure 8.12) convey by contrast endless anguish, as primary process overwhelms other psychological levels. There is no potential space. No third experience is reachable, despite desperate need.

There have been exceptional paintings by individuals with psychosis, such as the well-known work of Adolf Wolfli (see Figure 8.13), but psychosis is ultimately and fundamentally the antithesis of art.

Art, however, can help to heal psychosis, as can be seen in the work of art psychotherapy, which continues to retain a significant place in Western mental health services. I would like to make one final, brief comment on music, where form and content merge. Directness and accessibility of

Figure 8.12 "Horus dismembered."

Figure 8.13 "Kathedrale 1918" by Adolf Wolfli. Reprinted by permission of Audrey B. Heckler.

emotion and primary process imagery are the compelling features of music, in comparison to literature, painting, and sculpture. Interestingly, studies of the psychopathology and mental life of artists, musicians, and composers show that the lowest rates of mental illness and suicide are among musicians (cf. Arieti, 1976). I wonder whether the analytic forms of surrender to intuitive, unconscious dialogue, in potential and transitional space, of the kind I have described can be thought of as the psychoanalytic equivalent of musical composition. If there is truth to this, then ours is a work of *realization*, not only one of interpretation.

REFERENCES

Arieti, S. (1976). *Creativity: The magic synthesis*. New York: Basic Books.

Bion, W. R. (1963/1984). *Elements of psycho-analysis*. London: Karnac Books.

Brody, M. S. (2001). Paul Klee: Art, potential space and the transitional process. *Psychoanalytic Review*, 88, 369–392.

Deri, S. K. (1984). *Symbolization and creativity*. New York: International Universities Press.

Jackson, M., & Williams, P. (1994). *Unimaginable storms: A search for meaning in psychosis*. London: Karnac Books.

Lévi-Strauss, C. (1966). *The savage mind*. London: George Weidenfeld & Nicolson.

Lévi-Strauss, C. (1982). *The way of the masks*. Seattle: University of Washington Press.

Ogden, T. (1999). *Reverie and interpretation: Sensing something human*. London: Karnac Books.

Stitzman, L. (2004). At-one-ment, intuition and "suchness." *International Journal of Psychoanalysis*, 85, 1137–1155.

Turner, V. (1969). *The ritual process: Structure and anti-structure*. Chicago: Aldine Publishing Co.

Williams, P. (1998). Psychotic developments in a sexually abused borderline patient. *Psychoanalytic Dialogues*, 8, 459–491.

Williams, P. (2004). Incorporation of an invasive object. *International Journal of Psychoanalysis*, 85, 1333–1348.

Winnicott, D. W. (1971). *Playing and reality*. London: Tavistock.

Winnicott, D. W. (1988). *On Human Nature*. London: Free Association Books.

Chapter 9

"The central phobic position"

Notes on André Green's "new formulation of the free association method" and the analysis of borderline states*

André Green's paper "The Central Phobic Position: A New Formulation of the Free Association Method" was published in Part 3 (*IJP*, *81*, pp. 429-451), and was made available some weeks prior to publication on the *International Journal of Psychoanalysis*'s website for discussion. This chapter is based on a commissioned review of Green's paper for *IJP* and the discussion that took place over the Internet. The review and discussion were published in *IJP* and *Key Papers on Borderline States* (Williams, 2002). This chapter examines the clinical utility of Green's identification of a core phobic response in a certain type of borderline patient. I suggest that where there exists an incapacitating *core confusional state* deriving from a multiplicity of disturbing and traumatic experience (these may be inchoate, unassimilable part object relationships, psychotic anxieties, traumatic memories, or psychosomatic symptoms), the individual fears that the breaching of systemically organized defenses at any vulnerable point may lead to a "cascade" of overwhelming, traumatizing experiences leading to insanity or other mortal catastrophe. In this type of borderline organization, conflict and the use of aggression (so prevalent in borderline mental life) serves to defend against fears of concatenation leading to collapse of the ego into what is feared will be a psychotic (schizophrenia-like) state. Such patients are likely to exhibit the central phobic responses described by Green, and attention to chronic fears of engulfment and disintegration is necessary if the patient is to relinquish reliance on the systemic armor of continuously proliferating, overlapping defenses. Following a discussion of Green's paper I illustrate the nature of this clinical problem by referring to the analyses of two patients and their phobic responses to the analysis, which were designed to ward off fears of collapse.

---

* This chapter originally appeared as a paper in *International Journal of Psychoanalysis*, *81*, 2000, 1045-1060. Reprinted with permission.

THE CENTRAL PHOBIC POSITION

Green's paper refers to a quality of associative behavior observed in some borderline patients, and its role in maintaining a central defensive position, discernible in the use of the analyst and a particular functioning of the mind that Green terms "phobic." Through a clinical account of associative themes in a particular patient, Gabriel, Green delineates his concept of the central phobic position, and in so doing, the theoretical underpinning of his approach to psychoanalysis. His conceptualization implies a new formulation of the free association method. By constructing an analytic space in which free association and psychoanalytic listening are possible, the analyst can voice and link previously catastrophic ideas, quite unknown to the patient's consciousness, to help the patient create meaning and obtain relief from previously dominant, but unknown, terrors. Green concludes his paper by linking his clinical account to his ideas on temporality and negativity and to the relationship between oedipal and preoedipal elements. In the paper, Green begins by discussing disruptions of meaning in the free associative process, whether repressive or more evidently destructive of the ego. He refers to his interest in the work of the negative (1999b), especially forms of negativity that could not be interpreted in terms of their direct relationship with the destructive drives. In the transference with borderline patients, destructivity is directed predominantly, and first and foremost, at the subject's own psychic functioning. Green's ultimate concern in the paper could be said to be the "negativistic" manifestations that present themselves in such a way that it takes the analysand a great deal of time to recognize their function, and even then these manifestations do not stop once they have been recognized. He illustrates this through portrayal of certain stages of the analysis of Gabriel, who came to see Green because of chronic anxiety. Shortly after beginning treatment, something he apparently wanted very much, Gabriel said, "I can't hear you, I've got shit in my ears." During a session 10 years later, he again repeated, in connection with an interpretation that did not please him, "I can't hear you." He was expressing essentially the same opposition as in the past and this had remained a characteristic of his functioning, even after considerable progress had been made in the analysis. The difference lay in a capacity for reestablishing insight, the progress of which was not illusory, but the acquisition of such insight had to be preceded by a repetition compulsion designed to make Green lose his footing. Green's subsequent task was to move beyond the level of symptomatic behavior to discern what it was that gave Gabriel's current and repetitive behavior its specific oppositional character that stood in the way of analytic understanding. In other words, to understand the situation in which the meaning emerging from free association in the transference relationship became subject to what Green saw as jamming and quasi-systematic asphyxiation.

The analysis of the transference of Gabriel gave Green an understanding of what he now terms the central phobic position. For years, Gabriel's sessions were taken up with complaints of constant anxieties and what he had to say about these was highly confused. Green provides a summary of Gabriel's profoundly impoverished background, and the impact of this on Gabriel's capacity to think was certainly extensive. When Green managed to follow Gabriel—in other words, when Gabriel was experiencing himself as being understood—this contact led the patient to believe that Green was going to throw him out (in my experience this conflation of connection with traumatic loss of the object is one of the most common experiences in severe personality disordered and psychotic patients). Gabriel also often said, "I don't know," "I'm not sure," "I can't remember," "It's not very interesting, what I'm saying." These negativistic expressions had the power to kill representation and it is this clinical feature in particular that Green addresses. It took Green some time to understand that the feeling of periodically losing the thread of what Gabriel was saying was due to potentially meaningful ruptures of association. Rather than interruptions or changes of theme—which are part and parcel of associating freely—this was a discourse that seemed to be held at a distance and was based on generalities expressed in broken speech. The impact was to give Green the impression that he was trying to find his way in a dense fog. The more Gabriel continued talking, the more Gabriel felt in danger, as the communication between the parts of his discourse was increasingly felt to be insufficiently watertight and thus likely to fracture due to mounting incoherence. The express outcome Gabriel feared if his rupturing defenses lost coherence was a somatic illness or else madness. Green draws on links with elements of Gabriel's history during a confused, lonely childhood to illustrate the nature and persistence of his chronic, repetitive fears of disaster, to the extent that Green was ultimately able to grasp that Gabriel experienced a permanent state of torment, but to a certain extent *it was not he who was experiencing it.* His defensive activity had been facilitated by numerous temporary confusions of identity: between him and his mother, between him and a deceased paternal uncle whose first name he shared and, more recently, between his wife and his mother and, finally, between his son and himself. In reality, his mother had fostered extreme confusion during his adolescence to the point of introducing him to local people as her brother, and even at times as her husband. These were not identifications but temporary suspensions of his identity and the personality confusions that took place in his otherwise clear mind were a consequence of the mother's psychotic activity. Green explores the implications of such confusions for Gabriel's development, his eccentric behavior, and his analysis. The possibility of going mad turned out to be what Gabriel feared most of all, even more than succumbing to somatic illness. Gabriel was prevented from associating freely by fear derived from the anticipation of where it might lead him (insanity) and he desperately tried to avoid this. It was as if all of Green's interpretations might finally lead to a surge of traumas that would resonate with each other producing a catastrophic breakdown, and this had to be prevented at almost any cost. The effect of repression was not enough to explain what was happening. Gabriel's discourse was incessantly linear and constrained and displayed no capacity for imagining what might emerge or follow in any given direction. The quality of elaboration or growth normally seen in free associative thinking and speaking was missing.

Green continues with a discussion of the theoretical implications of his clinical account. He suggests that phobic functioning is not confined to the limits of a symptom manifesting itself primarily outside the session. Phobic functioning can become installed within communication itself and is thus a feature of the individual's internal world and hence language. The patient may then reveal a state of threat caused by the consequence of establishing meaningful links between a number of themes arising within the patient's mind. These themes are mutually potentiating; they do not simply accumulate in an exponential manner but are amplified grossly by coming into contact with each other. It is as though each trauma has remained in the mind, not simply repressed or isolated or dissociated, but "encysted." Each individual traumatic "cyst" contains its own latent danger, but when two or more encysted elements are threatened with exposure or mutual impingement, anxiety on a calamitous scale ensues. Notwithstanding this threat, patients produce, in spite of all their defensive maneuvers, an involuntary bringing together of the different traumas, without being aware of what is going on, thereby raising anxiety in order to counteract, to block, and eventually to stop the gathering diffusion of different threats that could lead to meaningful insight, but which are felt instead to lead to a disastrous outcome arousing terror. The patient's communications contain condensations, which Green likens to hubs (*"plaques tournantes"*) that offer a number of apparent "ways out" of the crisis; these devices are all alarming because they ultimately form a knot of encounters where different traumatic lineages intersect, increasing rather than decreasing the threat. Green examined the effects of the central phobic position on Gabriel through the core traumatic experience of his murder of the representation of his mother. The potential interaction of this with other traumatic experiences is a theme developed by Green, as is the ensuing denial by subjects of their own psychic reality. Green does not feel it is right in such circumstances to trace everything back to the earliest trauma; on the contrary, he stresses specifically that it is the grouping together of various traumas that is important to identify, each containing the potential (separately and/or linked) to signify catastrophe.

Green moves to a discussion of the associative process itself in light of the inhibitions revealed by the analysis of Gabriel. Free association makes use of narrative or grammatical structures without respecting their distinction between principal and subordinate elements ("side-cathexes"). Resistance makes a detour necessary, but this, in turn, is capable of enriching the possibilities of association, even when it changes the subject. We have become accustomed to the knowledge that it is possible for a new system of relations to emerge, but little or no attention has been given to the ways in which it is formed, Green argues. A new network implies that meaningful relations may exist between any of the elements uttered, whether they are a product of two semantically consistent ideas or of one idea semantically consistent with any other aspect of verbalization, incidental or contingent, belonging to side-cathexes uttered or linked by inference. This follows from the hypothesis Green advances that different side-cathexes may be related to a barred pathway that cannot be cleared (i.e., that which leads directly from a to b in Freud's model of the *Project*, 1950). The comprehension of one element, say, element d, of the network a, b, c, d, e, f, cannot reveal its function simply by its presumed reference to that which precedes it, c. Generally speaking, in its thrust towards consciousness, unconscious meaning seeks to open up a path for itself and, in order to find its way through, it has to make use of liaisons that do not bring the elements it is composed of into direct contact, or that cannot be inferred from mere relations of immediate proximity or of equivalent importance. In addition, Green sees the patient's communication as expressing an interplay of channels of significations, some representative, some affective, and others related to bodily states, acting out, reality statements, thought processes, and so on. The task of the analyst is to understand the complexity, structure, and function of the meaning underlying the overall discourse and to grasp the passage from one channel of communication to the next. In the apparent disorder of communication, it is the effect of mutually resonating chains of signifiers that increases the value of this functioning. Associations enable one to identify nuclei of what Green terms "retroactive reverberation": An element uttered acquires meaning if retroactive echoes are highlighted, revealing how the power of their meaning persists long after the discourse carrying them has died out. Retroactive reverberation and heralding anticipation (Green, 2000) act either in concert or alternately, indicating that free association gives access to a complex temporal structure that challenges the apparent linearity of discourse. Such functioning is suggestive of a network rather than of a linear structure. The associative discourse is marked at moments by what Green calls "the effects of irradiation." Particular moments in the discourse may often be understood only after the event. These moments are vehicles that give rise to dynamic effects; once pronounced, they irradiate and influence the intentions of the discourse. They will have a tendency to begin resonating, either with things already said (in a retroactive manner) or (sometimes simultaneously) with statements still to come that are not yet thought of but are potentially generative of themes that will enable one to notice new connections through what has been expressed. The unconscious has, in effect, the power to stimulate a virtual existence, giving it an unknown, stirring influence, especially if one thinks of it as the result of a process of potentialization in the manner Green has described.

The term "associative radiation" traces, by means of manifest discourse resulting from free association, lines of force running through it that constitute the veins of discourse. This makes it possible to follow, to resonate, to retroact, and to gather in advance the richness of meaning circulating along its pathways, the plan of which is based on coordinates of the unconscious marked by the hyper-cathexes and counter-cathexes that accompany them. Green, in addressing this complex, fundamental psychic process, is alluding ultimately to the key concepts and ideas around which the patient's mental universe is organized. He views it as deplorable that there is still no agreement among psychoanalysts in this important area. A task for the future will surely be to come to agreement on the subject, and he proceeds to review the components of the debate, as he sees them. He then concludes his paper by raising a number of metapsychological questions. How are we to understand what the central phobic position reveals in these patients? First, he links the well-known quotation on castration in the "Wolf Man" to what Lacan (1977) called "foreclosure": "This really involved no judgment upon the question of its existence [castration] but it was the same as if it did not exist" (Freud, 1918). This resonates for Green (1997) with Gabriel's denials, and highlights a paradoxical sense of guilt calling for interminable reparation, being the consequence of the primary murder, the ultimate aim of which is to carry out an "excorporation" of the abandoning object. Autoerotic activities are an attempt to fend off the void left by this evacuation. The superego, however, "knows" that there has been a primary murder and does not forget. Also, Gabriel's apparent empty-headedness (reflected in his use of language) reveals the trace of the presence of a maternal object that exists in the void in which it leaves the subject. If it happens to manifest its presence, its ghost can come to occupy the entire space and threatens to drive him mad. Corresponding to the primary murder of the object, there is the idea of a paternal power that has no choice but to give way, all the while deploring its own inability to free the subject from its fascinating imprisonment. Green engages in a detailed inquiry into the type of mental judgment involved in the creation of the above phenomena using, as a reference point, Freud's paper "Negation" (1925). Green concludes his paper on the borderline condition he depicts with the following:

> These patients know that analysis is the only place where they can express their madness and experience it without fearing too serious reprisals. Beyond their denial, their energetic attempts to ignore what is concealed by this old material that periodically resurfaces and beyond their struggles in the transference against recognizing the truth, where all means of defense are used, i.e., acts of forgetting, contradictions, blaming the analyst, repudiations, distorted reasoning,

the transference remains positive because they are indebted to analysis for the fact that they have remained safe, if not sound, thanks to the experience. Freud reminded us that no one can escape himself (p. 450).

THE INTERNET DISCUSSION

A moderated discussion followed. The comments in the summary below should be attributed to those who made them: Len Klein, Ruth Stein, Joseph Scalia, Claudia Vargas, Charles Spezzano, Donald Coleman, Marita Torsti, Per Roar Anthi, Loredana Micati Squitieri, Meir Perlow, Jean Arundale, Don Marcus, Juan Tubert-Oklander, Reyna Hernandez de Tubert, Matias Fernàndez, Lea Goldberg, Lester Goldfisher, William Young, Bjørn Sahlberg, André Green, and others.

While Green conceptualizes the central "defensive" position as phobic, some preferred the notion of dread of annihilation anxiety. One contributor cited a patient who was verbally inhibited unless there was a theme to be spoken of. Free association didn't take place; there were lots of silences and, as a result, much anxiety. Once the orientation to the presence of early infantile structures of trauma became part of the sessions, there was less silence and anxiety. Green's identification of guilt over "primary murder" indicates how the patient may either withhold speech or speak only in disjointed associations, so as not to allow anything to emerge that might point to the crime.

A questioner asked: "What is the level of the analyst's listening? Is it mostly based on the patient's chain of associations or is the field of listening that of transference and countertransference relations?" For example, when Gabriel intersperses his discourse with "I don't know ... it's not very interesting what I'm saying," and experiences the analyst as bored, are these phobic defenses against transgressive and/or traumatic material or transferential expressions of Gabriel's sense of unworthiness, as attested by his history? Green moves from describing Gabriel's verbalizations to stating, "I had no precise information about his history." An analyst subscribing to an object-relations position might take Gabriel's verbalizations as indirectly narrating a great deal about personal history. The "free association" analyst will go on looking for more associations, while the "object-transference" analyst might decide to reflect to the patient the affects of desolation and of being unwanted by the patient and/or by the analyst. The contributor felt that Gabriel's behavior could be seen as either resisting reaching a conclusive point that the analyst expects or, alternatively, enacting an object relationship or a fantasy of internalized objects.

The next contributor felt that Green's account displayed superb analytic work in the tradition of free association and evenly suspended attention.

Green's elaboration of one form of resistance to free association argues against the idea that such work cannot be carried out with patients who do not free associate. In response to the implication that Green's approach would not have worked with the patient cited by the first contributor, it was suggested that difficulties with certain patients may have to do with our not being able to listen and respond well enough within the kind of analytic space Green describes. Green's form of listening for the unconscious may be antithetical to the way many analysts, including some contributors to this discussion, theorize and work.

The next contributor stated that "preverbal preoedipal patients" may have verbal language, but this is not their main way of communicating. Why try to communicate with them through verbal language? Similarly, these patients don't have separate objects. Why do we treat them as if they see us as a separate object? One way of dealing with this problem is to develop the evident narcissistic transference—to let the patient see the analyst in the way the patient wants to. This can take time. Another is that interpretation is not used until the patient is ready for it. If the analyst is truly able to tolerate the feelings induced by patients, patients will come to feel accepted and realize they can have feelings no matter how terrible they are. Staying with the patient's feelings is not enough to "cure" the patient, but it is the beginning.

The next contributor contrasted two statements by Green: (1) "I sensed that a change was taking place within him so that he could accept an image of her that was less rigid than that which he presented during the analysis" (p. 439); (2) "For me, therefore, a productive session is one in which the analysand follows the fundamental rule while the analyst seeks to create the conditions for the patient to associate freely in an appropriate setting" (p. 441). There seemed to be a distinction between a productive session (freely associative) and the aims of analysis (shifts in internal images of key figures). The same distinction might be drawn another way: Internal object relations lead to the quality of the associative process, as when Green writes: "It was as if the representation of an object that was too absent created in his mind an excessive lack, awakening a degree of excitation that could not find any outlet" (p. 440). The excessive lack and excessive excitation would underlie the linkless associations.

The next contributor made a sizeable contribution, the essence of which was that he was disappointed not to hear more of what Green felt and thought about while listening to Gabriel. He suspected that Gabriel might not have felt particularly understood by Green and that Gabriel "had trouble getting Green to eat," that is, to listen, take in, digest, and grow in understanding of the intermediate space between them. The contributor concluded that Gabriel didn't know how to "play" properly but would unwittingly be the ironic and unreliable narrator who was "compliant" with his analyst's perceived interest in the dead mother complex. However, he felt that Gabriel's mother was alive and well in the inner theatre of his mind. He also thought that when Green told Gabriel that he (Gabriel) could not tolerate silence, Green might well have been dramatically enacting a rejection and refusal of Gabriel as a consequence of the way he was listening.

The first contributor to the discussion returned to say that he would listen differently compared to another analyst, including Green. There is a problem, however, if the elevation of a particular form of listening to the status of a truth usurps others. Referring again to the idea that some of Gabriel's associations might not have reflected a phobic position so much as an expression of Gabriel's sense of unworthiness, he could see no contradiction between this and Green's outlook. Gabriel was expressing his background but through dread of re-experiencing traumatic states that could drive him mad. The comment in the discussion that the "dead mother was alive and well in the inner theatre of Gabriel's mind" was questioned. The "dead mother complex" refers to experiences in infancy in which the mother may have been physically present but emotionally absent, or to a mother who is unable to remain engaged with her infant or to maintain an emotional investment in the baby. The internalization of such experiences brings about, in the developing mind, representational structures of the frustrating emptiness that the infant's emotional needs encounter. Green reports: "A major event in [Gabriel's] childhood was being put out to nurse, but at what age? It took me about eight years to find out that this had taken place from the ages of one to 3." Furthermore, during the time Gabriel was separated from his family, his mother never came to see him, never wrote to him, nor telephoned him. While this would qualify his mother as unavailable, it does not appear to suffice for the establishment of the "dead mother complex." However, his mother's behavior with him before he was sent away to a nurse would be critical. If we accept the report that she felt nothing and "she did not realize that her baby was crying like mad, was visibly wasting away, only absorbing the contents of a purulent and empty breast" (p. 432), then we would have a basis for suspecting the internalized dead mother complex. But how would we know that such an internalized organization is present in an adult? Since basic "rhythms of safety" are not likely to have been established, we would expect considerable anxiety and confusion, especially in relationships, where the "interrhythm" suffers from disjointedness and disconnectedness, just as Green found in the transference. When Green speaks of "'excorporation' of the abandoning object" (p. 447), the contributor thought he was referring to a later version of the mother than the "dead mother," and in fact the excorporation is in the service of avoiding any possible encounter with the "dead mother." That the excorporation may be interpreted as matricide by the superego is not unusual, where efforts at separation and individuation are seen by the superego as parricidal.

The next contributor was appreciative of Green's paper. When the analyst ceases to use associative thinking and decides to do something else, at that point psychoanalysis ceases. The unconscious reason for abandoning free association is always related to anxiety. Sometimes we project our own anxieties into our analysands and decide not to continue analytic work because understanding and associating further becomes impossible. We find ways of protecting ourselves by the methods we adopt when choosing our patients. The delicate touch Green displays at very deep levels with a difficult patient shows that he has both the capacity and the discipline to use the method of association thoroughly. The central phobic position is familiar in that it links to the concept of "integration anxiety" that derives from the fetal and newborn's strivings to preserve equilibrium (i.e., from the principle of constancy). These strivings, along with drive/object strivings, create a "ground map" for a multidimensional network of free associations.

The first contributor commented once more, this time asking: What is the nature of an object representation that can be excorporated? Such a representation must inhabit preconscious and conscious levels of functioning, but not the unconscious, where the object, in a variety of representations, persists within psychic structures Green calls "themes," which amplify one another once activated. The central phobic position, as developed in the paper, becomes more weighted on the rapprochement (borderline and oedipal) side of things than on the earlier organizing phase of infantile trauma and annihilation anxiety. What seems to make the present ego "precarious" is the exclusion of the maternal object through excorporation, depriving the ego of the use of the object in contexts necessary for thought activity.

The next contributor took up Green's implicit emphasis on the importance of paying attention to aspects of the patient's mode of associating and behavior in the analytic situation. Analysts lack a systematic rationale and terminology for analyzing the resistance manifestations Green describes. Although ingrained and often subtly split cognitive and affective patterns are difficult to grasp when they emerge, they nonetheless play a significant role in influencing the analyst's responsive feelings and countertransference (counterresistance). The contributor agreed with Green that tracing affects in itself is not a sufficient route to understanding the latent meaning of the patient's associations or behavior. But in contrast to Green, he gives priority to affects in the session. He found it difficult to follow Green when he seemed to maintain that an affect cannot be a representation. An affect is more than a metaphorical concept. It is often an authentic clinical fact containing psychic representations linked to objects, experiences, drive derivatives, mental states, and bodily sensations. Green's sharp distinction between affect and representation is therefore a problem.

A previous contributor took up how some had suggested that Green may not have been paying sufficient attention to countertransference experiences and not listening well enough. Green's attention to countertransference may not have been central in his paper, but it is quite clear that he is at home with it. Gabriel seems to have felt deeply, delicately, intricately understood, not misunderstood, as had been implied. The contributor was struck by the dearth of the discussion group's ability to "play" with the concept of the "central phobic position" and free association in the spirit in which Green had offered his ideas.

A new contributor suggested that the attack on psychic functioning by the borderline patient can be thought of as a defensive maneuver employing destructiveness, but it is not necessarily this. It is a particular kind of defense that hampers connections between experiences, or works to hold on to the state of nonintegration. Green mentions Gabriel's fear of somatic illness or madness. Some borderline patients seem to think that somatic illness will overwhelm them because of insubstantial boundaries, and that this affects their psychic organization. They flee from the risk of integration to the risk of somatic illnesses and then to the risk of madness. Their speech rhythms may become disorganized or mechanical, forcing the analyst to lose the thread. False connections succeed in keeping the spontaneous process of inner associations at bay. The analyst can feel isolated, inadequate, or dazed and may wonder: What's the matter with this patient, with me, with this relationship? Patients have two ways of conveying their mental state to the analyst: through unconscious communication and through verbal communication. Mental states related to preverbal experiences often find their way through the first channel via the "style" of associations, instead of content.

Another new contributor quoted Winnicott (1962):

> In my opinion our aims in the practice of the standard technique are not altered if it happens that we interpret mental mechanisms which belong to the psychotic types of disorder and to primitive stages in the emotional stages of the individual. If our aim continues to be to verbalize the nascent conscious in terms of the transference, then we are practicing analysis; if not, then we are analysts practicing something else that we deem to be appropriate to the occasion. And why not (pp. 169–170)?

At this point André Green responded, saying that he had the impression that he had failed to give a faithful impression of the kind of work he had been engaged in with his patient. He offered to present two analytic sessions to make his position clearer. This material was restricted to existing discussants. The author of the present paper studied the material, which comprises two sessions 4 years apart, the first after 6 months of analysis, both sessions being taken from around the time of the May holidays in France. In the first session Gabriel is confused and frightened at multiple levels, to the point of being "phobic" about the entire proceedings. Green works hard to contain Gabriel's pervasive anxieties, which center around being overwhelmed by the analyst, thereby losing his sense of identity, and a terror of destroying the analyst through the power of his hunger and need. The session has a primitive quality and demonstrates the patient's inability to differentiate himself adequately from his primary object. The second session indicates that a great deal of psychic development has taken place in the intervening years. Gabriel is calmer, more trusting, and voices his thoughts and feelings in a clearer, more reflective way. However, the session also reveals tremendous fear of coming properly alive in his feelings through engagement with others. Whereas in the first session it seemed that the patient had failed to be born psychologically, in the second session he was fighting against growing up, using anorectic-like defensive themes of long standing (Gabriel's mother, we are told, was anorexic). Another difference was that he was able to see more clearly what he was doing. Both sessions served Green's purpose well in illustrating the stubbornness of a phobic lacuna that dogged Gabriel, despite improvement. My own sense, however, was that because Green is dealing with such a major theme in his paper—offering, in effect, a paradigmatic shift —even this "earlier" and "later" material was not enough to give a clear picture of how Green's conceptualizing has evolved. What happened "in between" and how Green dealt with it would need to be understood to avoid the pitfall of the discussants' competing explanations of the etiology of Gabriel's difficulties, which had unfortunately come to characterize the Internet discussion. My response to Green's paper and subsequent material was to think that he was dealing with material for a book, not a paper, and this problem may have contributed to indigestion in some contributors. Green continued his response by saying that he felt that many discussants had preferred to argue their own alternative views rather than consider what he believes to be specific to psychoanalytic free association (retroactive reverberation, anticipatory announcement, irradiation of the signifier, etc.). Some questioned whether there was anything new in his ideas. Few seemed to have grasped the point of what Green calls the negative hallucination of one's mental state. Green criticized "easy" commentaries on his case, which arise when the reader is given the outcome of the story and fails to appreciate that more than 10 years of work was involved in facing continuous attempts at the "murder of psychic reality." Green felt strongly that had he told Gabriel that he experienced the analysis in the way he did because he felt "unworthy or unlovable" Gabriel would surely have thought or replied: "This is blah blah blah: I don't need to hear what I already know." Felt "unlovability and unworthiness" belong to consciousness. Green thought that there was a mix-up in the discussion between what the patient says, transference, countertransference, and the analyst's introspection and reactions to what occurs in the session. Transference is always guesswork in view of the modus operandi of the unconscious. Reference to the drives was also missing from the discussion, under the pretext that object relationships are enough to understand what is going on. Being understood, Green argued, does not mean expressing what the patient talks about using other words, but enlightening what is said and providing evidence that what is given back has traced the communication to its unconscious determinants, with the necessary transformational consequences. One must pay attention to the fact that as the evolving process gets nearer the patient's internal functioning, so body and mind become linked. Green did not take kindly to those who sought to teach him how to listen to patients, as though he had never thought of paying attention to interruptions and resumptions, which are elementary approaches to any material. He felt that in an optimal analysis the unearthing of an unconscious fantasy (which is always there) was necessary. How could we think of an object relationship whose final aim is not to understand the organizing role of unconscious fantasy? Green stated that he was aware that there is disagreement with his view that nothing has been found in infant observation that could help us in our understanding of the intrapsychic process. He did not think the pro-infant observation lobby was necessarily wrong; rather, that their position can have the effect of blocking our imaginative processes, as some comments in the discussion had shown, which is the worst thing that can happen to an analyst. Green felt it was a mistake to think that he was mainly concerned with words. Language is a mediator of feelings and other experiences in the session. Free association is the irreplaceable means by which patients introduce into the preconscious-conscious that which springs from their unconscious. It is designed to match or connect with the free-floating attention of the analyst. The result is that with certain patients, one has to give up the fact that a communication involving an interpretation can reach the preconscious; it will not secure direct access to the unconscious. Therefore, careful attention to free association is closer to primary thinking. Analysis is a permanent interplay between the intrapsychic and intersubjective, but it is the first that is the most difficult to accommodate. As a result, what frequently happens in contemporary practice is what Christopher Bollas has labeled an "undoing of psychoanalysis."

A new discussant then contributed with a query. Presumably the central phobic position also affects the process of internalization of the analyst at unconscious levels. How could the patient reach the stage that Green describes as "[On the couch, now, he was] able to feel very intense affects and, for the first time, to express his love" (p. 439), as this would suggest that the analysis had effected structural change beyond the "multiple and sometimes contradictory identifications" that he had had to resort to defensively on conscious and preconscious levels in his preanalytic personality?

One discussant expressed dismay at Green's attack on those who disagreed with him, but agreed with him that there was a difficulty inherent in discussions of clinical material when discussants tried to give the analyst supervision. However, on the basis of Green's paper and the supplementary sessions he could see no evidence that the patient was "crushing" or negating his own thought processes.

Another discussant noted how threatened Gabriel was by the analytic situation, and in spite of this, how he was able to seduce his analyst into nourishing him with penetrating interventions. In some respects the analyst's interpretations could be seen as a form of enactment. At one point Gabriel says, "I have the feeling of getting shot everywhere," but the analyst doesn't stop firing interpretations, and the patient seems to swallow them. The analytic dialogue becomes a kind of shadow-boxing in which Gabriel is unable to articulate his threatened feelings and underlying opposition to his analyst. Gabriel seemed to be trying to communicate to Green that he was neglecting what he, the patient, really felt. Perhaps the analyst failed to explore the meaning and implications of Gabriel's affects. Also, the patient's own ego was not drawn into the analytic process; rather, the patient's ego is overwhelmed. Consequently the patient is not able to investigate and integrate repressed fantasies as well as split-off experiences, traumatizations, etc. To what extent could "the central phobic position" as a specific form of resistance be co-constructed by both parties in the analytic interaction?

A previous discussant stated that the drives in psychoanalysis are themselves representatives (of body-needs and tensions) but can be talked about only by being represented, according to Kleinian theory, through unconscious fantasies (i.e., through higher-order representations). Neuropsychoanalysts agree that the experiential (clinical) accessibility of the drives is very difficult or nonexistent. Green notes the absence of drive-talk in his paper's discussion. This contradicts his own conception of unconscious fantasies, which are, clinically, both the necessary and sufficient reason for referring to the drives. The main disagreement between Green and this discussant is the latter's belief that it is necessary to provide the patient with feelings of being understood and of safety (including the interpretation of the patient's feelings of unworthiness). Gabriel's feelings of discomfort derive from his feelings about himself! For the analyst to face up to this, sometimes through the use of emotion, is neither easy nor unimaginative.

An earlier discussant acknowledged the discussion's failure to engage with the material Green had presented. The articulation of the arborescent and reticular nature of free associative networks, of principal semantemes and side-cathexes, of retrospective reverberation and heralding anticipation, is a lot to digest. Green had helped with the problem of not-yet-knowing, of latent meanings, and of not foreclosing. When the central phobic position is prevalent in a patient's communications, and tertiary processes are functioning poorly, a less complex rendering of the situation as "preoedipal" or "narcissistic" is not helpful; rather, the true complexity of the situation needs to be tolerated.

Two discussants saw Green's patient's ego as being overwhelmed by penetrating interpretations, rather than being drawn into the analytic process via interventions directed at his (or the ego's) self-reflective capacities. Another discussant thought that Green was attempting to extend the notion of phobia, traditionally regarded as a neurotic flight from prohibited desire, to borderline syndromes, where the destructive drives are phobically dodged in an effort to block them from destroying the ego. A central phobic position would appear to be a "midterm" between inhibition and this destructive activity. What Green adduces as explanation for its centrality is not convincing.

One discussant took issue with Green's comments on infant observation. The "blocked imagination" is what is responsible for not finding anything useful in infant observations, and not the other way around. Infant research provides manifest material for analysts to exercise their psychoanalytic imagination.

A new discussant suggested that Green's paper and the discussion calls attention to an ongoing problem in psychoanalysis. Green and some discussants believe that free association is not only possible, it is the essence of what makes a therapy psychoanalysis. Others believe that no association is free of the influence of the personality and the analytic style of the analyst. In addition, much that is communicated in analysis is nonverbal. Green, a man of strong convictions, is likely to have a powerful effect on his analysand's associations. Another analyst with a different personality and analytic style would have a different effect on the associations of the same patient. Our patients' associations are an amalgam of what is in their unconscious and their reaction to us.

A late entrant to the discussion found Green's paper brilliant and challenging. But what does he leave out of his theorizing? The discussant sorely missed reference to emotional experience. Green and similar thinkers seem to conceive of the human mind as a network of interrelated representations, signifiers, or symbols, whose meaning is derived from the complex structure of this gossamer cobweb, but they do not consider that this complex symbolic structure may represent anything but itself. Human discourse then becomes the reality to be studied, not a means of representing something else. The "reality principle" should include the recognition of affects as the true "inner reality."

Two discussants deplored the tone of Green's response to the discussion. Fundamentalism in psychoanalysis is regrettably usually the rule, rather than the exception, they remarked. It is both a manifestation of the traditional Western *Weltanschauung* that tends to frame all arguments in an "either/or" format, and a pathological manifestation related to certain universal human experiences of suffering. The future of psychoanalysis and of contemporary culture depends upon our capacity for developing a paradigm of human existence that complements the "principle of exclusion" ("either this or the other") with a "principle of inclusion" ("both this and the other"). Green is convinced that his understanding of psychoanalysis is the truth, and that any other point of view is misguided, superficial, uninformed, or simply wrong. He is committed to a principle of exclusion and this embodies a whole epistemology. Green believes—as Freud did—that there is some preexisting content "down there" in the patient's unconscious that is to be found by analytic enquiry and this implies an objectivistic theory of knowledge. Such a conception of scientific knowledge has been undermined by developments in physics, biology, and the human sciences. An alternative theory of knowledge may be framed as (1) knowledge is the result of the human being's ongoing efforts to develop a viable relation with objects; (2) the mental products we call "knowledge" are not preexisting, but are generated by this interaction; and (3) propositions about reality are neither true nor untrue, but only more or less useful in orientating our relationship with objects. On what bases do we choose between these two different epistemologies?

Another new discussant felt that a central phobic position may be a generalization because it cannot be applied to all types of borderlines. "Phobic" puts us into a diagnostic category and blurs the emphasis on avoidance as a predominant, not basic, mechanism of defense.

A previous discussant stated that contributors' collective calls for plurality and the chiding of Green for his alleged failure to heed that call may sorely miss the mark of their own culpability. He had found little evidence in the discussion of extending that same courtesy or acting in the same spirit as that which Green was decried for neglecting. Perhaps we all lose our way when we seek to protect or enlarge our own turf. All too often, we do not so much seek to understand one another as to presume that we already do and are therefore in a position to denounce the other's errors. Contemporary psychoanalysis is extremely challenged at this particular historical juncture. We wish to protect what we hold dear, yet find ourselves buffeted between the Scylla of autocracy and the Charybdis of anarchy. What is to be done when neither democracy nor pluralism appear to help?

The discussion was drawn to a close. While lively in some respects, this discussion threw more heat than light on the schizoid nature of mental functioning in severe disturbance and Green's complex articulation of a central phobic position. It is included in this chapter primarily to (1) highlight some of the issues for debate in trying to grasp Green's model of borderline functioning, and (2) to indicate the difficulty psychoanalysts have in talking to each other. The temptation to supervise and "know better" deriving from impassioned belief systems can be a contaminant of analytic debate. The need to tolerate pluralism is necessary if the risk of disintegration of psychoanalysis into subfiefdoms is to be avoided. Pedagogical and political disagreements are powerful and induce otherwise sensitive individuals into failing to listen to each other in depth. A tendency can arise to make "position statements" leading to a "ships passing in the night" quality of the kind that characterized the Green discussion. Is there a more urgent problem for our contemporary, pluralistic psychoanalysis to address?

Green's model can be useful, I believe, as it explores an area of ego fragmentation, discontinuity of psychic structure, and concatenation of incompatible unconscious elements that is not unusual in psychotic thinking. This forces the individual to strive, with varying degrees of success, to contain multiple traumatic experiences. The patient's primary terror of madness (breakdown leading to death) and the chronic confusion that precipitates this do not lend themselves to analysis from any linear developmental perspective or through a single, overarching causal explanation. Individuals who suffer inchoately in this way may create a "virtual personality" in order to effect an illusion of self-containment through the negation of the meaning of much of what they think and say. This virtual personality does not communicate in a way that reflects progressive integration of experience, but acts like a gatekeeper or frontier beyond which impingement must not proceed. From within, impingement may take the form of revival of individual traumatic events or from incompatible traumatic elements colliding with each other—these are experienced, in my view, as a confusion of part-objects that are felt to lay claim to the subject. From outside, assaults, mergings, and other potentially traumatic experiences must be warded off to prevent the dislodging of the precarious belief in sanity. Effort is invested in maintaining the intactness of the frontier to prevent the escalation of confusion. The "roaming vigilance" with which such individuals strive to protect their sanity gives rise to a heterogeneity of dispersed, layered, primitive activity (overlaid by conventional thinking and language) and it is the nature of this activity Green tries to identify in his patient Gabriel, taking as his departure point the strictures affecting free association. What the individual is protecting against will vary with the individual. In contrast to Green, I place greater emphasis on the object relations experience of these patients. I suggest that such individuals have a partial, limited hold on fragile, damaged objects (part-objects) that derive from traumatic conflicts or deprivations and neglect or both. These part-objects and their traumatic associations are experienced as multiple, divergent threats that singly or together are capable of inundating the vulnerable ego. Their overlap or concatenation is felt to be enough to precipitate tremendous *confusion* leading to fears of decompensation that will kill the patient. In this sense, confusional states in personality disorders may approximate to the traumatic, psychotic anxieties that Green identifies more than has been realized. Green opens up an original area of understanding in the patient's prospective and retroactive attitude to free association and the use of language, through which it is possible to identify the recurrence of the threat of downfall. I would add only one further element: that I have found the nature of this use of language to have an organic link to the type and prevalence of part-object experiences in the patient.

CLINICAL EXAMPLES

In my work with severely disturbed individuals, I have found Green's conceptualization to be useful in understanding latent confusion deriving from psychotic mental activity. I shall give two examples of "difficult to reach" patients. The first is reported elsewhere in this book in Chapter 2, "Some Difficulties in the Analysis of a Withdrawn Patient." Unfortunately, I came across Green's work on the central phobic position only after my patient quit analysis following considerable improvement. The second case I report below is ongoing. Both patients demonstrated an inhibited use of free association and an eccentric use of language. Their use of free association and language was designed not for the purposes of communication, but to act as a quasi-container for a range of traumatic experiences that threatened to implode, singly or multiply, precipitating madness. At the same time, the way both patients spoke had been deformed and reconstructed for the purpose of disguising this threat. The outcome of this inhibition in clinical analytic work is not the same as "resistance" or breaks in the free-associative process that might permit analysis of underlying lacunae. One is confronted by a systemic adaptation to traumatic mental events that structures the management of affect and object, both of which are needed and dreaded.

In Chapter 2 it can be seen how my patient, Alec, struggles in his analysis with a longing to make contact with me while at the same time warding off an ominous threat that remains ill defined. The patient's evident goodwill leads to work that delivers improvement, but both he and I are preoccupied (separately but not together) by the disquiet he feels about the fact of being in analysis, and the potentially catastrophic nature of the mental pain that he seems to increasingly fear will be unleashed as his trust in me develops. There is no single or overarching explanation for this man's terror of the revival of traumatic experiences. In the chapter I refer to his "putting on hold" his feelings and mental activity while attempting to communicate with me and others. I comment on his parthenogenetic fantasy with his mother as, in part, his form of engagement with her chronic depression. There is his negation of the role of his father, the effacement of his brother, the emotional deprivations of his childhood, his difficulties in managing his wife and in having feelings towards his own children, and there is the use of conflict and "surrender" as organized ways of relating to me. Taken together, these conflicts and deprivations might be thought of as having a damaging impact on Alec's sense of self or to have undermined his developing ego, leaving him prey to engulfment by anxiety derived from unconscious fantasies—or both. This is how I understood Alec. What I did not understand was the way in which Alec employed an elliptical, repetitively disfigured form of language and a partial use of free association to fend off an ever-present, cumulative threat of psychic collapse. The effect of this was to make me periodically lose my footing by having to confront, with some dismay, areas of potentially unmanageable impasse, often when I was beginning to feel that the analysis had taken genuine further "hold" in Alec. To view these deflating regressions as negative therapeutic reactions was useful but not adequate: With hindsight, they arose not in response to specific movements forward (although this sometimes occurred), but to a primitive, pervasive fear of the eventual consequences of *any* move forward, created at points where Green identifies the impact of "retroactive reverberation." One result of Alec's deformation of language was that I found myself losing faith in my own use of language, and more reliant on trying to grasp Alec's use of dreams and body language and my own countertransference experiences of regressions to what seemed like the beginning of the analysis. These sources of information were also useful but not enough to maintain hope of contact with Alec without language. I am not describing an unwillingness on the part of Alec to participate in the analysis by, for example, speaking less. On the contrary, he continued to talk genuinely of his difficulties, but his relationship to language was profoundly compromised. More important to him than his need for it was the noxious (retroactive) potential that dialogue harbored within it for unleashing confusion, traumatic memories, part-object confusion and, at worst, psychological death. It was as though each new unearthing in the analysis generated additional pain, not necessarily because of the topic itself (although this could be the case), but because the pain of *everything* we discussed, which was aggregated through multiple, part-object traumata, threatened a "composite" disaster. Failure to acknowledge this threat of composite catastrophe was, I believe, why Alec had to leave an analysis that was, to all intents and purposes, proceeding along the lines he consciously wished.

The second case I wish to discuss, Mr. X, illustrates the cumulative risk of traumatic collapse posed by free association, and Mr. X's strategy for dealing with this. Mr. X, 47, is a head teacher in a secondary school who has been married for 22 years and has one son, "C," aged 18. Mr. X's wife ("B") is 10 years older than him and suffers from depression and a range of psychosomatic symptoms that make it impossible for her to work. The son is at university; the son suffered a serious depressive collapse at 16, which necessitated brief hospitalization, and this was one of the factors that precipitated Mr. X contacting me. Mr. X experienced intense anxiety and guilt feelings evoked by his son's crisis, feeling he had not been a good enough father. Having failed to help him with his anxieties, he decided to seek advice and help for himself and his son. Mr. X was keen to take up the offer of analysis for himself without being able to indicate why. For most of the initial consultation, Mr. X's thoughts reverted to his need to discuss his son's problems—a veritable catalogue of troubles that seemed to have befallen the son without any sign of the son having participated in them. Mr. X had no suggestion as to how they might have arisen or how his son might be implicated in their origin. The mere thought seemed irrelevant to him. Mr. X had suffered anxiety attacks since the troubles began and could no longer concentrate. His wife could not cope with their son; Mr. X felt responsible for everything and everyone.

Mr. X's parents were schoolteachers. He described his father as strict and distant and his mother as passive and prone to mood changes: "... everything would be going along fine and then she would suddenly collapse and we wouldn't see her for days." Mr. X has a sister 2 years younger than himself who "went off the rails" as a teenager, dropped out, took drugs, and eventually cut her ties with the family. He has not spoken to her for several years. He understood her unhappiness to be due to feeling that neither parent had loved her (an opinion he stated strongly was wrong). She also harbored a grievance against her father for ignoring his wife's illness, which seemed to have been recurrent depression requiring occasional hospitalization and a life on antipsychotic medication. Mr. X refused to be affected during childhood by his mother's difficulties or his father's distant authoritarianism and concentrated on being an excellent school pupil, in which he succeeded. He was gregarious but made no close friends. He recalled only one unhappy time in adolescence when a boy with whom he had made friends was hit by a truck on a busy road and almost died; years later, after multiple surgical interventions, the boy became a chronic invalid. Mr. X "blossomed" at university and his ensuing teaching career went from strength to strength, culminating in him being offered the headship of one of the largest schools in London. Life at home seems to have been "normal," his wife's severe difficulties being treated by the family with fatalistic passivity. Mr. X's attitude to his wife's illness was tolerant and quietly dismissive. When pressed, he displayed anxiety and guilt that he had not been able to put things right for her.

From the outset of analysis Mr. X found talking about himself difficult, preferring to dissect the difficulties of others. He attended assiduously, used the couch, and behaved in all outward respects like an analytic patient. He brought dreams but could not discuss them. He spoke intermittently yet honestly, touching briefly on a topic only to leave it before moving on to another. Elaborating upon any theme or linking element that seemed potentially integrative was inhibited. If I raised this problem, his response was one of heightened anxiety, eventually accompanied by barely concealed anger at my attempts to undermine his best efforts. Mr. X seemed to need to keep me excluded from his mind, and provided he could achieve this he was willing to proceed. During the second year I told him that the strength of his controls prevented the possibility of the very analytic work he had sought out when he contacted me. He took this seriously and agreed with me, but it had little effect on his need to forestall loss of control. Eventually, I suspected that he felt I would throw him out if he were to reveal to me his thoughts and feelings, and again he agreed with this sincerely but it did little to reduce his vigilance. The first problem I discovered was that Mr. X had mastered a way of talking that was conversational (with seemingly appropriate affect); however, on inspection, his talk was nonspecific and the affect thin. He could appear to attend directly to any point made to him, and offered responses that seemed thoughtful and plausible. However, these responses were idiosyncratic in that they were directed to a specific aspect of what I had said to him—a secondary or tertiary point and not to the meaning of the main point being made. He free-associated in an apparently connected way but with an underlying investment in matters that were tangential and unconsciously overdetermined. Mr. X's responses were, I discovered, driven by an internally phobic attitude to a nonspecific, felt threat. I should stress the *organized* quality of Mr. X's discourse, which is also a different emphasis to the one Green gives in his paper. Mr. X was not able to respond (retroactively) with alarm to an interpretation that worried him and then discuss his anxieties—the "worry" needed to be effaced, as Green indicates—but the systemic organization of this activity was striking. The second problem I discovered was when Mr. X felt under imminent threat as a result of rising feelings of disorganization. He could regress sharply to a place where he would introduce a distress-filled, standardized form of speech. For example: "I don't like thinking about those things [*sharp, angry, distressed*]. I can't think about them. I get upset and confused," or "Yes, it's just that there's no point ... [*pause, distressed*] ... I think I should have protected myself more [*Pause*] Oh dear ... I am feeling upset and confused."

His statements about being "upset and confused" were infrequent and occurred only when the "gate-keeping" function of his deformed use of free association had been seriously compromised by anxieties overlapping and escalating into a confusional state. A negative hallucination of his mental state took place. The effect of the "upset and confused" states of mind was to take us back to states of mind from the beginning of analysis when he was often paralyzed and unable to think about conflicts. When Mr. X felt he was in relative control of the discourse we generated, he did not need to revert to the standardized "language of crisis." Over an extended period, it became more clear that Mr. X was terrified of collapse into a psychotic confusion comprising multiple disasters, one common factor of which was that he had no control whatsoever over the whereabouts, proximity, condition, or intentions of his objects. He felt that any catastrophe could plunge him into confusion and "objectless insanity" (abandonment and psychosis). His mother's illness; his rage against his unavailable, overbearing father; the wholesale dysfunction of his family that was never addressed let alone helped; and, above all, his bitter disillusionment at both parents' failure to be parents that underlay his ensuing omnipotent isolation that he felt had ruined his life—all were singly or in combination capable of destroying him, as he had believed them to be in infancy. As the meaning of these crises was investigated, so Mr. X's demeanor in the analysis changed radically. He became openly depressed, persecuted, and tearful, and often felt utterly hopeless. He also became bitterly oppositional in our work together, yet paradoxically more straightforwardly cooperative in our efforts to make sense of his "virtual" way of communicating in contrast to his underlying fears of an unavoidable descent into madness. Finally, the person whose representative had so fervently requested analysis years earlier had emerged.

CONCLUSION

Green's paper on the central phobic position is clinically useful as it opens up a way of listening which allows the analyst understanding of forms of negativity in certain borderline patients that cannot be interpreted in terms of their direct relationship with the destructive drives. They show themselves obliquely as nuclei of what Green terms "retroactive reverberation": an element uttered acquires meaning if retroactive echoes are highlighted, revealing how the power of their meaning (deriving from a core trauma) persists long after the discourse carrying them has died out. Identifying the presence of these traumatic elements and how, via "associative radiation," their phobic functioning can become installed within communication itself, allows for analysis of chronic anxieties that might otherwise remain obscured by what I have termed a "virtual" character structure. The temporal and transference implications for the nonlinear psychic presence of the reverberations of the core trauma and its impact on the patient's attitude to free association, and hence the relationship to the analyst, constitute an advance in the understanding of borderline thinking, an earlier outline of which can be found in Green's theory of borderline functioning (Green, 1975). A further implication of the problem of free associating that Green identifies lies in its capacity for identification of potential psychotic confusional states and their "echo" in unintegrated, unconscious part-object relationships.

REFERENCES

Freud, S. (1900). The interpretation of dreams. In J. Strachey (Ed. & Trans.), *The standard edition of the complete psychological works of Sigmund Freud* (Vol. 4–5). London: Hogarth Press.

Freud, S. (1918). From the history of an infantile neurosis. In J. Strachey (Ed. & Trans.), *The standard edition of the complete psychological works of Sigmund Freud* (Vol. 17). London: Hogarth Press.

Freud, S. (1925). Negation. In J. Strachey (Ed. & Trans.), *The standard edition of the complete psychological works of Sigmund Freud* (Vol. 19). London: Hogarth Press.

Freud, S. (1950). Project for a scientific psychology. In J. Strachey (Ed. & Trans.), *The standard edition of the complete psychological works of Sigmund Freud* (Vol. 1). London: Hogarth Press.

Green, A. (1975). *On private madness*. London: Hogarth Press

Green, A. (1997). The intuition of the negative in playing and reality. *International Journal of Psychoanalysis*, 78, 1071–1084.

Green, A. (1999a). *The fabric of affect and psychoanalytic discourse*. London: Routledge.

Green, A. (1999b). *The work of the negative*. London: Free Association.

Green, A. (2000). The central phobic position. *International Journal of Psychoanalysis*, 81, 429–451.

Lacan, J. (1977). On a question preliminary to any possible treatment of psychosis. In *Ecrits* (pp. 179–225). New York: Norton.

Williams, P. (2002). *Key papers on borderline states*. London: Karnac.

Winnicott, D. W. (1949/1957). Birth trauma, birth memories and anxiety. In *Collected papers* (pp. 174–193). New York: Basic Books.

Winnicott, D. W. (1962). The aims of psycho-analytical treatment. In *The maturational processes and the facilitating environment* (pp. 166–170). London: Hogarth.

Chapter 10

Freud-baiting*

Paul Williams, a psychoanalyst and anthropologist, examines the witch-hunt against Freud and psychoanalysis. Is truth now up for sale in the free market economy?

Since the late 1970s, and the publication of the scholarly critique of psychoanalysis by Adolf Grunbaum in the 1980s, together with the release of much of Freud's personal correspondence from the Freud archive, the number of experts on Freud has proliferated. Many, like Grunbaum, are serious scholars attempting to grasp Freud's place in our modernized world. Others, like Frederick Crewes, Jeffrey Masson, Robert Wilcocks, Allen Esterson ("The Culture Essay," May 29), and Gloria Steinem, to name a few, are noteworthy for their efforts to denigrate and, if possible, to undermine Freud's reputation. Why are these people so bitter? I shall argue that there exists a misguided campaign of vilification against Freud, which derives not only from intellectual rivalry, but also an ideological worship of the idea of certainty in "science" (a characteristic of our era) alongside a profound ignorance of psychoanalysis, especially the workings of the unconscious mind.

To say that Freud exerted enormous influence on 20th-century culture is so obvious as to seem banal. His ideas concerning the power of sexuality on the formation of our identity and the way we relate to ourselves and others (from infancy onwards), and his studies of the complexities of the unconscious mind, have rendered "the internal world" an accepted currency among clinicians, philosophers, scientists, writers, artists, and the public. At the same time, psychoanalysis has been subjected to much criticism. This is usually along the lines that it is not proper science. The criticism comes in

---

* This essay was produced in 1994 at the request of *The Sunday Times* in London in reply to Allen Esterson's "Culture Essay" in *The Sunday Times*. Esterson, a writer and critic, portrayed Freud as a scientific fraud, dissembler, hypocrite, and liar. His essay appeared at the height of the "Freud-bashing" era in the 1990s. The opinions given in this reply are mine, and I informed the publisher that I was speaking on my behalf only. I was asked to write the piece in the style of "elevated pub conversation."

sporadic waves (many will remember Eysenck), and we are currently enjoying a bout of it, of which Esterson's article is an example, albeit of a personal and rather unpleasant variety. These assaults are not, as they would have us believe, solely concerned with questions of scientific respectability. Their objective bears more widely on our ideas of freedom of expression and intellectual democracy, in an age when the power of science and access to control over knowledge have never been more prized. Those who wish to smear and dismantle Freud's work seek opportunities to define and manage what the rest of us think and believe about the ways our minds and bodies function. Freud-baiting is a *political* activity. Groups representing certain (often reactionary and ideologizing) branches of science, literature, and politics who spare no effort in their attempts to legitimize and monopolize "truth" view Freud is a special target, not just because he overturned certain preconceptions of conventional science, but because he had the audacity to try to demonstrate how human minds work—something orthodox science, including medicine and psychiatry, has failed to achieve. In addition, he was a literary master who also had a brilliant translator in James Strachey, to the dismay of certain literary professionals. In order to distinguish more valid criticisms of Freud from institutional and political bigotry, we must examine the charges these critics make against psychoanalysis.

FREUD IS NOT SCIENTIFIC

This chestnut could have been heard cracking in any Viennese drawing room fire a century ago. How valid is the charge? Grunbaum's critique of the psychoanalytic scientific method is the most impressive ever undertaken. He concluded that although Freud's theories are capable of meeting the requirements for falsifiability laid down by Karl Popper (criteria justifying the title "scientific"), these cannot be confirmed within the clinical psychoanalytic setting. This is significant criticism (physics has suffered from comparable difficulties), yet few psychoanalysts would argue with it, let alone feel abashed. This is because Grunbaum's study did not set out to address the hermeneutic complexity, in addition to the empirical rigor, with which psychoanalysis observes and interprets mental phenomena. In addition, analysts know that psychoanalysis has come a long way since the time of Freud. Existing theories have evolved, new theories have emerged, and many of Freud's ideas have been proven to be true through overwhelming clinical observation, while others have not. Psychoanalysts themselves have been lax in presenting the substantial body of evidence that now exists to support the scientific validity of psychoanalysis. It is within their capacity to do so and it would help their cause.

If critics of Freud know that modern psychoanalysis is not the same as Freud's original work, why do they get so worked up? Their witch-hunt is not merely about *how* Freud worked but about *what* he discovered. By attacking the founder of psychoanalysis, they hope to destroy the discovery that has enabled human beings to radically alter the way they think about themselves and the world. Freud struggled to approach an astonishing domain of human existence—*the unconscious mind*—for which no systematic explanation was available. Of course, the unconscious mind existed before Freud, but he was the first to try to properly explain it in psychological terms. Think of your own fantasies, grudges, daydreams, sexual and aggressive imaginings. These are *conscious* thoughts, and unpredictable enough, you might say. What of that subterranean, mental cinema-complex where anarchy reigns, known as your unconscious? One night, you dream you're the boss at work, chairing a meeting, when your mother walks in and says, "He really is quite hopeless, you know." The next night you are wandering along the streets of your childhood, when a policeman tells you that a half pound of butter is missing from your bank manager's briefcase. What on earth is going on? Unconscious images depict, in primary form, our emotional and mental lives. Images join up to form unconscious fantasies. These may take the form of dreams, and they can influence waking life. Some unconscious fantasies can last a lifetime. If they are damaging, they can give rise to illness, even to the abuse of children, rape, or murder. Other people may spend their lives searching for Mr. or Mrs. Right, or convinced everyone hates them, and so on. We *all* have unconscious fantasies, and they are discerned through dreams and ways in which the unconscious "leaks" into consciousness and behavior.

Freud studied consciousness and the unconscious in the spirit of 19th century scientific inquiry. After failing to account for psychological functioning along neurological lines he created a new vocabulary—*psychoanalysis*—forged from conventional scientific observation and hermeneutic inquiry. The hermeneutic method involves interpretation of phenomena not always immediately apparent to or measurable by the observer, in order to acquire knowledge of their meaning(s). This branch of science has a long and respectable history, and is used by philosophers (Schopenhauer, Nietzsche, Heidegger, Husserl, Habermas, etc.) and by social scientists to study culture and morality (Weber, Goffman, Foucault). It is taught in most universities today. Certain scientists and academics consider that anything other than "pure" science is suspect. Contemporary, "pure" science has grown in iconic appeal over recent years due to its seductive promises of certainty, thereby increasing the numbers of people who have turned to its high-tech truths for intellectual security.

What led Freud to use the methods he did? He and subsequent analysts found the unconscious to be immensely contradictory and labile. It can say one thing, then promptly deny it. Black can become white, white black. Life can feel wonderful (even though you're depressed), good can feel bad, bad good. Your own dreams can confirm this. Empirical observation and hermeneutic study by Freud and generations of psychoanalysts have revealed specific laws governing the operations of the unconscious. Freud-baiters cannot deal with this evidence. They insist upon a solely intellectu-alist appraisal of psychoanalysis and the unconscious. A strictly rationalist critique is, however, inadequate to account for the surreal, elusive phenom-ena of the unconscious. An inability or unwillingness to join in any meth-odological debate concerning the unconscious forces critics to remain mute regarding its existence and meaning. "Pure" science cannot define it; Freud's methods are discounted using truth criteria employed élitistly. Meanwhile, the unconscious continues to exist, dreams are dreamt, patients suffer, and psychoanalysts try to help them.

FREUD WAS A LIAR

Here enters a shrill, last ditch argument, often voiced by literary Freud-baiters in particular, who leap on Freud's "change of mind" regarding the seduction theory. The correspondence regarding his case histories is used as evidence against Freud. These charges are specious: Freud may have had many of the faults of a Victorian patriarch, but he was no liar. He believed his female patients to have been seduced. He later believed that fantasies of seduction occurred, and he was open about it. Intellectual honesty and a willingness to review unflinchingly his previous theories were characteris-tics of Freud's work throughout his life. Analysts, and many other mental health workers, know that many patients experience fantasies of seduction. They also know that many patients have been seduced and abused, difficult though this may be to prove. The two groups are not coterminous, and discerning the truth of abuse in a given case is a delicate undertaking that takes into account factors other than fantasies (a factor of importance in the "false memory" debate). Extensive research over the past 20 years has confirmed this, and yet despite this valuable work, the psychoanalyst may never know with certainty the full truth.

Freud "the liar" is accused of claiming therapeutic successes that were later proved not to be so (Anna O. and Serge Pankejeff, "The Wolf Man," are sometimes cited). Has a clinician never before believed a patient to be improved, even cured, only for the patient to fall ill again, often years later? Does this constitute an ethical scandal, or a lie? To suggest, as Esterson does, that Freud should have had the clinical knowledge we have today to enable him to discern his patients' more complex pathology (or more absurdly, that he had it and didn't use it) is like castigating the inventor of the horse and cart for not having come up with the motor car while he was at it.

The "Freud the liar" argument derives from a limited, *cognitive*-based appraisal of Freud's work by literary critics, an approach which paral-lels in narrowness the objectivism of some "pure" scientists. Both groups insist on remaining oblivious to the dimension of unconscious mental life, including, it would seem, their own. The result has been a series of shallow, one-dimensional, partisan critiques that sound more like mechanical descriptions of a Cézanne or a Vermeer than the paintings themselves. A list of colors, chemical compounds of the paint, and number of brushes used are given, from which the work is judged. Absent is any embrace of the forces that impel these creations in the first place, or of the technical achievements involved. Practicing psychoanalysis is akin to restoring a painting, in fact. Patient and analyst attempt together to lift the grime and wear of the years without damaging the original underneath. Where damage appears, repair is carefully undertaken in accordance with, as far as is possible, the intentions of the creator—the self of the patient. The process is a science *and* an art.

PSYCHOANALYSIS DOESN'T WORK

This brings us to the final criticism by the Freud-baiters, and one that is not only erroneous but offensive to analysts and patients. It would be foolish to say that there are not bad analysts or failed analyses—of course there are, as there are failures in any professional group. However, in competent hands psychoanalysis is, for many patients, a very powerful and successful treatment method. In addition, Freud and psychoanalysis effectively invented the "talking treatments" which, in the last 50 years, have acquired a central place in psychiatry around the world, including in the British National Health Service. We now *talk* to people about their disturbed behavior and their mental problems.

Human beings grow and flourish psychologically when their inner selves experience and assimilate the deepest emotional truths that being alive arouses. They need to be bonded to others to achieve this. To acquire psychological health is no less than a creative *oeuvre*, requiring an appropriate setting. For many this is the home. Others, whose formative years fail them, never settle in their personalities until they re-find themselves. The careers of many artists, scientists, and ordinary people are testimonies to this search. It can be a difficult and painful undertaking, which many people avoid. In the past 15 years, reactionary politics, behaviorism, "pure" science, and high-speed, high-tech consumerism have striven to deter us from the complex task of maturing. Illusions of immediate gratification and success are commodities peddled to maintain this deception, and they can now include "truth," whether religious, scientific, or political. The commercialization of everything affects knowledge as much as any other area of life. In reality, understanding the world and oneself is immensely difficult. Psychoanalysis is committed to this task using scientific skills of an observational and interpretive nature, art and, unfashionably, patience.

WHY ARE SO MANY ATTACKS ON FREUD OCCURRING NOW?

I think the period since 1989 has been horribly sobering. Take away the Cold War and what do you get? Peace? Fraternal love? Generosity of spirit? No, you get, as Freud observed, the return of the (literally and militarily) repressed. We are now having to face in more complex forms the destructive, ungenerous, and murderous side of human nature. The desiccation of compassion is apparent in the escalation of drug abuse and drug-related killings, mass and serial murders, the Jamie Bulger case, the annihilation of children on the streets of Brazil, Jeffrey Dahmer, Frederick West, the Soviet and East European Mafia, Yardies, and so on. Remove an evil empire as a scapegoat in which to locate everything negative, and you must face up to the destructive impulses of your own country, your region, your city, your neighborhood, your ethnicity, your kids' school, yourself. I think this arduous self-reflection leads to a hatred of the way of thinking that has the most to say about these things—psychoanalysis. So let's get Freud. He brought up all this stuff. He said that civilization was a veneer over polymorphous perversity, incest, rapaciousness—man as a wolf to other men. He said neurosis was the price of civility, God damn him. He must be a cheat, a liar, and anyway all his followers f... their patients, don't they? The analysts and therapists are held responsible for evoking those things *that I cannot bear to know about my friends, my family, and myself.*

Unless the Freud-baiters can provide a coherent critique of psychoanalytic methodology, particularly in relation to the unconscious mind (and propose their own alternative at the same time) they should, in time-honored fashion, put up or shut up. Otherwise, their legacy will come to be seen as a brand of unbridled, narrow moralizing which too often characterizes the age in which we live.

Chapter 11

Notes on "notes upon a case of obsessional neurosis" (Freud, 1909)*

This chapter reviews Freud's famous paper on the "Rat Man," placing it in context with regard to the subsequent evolution of psychoanalytic concepts. The origins and fate of Freud's ideas on obsessional-compulsive thinking in contemporary psychoanalytic thinking are discussed, including some comments on the author's clinical views of obsessionality.

"Notes upon a Case of Obsessional Neurosis" occupies a particular place in the psychoanalytic literature as it is one of the earliest full accounts of a psychoanalysis produced. It is of great historical interest in that it provides a picture of the theoretical and technical development of psychoanalysis in 1907 (when Freud began the case), but interest in the paper goes beyond history. The account is captivating due to its detail and to Freud's prescient attention at the time to small amounts of data, the importance of which would only become properly understood in the light of subsequent theoretical developments years later. It is also true that as a literary account of the internal world of an obsessional individual, the paper makes for compelling reading. This is in part because it was conceived of as a "demonstration" by Freud of how to understand the meaning of obsessional-compulsive neurosis, something that had hitherto eluded medicine and psychology. The paper, along with the original record of the notes on the case made by Freud (which appears immediately after the paper in the *Standard Edition*), conveys the quality of the relationship between the analytic couple, their respective characters, the patient's internal world, the analytic setting and atmosphere, the methods by which analysis was conducted, and what Freud made of a mass of confusing information. It is therefore informative at many levels.

Because of the place of this case in the developing theory of psychoanalysis and the fullness of its clinical record, it has been subject to scrutiny and interpretation by a range of commentators. There has also been criticism as well as appreciation. In particular, some castigated Freud for what appear to be

---

* An earlier version of this chapter appeared in R. J. Perelberg, *Freud: A modern reader* (pp. 177–188). © 2005 Routledge.

departures from "classical" technique through his use of supportive, social, and didactic ways of communicating. Others defended Freud's actions, and both sides of this argument will be considered. Freud has also been charged with claiming a level of improvement in the patient that was not sustained, although it will be argued below that this is a less tenable criticism.

THE MAIN THEMES IN THE CASE OF THE "RAT MAN"

The pseudonym "Rat Man" carries unfortunate, pejorative overtones for someone with a crippling obsessional illness. The patient was Paul Lorenz; in his 20s he came to see Freud with symptoms that he had suffered since childhood, and which had grown in intensity during the previous 4 years. The theme of his troubles had for a long time been a fear that something terrible would happen to his father and a woman he (Lorenz) loved. Lorenz had found himself caught up in a temptation to marry another woman, instead of the woman he loved and had planned to marry. This conflict created indecision and torment in him and he became trapped by an impossible choice, as he saw it, between following his parents' (particularly his father's) wishes and his own desires. He was also sorely troubled by anxieties over an aunt who had died.

Lorenz had experienced disturbing impulses such as a desire to cut his throat or to commit suicide in other ways, and he had imposed prohibitions on himself that restricted his life to the point of despair. Freud was confronted by a bright, shrewd young man whose emotional, sexual, and social development had been stunted by obsessional thinking, the roots of which appeared to stretch back into infancy. The analysis began and, under instruction from Freud to speak frankly, Lorenz proceeded to recount his troubles. He talked of his longstanding low opinion of himself, and of how he had sought support from his peers to try to get help with this. He mentioned a young man who had befriended him: This friendship was a ruse, it had turned out, as it was designed only to gain access to Lorenz's sister. Lorenz had felt betrayed, describing it as the "first great blow of my life." He also described his precocious sexual life, beginning at age 4 or 5 when he had undertaken clandestine explorations of his governess' genitals. His interest in the female body intensified during childhood through numerous voyeuristic incidents and occasions of sexual contact with servant girls. Freud notes that "looking was the same as touching" for Lorenz, and this is interesting in the light of Freud stating later that avoidance of contact and personal touching lie at the center of obsessional neurosis. Lorenz experienced erections from the age of about 6 and felt anxious about these and his persistent desires to see women naked. He worried that his parents knew of his thoughts and wishes, and was already (by 6) terrified and depressed by the notion that his father might die. Katherine, his sister, had died at the height of his infantile neurosis and this was clearly a severe loss.

Lorenz proceeded to recount to Freud his many adult fears, the crisis over the two potential spouses, and his fear of contravening his father's wishes, the latter having occupied a central place in his narrative. He spoke of a bizarre incident that was to become a motif of the analysis. It had taken place during military exercises in which Lorenz had participated prior to starting his analysis. On an occasion before a march, Lorenz had lost his *pince-nez*. He had contacted his optician for another pair rather than delay his colleagues but then, after the march had begun and the soldiers had stopped for a break, Lorenz had sat between two officers, one of whom (a captain) recounted a particularly gruesome punishment of criminals in the East. With difficulty and much encouragement from Freud, Lorenz revealed the details of the punishment. The criminal is tied up and placed face down; a bucket is put upside down on his buttocks and rats are placed in it. Gradually they bore their way into the man's body through his anus. Freud comments in his paper on Lorenz's horror of the pleasure he (Lorenz) unwittingly took in recounting the story. Lorenz revealed to Freud that he had had a particular thought as the officer had been describing the punishment: that the torture was happening to someone very dear to Lorenz, possibly to the woman he loved. He added that on the evening of the day he had been told the story, the same officer handed him a package containing his new *pince-nez*, saying that another officer had paid the charges and Lorenz should reimburse him. Unaccountably, Lorenz became convinced that he should *not* reimburse the officer, or else the rat torture would happen to his father or the woman Lorenz loved. This was in turn followed by making a vow that he *must* pay back the money. Lorenz tried to pay back the money but his ambivalence gained the upper hand and he failed. When he eventually did speak to the officer who had paid the charges, he was told by him, most confusingly, that in fact *another* man had paid the charges. Lorenz resolved his dilemma in concrete fashion by deciding to go with *both* men to the post office, give the money to the young woman behind the counter, and she would give it to the second man who had paid the charges. Lorenz would then pay the *first* man the same amount, thereby keeping his vow. Freud makes an interesting comment about the session in which this disturbing material arose: At one point Freud reassures Lorenz that he (Freud) is personally not fond of cruelty like the captain and has no wish to torment his patient. Freud adds that Lorenz referred to him as "Captain" during the session. As will be seen, the transference implications of Freud's comment had powerful repercussions, not all of which were taken up by Freud.

In subsequent sessions Lorenz elaborated the story of his obsessional vow to repay the money. There is a long, complex account of his unresolved ruminations, and a recovery of a memory that complicated the issue further. Lorenz had been told by yet another officer *prior to* the day he heard the rat-torture story that it was actually the woman at the post office who had paid the mail charges. The "cruel" captain had obviously been mistaken and somewhere in Lorenz's mind (given the timing of these events) he must have known this but he had nevertheless proceeded to make his vow on the basis that the captain's version was correct. This distortion of reality resulted in endless self-torment. In the ensuing weeks and months after hearing about the rat-torture, Lorenz was haunted by his insistent (misplaced) vow to repay the officer, to the point of ingeniously developing the idea that if he could show the officer a doctor's certificate stating that Lorenz's health was at stake if he didn't repay the money, this would persuade him to accept it. It was while caught up with this notion of getting a doctor to support the contention that he was ill that Lorenz found his way to Freud's office. These bizarre, baffling events were followed by a lengthy report to Freud of Lorenz's father's emphysema, which had finally killed him 9 years earlier. In particular, Lorenz mentioned a conversation with the family doctor at the height of his father's illness. He had asked the doctor when the danger would be over and was told "the evening of the day after tomorrow." Thinking his father would be better by then, he rested only to be woken up a short while later to be told that his father had died. He reproached himself for not being present and subsequently found himself denying the reality of his father's death. His obsessional self-accusations became worse, culminating in incapacitation, thoughts of suicide, and fears of what would happen to him in the next world. In the analysis, Freud makes a point of taking extremely seriously Lorenz's guilty feelings, but emphasizes to Lorenz that the source of his guilt must lay elsewhere, as they both knew that he had not committed any criminal or cruel act against his father. In fact, Freud gives Lorenz what amounts to pedagogical instruction in the difference between unconscious and conscious thinking, linking these to Lorenz's history of oedipal anxieties, his preoccupation with his father's death, and the violently conflicted feelings underlying these. Lorenz was fascinated by and resistant to Freud's ideas, but his need to confide his troubles and his positive transference to Freud helped him to overcome much of his wariness and he continued to disclose his childhood anxieties. These included falling in unrequited love at the age of 12 with his sister's friend and imagining that if she knew of a misfortune he'd suffered (e.g., his father's death) she would be more affectionate towards him. Freud pursued the possibility of this potential misfortune being a wish as well as a fear in Lorenz's mind, and Lorenz proceeded to divulge other examples of similar oedipal constellations of thoughts. Freud and Lorenz discussed in detail his childhood wishes and fears as they emerged in various guises and in different relationships. In the process, Freud built up a picture of Lorenz's strongly ambivalent feelings towards his father. Freud realized that when Lorenz's father did actually die, his obsessional symptoms worsened because the death became unconsciously indistinguishable for Lorenz from the fantasized consequences of his wishes to see his father dead. In all, the analysis, Freud reports, lasted 11 months and was a painstaking effort by both partners, but particularly by Freud, to unravel an array of infantile ideas and distortions of reality that had rendered internal and external reality impossibly confusing for Lorenz.

FREUD'S THINKING

Freud's summary of the case, of which the above is the briefest outline, was used by him as a platform to demonstrate his thinking and ideas, as much it was to record a clinical case of analytic treatment. This is reflected in the structure of the paper. Having presented an account of the history of the patient's difficulties and Freud's own understanding of them, he moves to a more discursive examination of the psychological phenomena of obsessional ideas, and in the final section provides a theoretical overview of obsessionality and its place in analytic thinking. We are led from the clinical detail "ever upward" towards a broader perspective that culminates in a theoretical contextualization of the meaning of symptoms otherwise deemed to be incomprehensible—a veritable *tour de force* of psychological and literary exposition.

Freud employs a variety of interrelated concepts in discussing the meaning of Lorenz's illness. His concern is to render comprehensible symptoms that appear to have neither motive nor meaning. He does this by bringing disturbed ideas into a temporal and experiential framework—when, how, and under what circumstances did the symptoms arise? An example is Lorenz's impulsive wishes to kill himself. Freud notes how these related to feelings of loss and rage when separated from the person he loved (his girlfriend in particular). There were also indirect wishes to commit suicide, one of which was linked to a period when Lorenz decided he was too fat and underwent drastic exercise to get slim. During runs in the mountains he occasionally felt the impulse to throw himself off a cliff. Analysis uncovered that his disturbed thinking was linked to an English cousin, Dick, who had at one time been attracted to Lorenz's girlfriend while on holiday in the same location. It transpired that sexual rivalry underlay these particular suicidal impulses (interestingly, *dick* in German means "fat"). Lorenz's obsessional thinking took other forms. For example, he could overprotect his girlfriend, including from fantasized accidents that might befall her. When apart from her for any length of time he became at one point obsessed by a need to understand each syllable spoken to him by others, as though he risked losing a priceless treasure (it is not difficult to imagine this to be, among other things, an echo of the loss of his sister). The problem turned out to be linked to having misconstrued or distorted something his girlfriend had said: He believed (wrongly) that she had indicated she no longer wanted to have anything to do with him. When he was corrected he vowed never to misunderstand anyone again, in order to avoid such mental torment. These doubts, protection fantasies, and fears of accidents and death were, Freud argues, the products of disavowed hostility towards his girlfriend. Lorenz experienced feelings of unmanageable hatred alongside his love and avoided recognition of this by keeping the affects apart and through use of intellectual rationalization. The conflict between love and hate was of prime importance in all Lorenz's relationship difficulties.

Reflecting on the precipitating causes of Lorenz's illness, the significance of which had been lost on the patient (although he had not forgotten the circumstances), Freud comments on an important difference between hysteria and obsessionality. In the former, "it is the rule that the precipitating causes of the illness are overtaken by amnesia no less than the infantile experiences by whose help the precipitating causes are able to transform their affective energy into symptoms" (1909, p. 195). The amnesia is the consequence of repression. Obsessional neuroses do not exhibit the same erosion or loss of impact on consciousness. Although some amnesia may mask the infantile precondition of the illness, the precipitating causes and their circumstances are retained in the memory. Patients remember something of the start and course of the illness, and may, by recounting their self-reproaches, provide indicators of the unconscious origins of their troubles. The principle of a relationship between manifest and latent content is fundamental to psychoanalysis, but Freud is noting here how in obsessional neuroses the links are more accessible through patients' conscious awareness of symptoms and their associations to them.

Lorenz's recounting of a conflict between his desire for a particular girl and the woman he planned to marry (his wealthy young relative) signaled, to Freud, the point at which Lorenz had become most seriously incapacitated. Freud was very interested in the conflict between Lorenz's desire for the girl and the persisting influence of his father, as it not only reflected Lorenz's oedipal difficulties but also mirrored the way in which the father himself had married into the same wealthy family. Lorenz had found himself paralyzed by indecision and unable to work, and Freud points to the symptom not merely being a consequence of the illness but a *cause* of it. Freud suggests that Lorenz was identified, through his incapacity, with his father who had been in a similar position. Lorenz's conflict with his father was, at the same time, an ancient one as could be seen from Lorenz's precocious sexual life. Although he had by and large got on well with his father, despite a few overt conflicts, his persecuted sexual fantasies as a child (e.g., that his father would die and that he [Lorenz] would thereby secure the attentions of a certain little girl) indicated to Freud very long-standing oedipal problems. Interestingly, in the transference, a fantasy of marrying Freud's daughter "for her money" arose within a short time of beginning the analysis.

Freud pieces together Lorenz's "Father Complex," including its relation to the rat torture, in a series of steps that take into account Lorenz's
masturbatory fantasies, his longing for his father and his battles with him
(especially over his choice of a girl), and a complex story of a beating by the
father in which Lorenz had flown into a fury and following which, he told
Freud, he had "become a coward," fearing physical violence. Freud was
further able to grasp the father-son relationship in the transference through
Lorenz's fear that Freud would turn violently against him. Another source
of conflict with his father was discovered via a memory of how his father
had once not repaid a debt from his time in the army. Its identificatory
significance in relation to Lorenz's own obsessional guilt about repaying
the *pince-nez* postage money was not lost on Freud. Lorenz had long felt
feelings of condemnation towards his father for not settling his debts, and
was again identified with him. To complicate matters further, it turned
out that the confusion surrounding the two officers was also linked to the
earlier confusion in Lorenz's life between the two girls with whom he had
been involved.

In the midst of all this ambivalence and sexualized thinking, the rat-
torture story (imparted to Lorenz by a male figure of authority) had a profound impact on his imagination. Freud states that the story stimulated
a number of instincts, the most important of which was *anal erotism*,
which had been active in Lorenz since childhood. The rats were endowed
with multiple symbolic meanings that were associated to by Lorenz: These
included money, "installments" (*raten* in German), gambling debts (*spiel-
ratte*), syphilitic infection (reflecting Lorenz's fantasies of his father's life in
the military), penis, worms (Lorenz had suffered a roundworm infection
as a child), anal intercourse, marriage (*heiraten*), the Rat-Wife from Ibsen's
Little Eyolf, children, and biting cruelty (an association to the gnawing teeth
of rats). Lorenz had himself bitten people as a child and had experienced
many sadistic impulses—not least, of course, towards his father. Rats as a
symbol of children (including himself) and of cruel wishes and lascivious-
ness became a hallmark of the analysis. Freud links all these associations in
a brilliant reading of the psychological significance of obsessionality in the
context of the precipitating circumstances, the patient's unconscious and
affective life (particularly his conflicts with the figures close to him), and
his childhood fantasies (including infantile theories of childbirth).

THE ROOT OF THE IDEAS IN FREUD'S THINKING

In the final section of Freud's paper (preceding the addendum comprising
the notes on the case), Freud provides a series of theoretical reflections that
follow from the material of the case. He begins, however, by criticizing his
own earlier views on obsessionality as being over-inclusive. He had linked

them, in 1896, to repression and sexual activity in childhood, but revises this in light of the heterogeneity of psychic states that can be gathered together in obsessional thinking. Almost anything may be drawn in to suit the obsessional's agenda. He comments on the delirium-like hybrid nature of the mental opposition that accompanies obsessionality—patients, in their fight against their obsessional thoughts, both reject and accept aspects of the disordered thinking, and this leads to chronic conflict and indecision. This struggle takes place at a conscious, secondary level but also at a primary level, as can often be seen in obsessionals' dreams. Mishearing, misrepresentation, and distortion of language and ideas characterize obsessionality, Freud argues, and the means of self-deception involve elliptical thinking and "forgetting" (the omission of ideas so as to avoid recognition of conflict—"errors of memory" as Freud calls them). Superstition and chronic doubting are further outcomes of these maneuvers. Freud does not explore in any detail unconscious processes of thought in obsessionality, partly because of their obscurity and complexity. He deals mainly with the phenomenology of the condition, its mental characteristics, and its instinctual sources. His argument as to *why* obsessionality arises is, as outlined earlier, that there is a withdrawal of affect from the causes of the original conflict, which is felt to be unmanageable. This does not lead to amnesia but to severance of mental connections; nevertheless, these connections persist in making themselves felt in shadowy form, via projection onto the external world.

Freud makes reference to omnipotence of thinking in obsessional neurosis—not omnipotent to the extent of generating delusions, but expressed as an overestimation of subjective powers. This exaggerated thinking is viewed by Freud as a residual megalomania from infancy. One manifestation of this in Lorenz, and in other obsessional patients, is a preoccupation with death: either worrying about how long they or someone else will live, a fear that someone loved will die, or idiosyncratic superstitions around death. Freud links this to Lorenz's confused, unresolved conflicts of love and hatred in relation to his girlfriend and his father, and in turn contextualizes these within the framework of instinct theory. Freud places emphasis on Lorenz's disavowed hostile feelings towards his father as having greatly intensified his obsessional illness. At the same time he discusses how persistent conflict involving loving and hating could have come about during what he calls the "prehistoric" period of infancy when the two opposing attitudes may have been split apart and one of them (the hatred) is repressed. Only such an early conflict between love and hate could account for the scope and chronicity of Lorenz's symptoms, Freud suggests.

Freud's concluding theoretical remarks are concerned with the obsessional's pervasive uncertainty and compulsion to override the uncertainty. Freud's ideas are grounded in his theory of instincts and he uses this to explain the certain psychological forms obsessional neurosis takes. The sexual instincts, particularly the scopophilic and epistemophilic instincts, are invoked as driving forces behind the obsessional's conflicts. This instinctual pressure leads to processes of distortion and generalization that disconnect the primary conflict from its representational forms. Analysis of psychological deformations of thinking inherent in obsessionality is a potentially productive research path, and an under-investigated one, Freud believes.

We can see from this cursory examination that Freud's theoretical and technical thinking reflects the developmental stage reached by psychoanalysis in 1907–1909. Freud makes maximal use of his theories of sexuality and the role of the sexual drives in shaping the representational forms of obsessional conflicts. Sadism and ambivalence are conceptual tools employed to understand the hostility in obsessions, but Freud remarks that "the relation between the negative factor in love and the sadistic components of the libido remains completely obscure" (Freud, 1909, p. 240). He will take up this problem again in "Instincts and their Vicissitudes" (1915) and in Chapter 4 of "The Ego and the Id" (1923). Freud's elaboration of the father-son relationship in Lorenz's analysis derives from sexual conflicts he saw as underlying the relationship. One of Freud's key reconstructions in the analysis was that Lorenz's memories of being castigated and beaten by his father were due to his having masturbated. Obviously, this could not be proven conclusively, but he used it to link the sexual and sadistic aspects of the conflict more closely. Freud was able to interpret transference activity towards the father but certain aspects were to escape him. As Mahony (1986) suggests, this is because Freud had understood the connection between obsessional character and anal erotism but not the link between the latter and obsessional neurosis. Freud knew well that it was not only a conflict between love and hate that drove Lorenz's illness; it was made particularly complex by pleasure, shame, and disgust at the feelings and ideas associated with the conflict. Psychoanalytic theory at this point in its development could not account for the regressive, primitive nature of these states of mind.

We can also see how Freud employs a topographical model of the mind to understand Lorenz, dividing him into a personality that had disintegrated into three areas: an unconscious comprising suppressed passionate and cruel impulses, a conscious that is plagued by symptoms, and a preconscious engaged in creating the superstitious and ritualistic behavior designed to counter his unconscious impulses (cf. Holland, 1975). Finally, reconstruction plays a central role in Freud's theory of technique. In other words, Freud sets out to identify gaps in the history of Lorenz and proceeds to fill them in, building up his explanatory schema as he continues. The evolution of a transference neurosis, which would be of central importance to analysts today, was recognized by Freud only in part and played a much more subsidiary role in the treatment than did reconstruction.

THE FATE OF THE IDEAS IN FREUD'S THINKING

Freud's linking of obsessional thinking to anal erotism is a clinical insight that should not be underestimated, especially as knowledge of the connection between obsessive-compulsive neurosis and anal regression only emerged in 1926—20 years after Lorenz's analysis. The absence of a theoretical or clinical understanding of the implications of the maternal transference in the paper reflects the point psychoanalysis had reached by 1907. Freud placed relatively little emphasis on the mother-child relationship in the Lorenz case, although there are references to the mother in the full case record. Pregenital psychological development and libidinal organization were to occupy more of the psychoanalytic stage as Freud began to develop his ideas around the occurrence of fixation points that lead to regression and symptom formation. To contemporary readers endowed with the benefit of hindsight, it is possible to interpret the scale of Lorenz's experiences of loss of the object, his rage at these losses, and the concomitant superego activity (often projected into Freud) as evidence of his profound ambivalence in relation to the primary object. This is not to diminish Lorenz's oedipal difficulties, but to note a level of narcissistic injury linked to splitting of the object and the ego, and to projection and ensuing persecution. Another way of thinking about this crisis is to consider the extent to which Lorenz was preoccupied by ridding himself of bad things and preventing their intrusion into himself (Holland, 1975, p. 163). This struggle pervaded his life. Today we might think of splitting and massive projective identification as mechanisms used to forestall a sense of disintegration related to loss of the object. Such vulnerability of the ego and diffusion of the sense of identity began to be addressed more fully by Freud in "Mourning and Melancholia" (1914) and On Narcissism (1915), where he discusses the damage to character that identification with the lost object can create. The developmental implications of these crises have occupied psychoanalysts ever since.

It has been noted how Freud is aware of, and sensitive to, the transference to him, particularly in terms of Lorenz's internal image of his father. However, it would be incorrect to say that Freud had at this point grasped the need for a dynamic analysis of the immediate transference. He did not yet appreciate the extent to which memories of the past are inextricably linked to attitudes in the present, especially to the analyst. Lorenz sees threatening authority figures everywhere, and Freud is no exception, but some commentators (e.g., Kanzer, 1952; Gottlieb, 1989) have criticized Freud because he did not pay sufficient attention to this transference (poor attention to the maternal transference is an unfair charge given the theoretical stage Freud had reached). Mahony (1986) suggests that at that point in Freud's thinking about the case, transference liquidation was not a goal in the analysis, reconstruction and education being the predominant objectives (p. 240). Freud has also been accused of behaving antitherapeutically by reassuring

Lorenz of his benign intentions and of attempting to influence the patient positively using didactic methods. The example of Freud distancing himself from the captain's cruelty while not properly addressing Lorenz's transference picture of him *as* the cruel captain is often cited. Freud also burst out laughing when Lorenz told him that Freud's brother was a murderer who had been executed in Budapest, assuring Lorenz that he had had no relatives living in Budapest. This occurred during a period when Lorenz was terrified that Freud might harm him physically. There is a further, well-known example of Freud providing Lorenz with a meal. Why was Freud unable to address these tense interactions in more depth? The answer may lie in insufficient transference interpretation, but Gottlieb (1989), among others, identifies countertransference tensions in Freud that he was neither theoretically nor technically able to properly address at that stage of his development. The brother-murderer accusation by Lorenz, for example, is viewed by Gottlieb as a variant of a central transference fantasy that pervades Lorenz's analysis, but that this version triggered in Freud particular anxieties linked to having had an uncle who was arrested for criminal activity. Gottlieb pieces together an intriguing argument to support his view (pp. 46–58). Whether or not Gottlieb is correct, it is not unreasonable to infer that Freud's extensive use of explanation and instruction in the reconstructive narrative he created with Lorenz, and some of his spontaneous, nonanalytic actions, were at least in part a response to the countertransference impact of a disturbed and subtly destructive patient. This observation should not be used to compare Freud's standard of work in 1907 to a technical standard of subsequent periods. Lipton (1977) went to some lengths to defend Freud from criticism of his treatment of Lorenz, although Lipton himself has been accused of lapses into polemicism. Two important points made by Lipton are that much of the technique employed by Freud in the Lorenz case later became codified as standard technique in his later papers on technique, and that modern technique expanded greatly in order to deal with the complexity of the analyst-patient relationship, including reducing personal influence and attempts at "corrective emotional experiences." It is therefore inappropriate to compare modern technique with Freud's technique of the time.

CONCLUSION

The case of the Rat Man is best understood today as the presentation of a coherent, compelling narrative account of the form and symptoms of a chronic obsessive illness explored in the context of the development and life history of the patient. The case history has been described as an "aesthetic object" constructed according to study of the central identity theme of the patient (Holland, 1975, p. 168). Although Freud wished to present the paper as a formal scientific account of a psychoanalysis that laid bare the origins of obsessive-compulsive neurosis (his presentation of the case in Vienna was extensive, taking 5 hours), it is more plausible to think of the account as a piece of original, integrative thinking that stretched to the limits the conceptual and methodological tools available to Freud at the time. The scale of the undertaking and the availability of detailed clinical records have inevitably stimulated psychoanalysts from all schools to review the case as psychoanalytic methodology has evolved: Gottlieb (1989), Grunberger (1966), Holland (1975), Reed (1988), Sherwood (1969), and Zetzel (1996) are notable examples. At the time of this writing, an original contemporary contribution that takes as its departure point the transference problems of the "Rat Man" case is a study of ways in which unconscious fantasy and projective identification actually work (Lear, 2002). We need to be grateful to Freud for his insights into Lorenz's difficulties and personality, and for the access we are given to Freud's technique which demonstrated, among many things, an intuitive capacity to "feel into" the world of his patient while retaining analytic objectivity (the way in which Freud "aligns" his thinking and language to Lorenz's is discussed by Mahoney, 1986). We need to be cautious about reaching too swiftly to condemn transference and countertransference failures that were yet to be understood by psychoanalysis. It seems likely that the vicissitudes of countertransference and Freud's explanatory, somewhat didactic technique at the time combined to produce an analytic stance that subsequent generations of analysts would come to regard as insufficiently neutral. A similar qualification applies to Freud's claim that Lorenz was "completely cured." There may have been exaggeration in this claim in order to impress scientifically, but it is likely that, by the standards of the day, the improvement in Lorenz's condition was as significant as Freud claimed to both analyst and patient. With the benefit of hindsight it is possible to argue that a considerable portion of Lorenz's improvement could be attributed to a transference cure. The Rat Man case is a product of its time, but one that reveals analytic skill and insight of a remarkable order. Perhaps the most interesting aspect for readers today is to think about the case in the context of Freud's earlier and later intellectual development. It allows us to participate in the evolution of fundamental psychoanalytic ideas as they emerged.

What of the analytic treatment of obsessionality today? Many analysts do not treat obsessive individuals because of the perceived intractability of the condition. Others, while cognizant and accepting of Freud's insights, pay careful attention to the nature of the chronic anguish that characterizes the obsessional's relations with objects. The potential for contamination and destruction of objects, as far as I have been able to assess in my own work, is often closely allied to powerful traits of omnipotence and omniscience that betray severe anxieties about the fate of objects, and hence of themselves, that underlie the obsessional's elaborate fantasies and fragile self-esteem. The obsessional's controls in relations to objects can, if analyzed systematically from their *emotional meaning*, allow for what I believe to be the affective crisis at the heart of what is a characterological disorder. Rice (2004) put it as follows: "… all of the phenomena of this illness have an inherent meaning and unity of their own and are part of a total and purposeful drama" (p. 23–44). It is the analysis of the life of obsessionals, not of their symptoms, that holds the key to relief of these patients' crippling symptoms, as Freud understood.

REFERENCES

Freud, S. (1909). Notes upon a case of obsessional neurosis. In J. Strachey (Ed. & Trans.), *The standard edition of the complete psychological works of Sigmund Freud* (Vol. 10). London: Hogarth Press.

Freud, S. (1914). On Narcissism: An Introduction. In J. Strachey (Ed. & Trans.), *The standard edition of the complete psychological works of Sigmund Freud*. Vol. 1914–1916, pp.67–102. London: Hogarth Press.

Freud, S. (1915). Instincts and their vicissitudes. In J. Strachey (Ed. & Trans.), *The standard edition of the complete psychological works of Sigmund Freud* (Vol. 14). London: Hogarth Press.

Freud, S. (1917). On Narcissism: An Introduction. In J. Strachey (Ed. & Trans.), *The standard edition of the complete psychological works of Sigmund Freud*. Vol. 1914–1916, pp.237–258. London: Hogarth Press.

Freud, S. (1923). The ego and the id. In J. Strachey (Ed. & Trans.), *The standard edition of the complete psychological works of Sigmund Freud* (Vol. 19). London: Hogarth Press.

Gottlieb, R. (1989). Technique and countertransference in Freud's analysis of the Rat Man. *Psychoanalytic Quarterly*, *58*, 29–62.

Grunberger, B. (1966). Some reflections on the Rat Man. *International Journal of Psychoanalysis*, *47*, 160–168.

Holland, N. (1975). An identity for the Rat Man. *International Review of Psychoanalysis*, *2*, 157–169.

Kanzer, M. (1952). The transference neurosis of the Rat Man. *Psychoanalytic Quarterly*, *21*, 181–189.

Lear, J. (2002). Jumping from the Couch: An Essay on Phantasy and Emotional Structure. *International Journal of Psychoanalysis*, *83*, 583–595.

Lipton, S. (1977). The advantages of Freud's technique as shown in the analysis of the Rat Man. *International Journal of Psychoanalysis*, *58*, 255–273.

Mahony, P. (1986). *Freud and the Rat Man*. New Haven, CT: Yale University Press.

Reed, G. (1988). Freud and the Rat Man. *Psychoanalytic Quarterly*, *57*, 238–241.

Rice, E. (2004). Reflections on the obsessive-compulsive disorders: A psychodynamic and therapeutic perspective. *Psychoanalytic Review*, *91*, 23–44.

Sherwood, M. (1969). *The logic of explanation in psychoanalysis*. New York & London: Academic Press.

Zetzel, E. R. (1966). Additional notes upon a case of obsessional neurosis, Freud 1909. *International Journal of Psychoanalysis*, *47*, 123–129.

Chapter 12

Unimaginable storms
Introduction and conclusion*

DECTORA: Does wandering in these desolate seas
    And listening to the cry of wind and wave
    Bring madness?
FORGAEL: Queen, I am not mad.
DECTORA: Yet say
    That unimaginable storms of wind and wave
    Would rise against me.
FORGAEL: No, I am not mad—
    If it be not that hearing messages
    From lasting watchers, that outlive the moon,
    At the most quiet midnight is to be stricken.
DECTORA: And did those watchers bid you take me
    captive?
FORGAEL: Both you and I are taken in the net.

—Yeats, "The Shadowy Waters" (1906)

The book *Unimaginable Storms: A Search for Meaning in Psychosis* is a clinical account of psychoanalytic work done on a unique ward for patients with psychosis at the Maudsley Hospital in London, the United Kingdom's leading psychiatry training hospital. In the early post–World War II period the theories of psychoanalysis were accorded importance in the teaching of psychiatry. Sir Aubrey Lewis, professor of psychiatry at the Institute of Psychiatry and the Maudsley Hospital, was of the opinion that psychoanalysis should have a place in all psychiatrists' training (Lewis, 1967). His successor, Sir Denis Hill, was even more active (Hill, 1970, 1978), setting up a unit in the Maudsley Hospital for the application of psychoanalytic ideas to the treatment of psychiatric inpatients on a general psychiatry ward. When John Steiner, the first consultant appointed to this unit, eventually

---

* These originally appeared in M. Jackson and P. Williams, *Unimaginable Storms*. © 1994 Karnac Books. Reprinted with permission.

moved from the Maudsley to the Tavistock Clinic in 1975, Murray Jackson was appointed his successor, and for 13 years directed the unit in cooperation with Robert Cawley. Another colleague at the Maudsley whose work influenced the ward significantly was Henri Rey. I joined the ward in the early 1980s and together Murray Jackson and I recorded the ward's work for publication.

Unimaginable Storms contains 10 clinical chapters comprising interviews with a range of patients and covers the main psychotic conditions. The interviews are followed by transcripts of the staff discussions about what had emerged during each interview. What follows below is an extract from the introduction to the book followed by an extract from its conclusion. The purpose of these extracts is to underline two things. First, that the emotional forces involved or released in the course of psychotic illness can at times be of such magnitude, and find expression in such inappropriate and damaging action, that they are often beyond the capacity of the individual psychotherapist to withstand and utilize therapeutically. The individual psychotherapy of such seriously disturbed patients is best approached as the undertaking of a team* comprising complementary skills. The combined abilities of such a team are emphasized in the book because they can create a milieu in which patients discover a container for their disturbed self and from which, in the best cases, they may progress towards an autonomous existence. At the very least they will retain a base in the event of crisis. The sooner patients receive and respond to this constructive assistance the better will be their outlook. In a clear-cut, first-onset case of psychotic disturbance it is usually not difficult to discern the major psychotic preoccupations, prodromal processes, and precipitating events. Tentative reconstruction of the developmental difficulties that have contributed to the patient's predisposition to a psychotic reaction can be undertaken, and a treatment plan to deal with the prevailing crisis can be prepared. However, the longer patients are denied this perspective the more difficult it is likely to be for them to recover from the attack, integrate its place in their life history, and make therapeutic use of its meaning. Of great concern to many clinicians today is the decline in recent years in the provision of such treatment for persons with psychosis. Under the guise of economic rationalization, advances in pharmacological treatments that control symptoms; newer, "quicker" psychological therapies that claim to alter behavior; and the ideology that patients with psychosis are best kept out of the hospital, comprehensive psychiatric and psychotherapeutic

---

* "Team" has become a fashionable term that can at times be used to conceal work of questionable quality behind a facade of collaboration. True teamwork involves the cooperative deployment of different skills in order to reach the best possible decisions and most appropriate treatment. At best it is a sophisticated and psychodynamically complex activity that is more difficult to achieve than is usually recognized (similar considerations apply to the use of the term "group").

treatment for those who might benefit from it is now, regrettably, a rarity. It is important not to decry advances in specific psychiatric treatments that have brought benefit to patients. It is surely essential to decry a situation in which individuals who experience psychosis are increasingly denied the opportunity to talk about their illness so that they may discover its meaning and integrate this into their personality in order to achieve a durable recovery. The author of the book views this situation, which, at the time of writing, is getting worse, not better, as a mental health scandal.

INTRODUCTION

Psychotic disorders bring immense suffering to victims and relatives and constitute the heaviest burden on mental health services throughout the Western world. Although a great deal is known about the nature of these devastating disorders, many conjectures are still to be confirmed or refuted and much remains to be understood. The precise mode of action of biological methods of treatment has yet to be elucidated, and claims for psychoanalysis and its offspring, psychoanalytic psychotherapy, as effective treatments for psychotic disorders have not been substantiated at the level of formal scientific proof. While the definition of psychosis is generally agreed upon, the same cannot be said for the controversial category of schizophrenia, and these two orders of classification bear examination. Psychosis encompasses a wide group of mental disorders, which have in common a serious impairment of the individual's capacity to remain in contact with reality. They are often accompanied by confusion and disorders of thought and perception, which can find expression as delusional thinking and hallucinatory experiences. The causes of an individual psychotic episode or of long-term vulnerability are to be sought in biological, social, or psychological factors. Each of the related disciplines has its own language and method of investigation. Bridges, conceptual and operational, between these disciplines may be difficult, sometimes impossible, to construct. Yet each discipline is relevant, individually or in combination, to the acquisition of a deeper understanding of the nature and treatment of psychosis. The cooperation of different specialists is also needed if the needs of the psychotic individual are to be met fully. It would seem reasonable, under these circumstances, to expect practitioners skilled in particular specialties or subspecialties to acquire a level of general understanding of, or contact with, other disciplines to permit constructive debate to take place. In practice, cooperation appears to be the exception rather than the rule. A change in this position is long overdue, and meanwhile patients pay the price for this delay.

The term "schizophrenia" remains the subject of continuing and growing controversy. Schizophrenia is regarded as a disorder, or group of disorders, within the broader category of psychotic conditions. It is characterized by the prominence of negative and positive symptoms with associated tendencies towards passivity and withdrawal, and activity. Disorders of thought and perception also prevail. The illness seems to arise on a basis of a predisposition, manifested as a vulnerability of biological or psychological origin, or both. It tends towards a chronic course, although recent studies have shown that the long-term outcome is better than has been believed. The presence of structural brain abnormality in a large proportion of cases has been demonstrated by modern neurophysiological research using noninvasive methods which permit direct observation of brain function (for example, see Rubin, Karle, & Moller-Madsen, 1993; McNeil, Cantor-Grace, Nordstrom, & Rosenlund, 1993). Abnormality of biochemistry has been demonstrated in many cases, and although the nature and origin of this is not fully clear, the dramatic suppression of positive symptoms such as hallucinations by antipsychotic drugs during an acute attack is open to no other explanation. Recent advances in the theory and technique of family therapy have brought benefits to many schizophrenic patients and their families. In addition, research and clinical practice in the early detection of patients at risk of breakdown,* of the education of patients and families in methods of stress management,† and of psychological treatments embodying cognitive and behavioral techniques represent major, permanent improvements in the care of schizophrenic patients. The antitherapeutic aspects of traditional mental hospitals are now recognized (Pylkkanen, 1989), and the therapeutic possibilities of care in the community have been accepted. (The wholesale manner in which community care programs have been implemented in many countries at the expense of hospitals has, however, created many problems, not least the difficulty in containing patients sufficiently in order for them to be able to benefit from psychological therapies, where available.) Improving aftercare programs and more professional case-management methods have brought the hope that the isolation and abandonment that faces most schizophrenic patients after discharge from the hospital may one day end. Notwithstanding these impressive developments, the deficiencies in community care provision cited above and an overall neglect of the core problems of the severely mentally ill continue to be reported in the national, international, and medical press as a disgraceful and unnecessary state of affairs. Research into the development of more effective and less potentially dangerous psychotropic and antipsychotic drugs is being zealously pursued by major Western pharmaceutical firms. Despite the overoptimism that frequently accompanies the arrival of these new products, and the well-known toxic consequences of overprescribing,

---

* See Falloon, Boyd, and McGill (1984).
† A field opened up by the work on expressed emotion (EE) of Leff, Kuipers, and Berkowitz (1982).

psychopharmacology has made an inestimable contribution to patient welfare. In the process, public awareness and expectations of more rapid treatment have increased. This expectation is understandable and reasonable; however, it has also contributed to reductionist thinking and a denial of the psychological complexity of psychotic attacks (and hence a need for in-depth treatment). Inadequate government funding for the provision of treatment and aftercare for psychotic patients has frequently generated financial support for charitable organizations operating in the sphere of mental health. These private charities tend to pursue specific ideological and scientific goals, and one, in the United Kingdom, has initiated the foundation of a research center to investigate neurobiological and psychosocial aspects of schizophrenia.* This kind of research and the growth of public concern for the plight of the schizophrenic are widely believed to justify an optimism that it will bring a breakthrough in the understanding and treatment of psychotic disorders in general and of schizophrenia in particular, a hope that tends to be couched in terms of biological and psychosocial advances. It is often associated with a devaluation of psychoanalytic concepts, and of the relevance of psychoanalysis and its derivative, psychoanalytic psychotherapy. Such views have found increasing expression in the popular media and in psychiatric publications. Since psychoanalysis and psychotherapy have long been applied to psychotic conditions in the United States, although now much less so, criticism there is more vocal than in the United Kingdom where psychotherapy has rarely been regarded as of any relevance to psychotic illness. Studies of the outcome of psychotherapy with schizophrenic patients have at times been used to conclude that psychoanalytic psychotherapy is of little or no value in the case of psychotic patients. Although often inaccurate and even misleading, these inferences succeed in damaging opportunities for collaboration between potentially complementary disciplines (for example, see Mueser & Barenbaum, 1990). The 1990s, hailed as the "Decade of the Brain" (Gabbard, 1992), gave rise to such headlines in the United States as "Pills for the Mind," "The Eclipse of Freud," and "Is Freud Dead?"† In our present intellectual climate, which tends too readily towards polarization and, worse, reductionism, the rise of this kind of polemicism in the reporting of mental health treatments seems more calculated to stimulate circulation figures and the sale of pharmaceutical products than to generate informed debate.

The view that schizophrenia is a neurodevelopmental disorder of organic origin is based on research findings that are impressive. However, the application of these findings as general truths about the nature and treatment requirements of schizophrenia can be quite misleading. Studies of brain pathology reveal statistical significance only, and the common structural

---

* SANE (Schizophrenia: A National Emergency).
† *Time International*, July 6, 1992, and November 29, 1993.

disorders detected in the "schizophrenic brain" are by no means confined to schizophrenia. It is not yet known how frequently such structural disorders occur, or how often they have pathological consequences for personality development and psychological functioning. Genetic studies of schizophrenia have proved to be far more complex than many had imagined. The essential fact that genes represent *tendencies*, and thus may be modifiable by favorable early environmental conditions, has been demonstrated by studies showing that where a genetically predisposed infant is born into a secure and mature family the genetic effects may be neutralized (Tienari, 1992a, 1992b). Lewontin (1993), speaking of the "doctrine" of DNA, criticizes the tendency to overemphasize the role of genetics in human development. He points out that "genes affect how sensitive one is to the environment, and environment affects how relevant one's genetic differences may be" (p. 30).

This book emerged from work undertaken at the Maudsley Hospital in London, which operates within the British National Health Service, and which offered a work environment free from many of the stresses imposed on psychiatric staff in traditional mental hospitals. This freedom offered the opportunity for long-term, intensive psychodynamic study and treatment of a significant number of first-episode and relapsing psychotic conditions. The individual psychotherapy of such seriously disturbed patients is best approached as the undertaking of a team comprising complementary skills. The *combined* abilities of such a team can create a milieu in which patients discover a container for their disturbed self and from which, in the best cases, they may progress towards an autonomous existence. In cases that follow a remitting or chronic course, psychotic processes are likely to assume growing control over the patient's mental life and make recovery increasingly difficult. Concern for such patients, as I shall try to demonstrate in the ensuing chapters, does not imply idealization of the task or sentimentalizing the activities of listening and caring. Meaningful aggressiveness, for example, felt by the patient to be in the interests of survival, must be distinguished from destructiveness deriving from various forms of hatred that are the product of illness, abuse, and unmanageable distress. By the same token, genuinely reparative wishes must be recognized and respected for what they are.

CONCLUSION

The aim of this book was to demonstrate the value of a psychoanalytic perspective in the understanding and treatment of psychotic disorders, and of the importance of making emotional contact with afflicted individuals from the first opportunity. I have illustrated the significance of a psychodynamic evaluation when breakdown occurs or appears imminent. The greater the sensitivity of the assessor to the patient's emotional reality and the better the assessor's understanding of psychodynamics, the more profound and accurate will be the evaluation.

A treatment plan may then be formulated and implemented in accordance with the patient's needs and capacities, which may vary at different periods over time. Such a plan coordinates psychodynamic, psychosocial, neurobiological, and pharmacological methods so that each occupies its appropriate place within a comprehensive, flexible grasp of the patient's problems. An attempt to reach patients emotionally from the earliest moment involves exercising empathy, discerning the nonpsychotic part of their personality, attempting to understand their life (external and internal, present and past), searching out the meanings of their disturbance in relation to their history and prevailing fantasies, considering their experience of the interviewer, and providing them with the experience of being understood. Such a formidable list indicates a specialized activity in which competence can only come with training and experience. However, even in inexperienced but supervised hands, a basic knowledge of psychodynamic principles coupled with an attitude of respectful curiosity and a belief in the patient's resources and reparative capacities can prove to be of great benefit. If this attitude is carried over into long-term individual psychotherapy with an experienced therapist, impressive results can follow (see Levander & Cullberg, 1993). By comprehending psychotic patients' experiences in *their* terms, we can discover an existential coherence and emotional logic to their communications. These communications may be confused or hard to follow, but they are the patients' own ways of expressing their crisis. If we succeed enough in understanding these patients we reach *levels of meaning* that offer significant explanations of the phenomena under observation. "Understanding" in the way we describe takes many forms, not least unconditional acceptance, tolerance, and the withstanding of the patients' communications. It is shorthand for the practitioner's progressive recognition of patients' authentic experience, its relation to their life story, and of the way they have needed to control their severe underlying anxieties. Control requires the use of unconscious mental defense mechanisms to deal with otherwise unmanageable feelings arising particularly when they try to achieve emotional closeness to or dependence upon others. In severe psychotic conditions these mechanisms have been active since infancy and they may have led to structural changes within the personality. These can appear obvious when the onset of psychosis is early, or they may be slow and insidious, or present as limitations of personality that may not be immediately apparent. Any improved awareness of their life problems and the causes of their limitations will help patients integrate the meaning of their psychosis and thus acquire a greater sense of agency in living life. The search for meaning and understanding may be thought of as an attempt to help a sane and cooperative part of the patient's mind to acquire an interest in how the patient's mind works. We must try to find out why a part of the patient's mind has become psychotic, and why the patient feels obliged to maintain a preference for the psychotic world with all its confusions and sometimes terror, to the pains of the world of dependent human relationships. Important contact can sometimes be achieved at the first encounter, as I have demonstrated, depending upon the evolutionary stage of the psychosis. If a high degree of integration is subsequently acquired as the result of long-term individual psychotherapy or psychoanalysis, the quest for self-knowledge can become an enduring motive for the patient, and an unswerving ally of sanity and stability. The notion of seeking out a sane part of the personality may sound didactic, referring as it does to patients' cognitive appraisal of their mental life. However, if employed in a trustworthy, long-term therapeutic relationship, this should never have the quality of intellectualization. It is a dialectical, educative interplay between cognitive, emotional, and unconscious forms of mentation and is expressed as a reflective state of mind to be pursued according to each patient's and each psychotherapist's ability. Intelligence and psychological-mindedness are widely recognized as prerequisites for the acquisition of "insight." Clinicians would be wise to remain open minded about any particular patient's potential for insight, as it occurs more frequently than is realized. Even with chronic patients it is not uncommon for the interviewer to be asked such questions as "Why do I have such crazy ideas?" or "I know I am pregnant but I am a man and can't be. I can't stand the confusion!" or "Why do I see my mother as a cockroach instead of something else?" Unfussy explanations, perhaps using the analogy of dreamlike thinking invading waking life, can be extremely relieving, as well as help the patient begin to integrate inner and outer reality.* The degree to which psychotic patients appreciate a clear framework to begin understanding their experiences should not be underestimated.

Much has been written about the clinician's need for understanding and the importance of the psychotherapist's attitudes of warmth, empathy (see Pao, 1983), and concern. It is often thought that treating the psychotic is a very different matter from treating the neurotic; however, the difference in the severity of pathologies should not be allowed to induce unnecessary caution in the clinician. For example, the psychoanalytic dictum that direct interpretation of symbolic processes is inadvisable and hazardous need not be true for many psychotic patients. The advocates of supportive psychotherapy argue, understandably, that it is safer to help the psychotic individual to acquire a sense of existential security rather than reveal unconscious symbolic meanings (e.g., Killingmo, 1989) that might seem disturbing. Yet many psychotic individuals deeply appreciate interpretations of hidden

---

* Matte-Blanco (1988) points out that we live in two worlds at once, but usually only notice one of them in dreams, or psychosis, and that they each have their own distinct systems of logic.

meanings, and often respond with constructive understanding. One reason for this is because the patient's illness is already out in the open for both patient and clinician to identify. Provided communications by the clinician are offered in a clear and tactful way to the sane part of the mind at an appropriate developmental level, they are safe. The reason they are safe, and often highly effective, is because they are directed towards a more realistic, thoughtful component of the mind that is actively capable of promoting reflection and emotional contact. At the same time, such communications avoid assault on the psychotic part of the personality. Tact is essential because the experience of feeling understood can bring intense pain, not least shame, to a person who is experiencing psychosis. Haphazard or uninformed use of interpretations of symbolic meanings can risk doing severe harm. Experienced psychotherapists know that as integration proceeds, so the neurotic patient's capacity for absorbing complex symbolic understandings increases. What is less well known is that this is also the case for many psychotic patients, provided interpretations of unconscious, symbolic life are always addressed to the aspect of the patient's mind that is functioning in a sane way.

The recovery of imagination

The "unimaginable storms" of this chapter's title, taken from Yeats' poem, is a metaphor for psychotic mental storms, which signify an all-consuming, immediate engulfment of the rational mind. Such a massive loss of contact with reality can induce panic anxiety and a disappearance of the sense of an ongoing, identifiable self. Not all psychotic individuals endure this extremity of distress, but those who do survive a quality of existence that is difficult, if not impossible, for the more sane person to imagine. If some form of representation of the psychotic experience can be achieved in the imagination of the afflicted subject (to achieve this requires psychotherapists to also be open to experiencing their own version of this), then an emotional distance can be established between the inundated self and the storm, and reflective—*symbolic*—thinking about the storm becomes possible. When psychotherapy succeeds, individuals recover, or discover, the capacity to think about experiences symbolically. They may come to understand that what they regarded as reality was, in fact, metaphor. For example, the belief "I am the Messiah" may be comprehended as "I wished to be omnipotently powerful, bigger than my father, because only in that way could I hope to gain control over the catastrophic events that have overwhelmed me." Or, "I am the Devil" may be recognized as an omnipotent belief that certain aggressive wishes are omnipotently destructive and generate unbearable guilt that must be controlled. Similarly, paranoid delusions may come to be seen as arising in the mind rather than emanating from the radio, passers-by, or distant stars. The patient's dream life, in itself a visually observed experience involving a degree of distance and perspective, may begin to provide a helpful focus for a search for meanings. Acquiring a manageable psychological space to permit thinking to occur can be supported nonverbally through the use of graphic or plastic materials; in creative art work; in body movement, dance; or in music. These media facilitate a point of departure for rational understanding and transformation, via the imagination, of upheavals that would otherwise need to remain under psychotic control.* When such growth processes occur the psychosis becomes contained, its levels of meaning become approachable, and individuals can feel some rational control over their mental life. Unmodified, psychotic processes create a susceptibility to a quality of anxiety, sometimes like nightmare, variously described as "unthinkable anxiety" (Winnicott), "disintegration" (Kohut), or "nameless dread" (Bion).

Fast-food psychiatry

The situation facing individuals with psychosis is a parlous one, as has been made clear. The situation has gotten worse, not better, since this book was written. Many patients who urgently need hospitalization don't get it. By contrast, many other patients can spend unnecessarily long periods in hospital. The idea that admission rates can be reduced without diminishing the quality of care remains a chimera. If the quality of care in hospital is poor, time spent there can be of little long-term value, and at worst it is a damaging experience and a waste of money. Short-term government policies, the unconsidered pursuit of quick cures and cost-cutting programs, have accelerated the decline of public hospital psychiatry, a situation that is being increasingly criticized.† Bad hospital psychiatry, of course, gives good hospital psychiatry a bad name, but even allowing for the efforts of good psychiatrists the preservation and improvement of hospital psychiatry has been significantly impaired by poor government commitment over many years. Similarly, gross inadequacies in community care for the mentally ill are now widely recognized, in particular for psychotic patients previously installed, for better or worse, in mental hospitals. There is a view that the remedy is merely to increase funding. The desirability of such a move may seem obvious, but on what should such funding be spent? If spending is not accompanied by a coherent mental health policy that includes recognizing the role of the psychiatric hospital as a unique vehicle capable of adopting an integrated approach towards a psychotic patient, the quality of care for these patients will remain inadequate or continue to decline. The task of

---

* See Rycroft (1968), Grotstein (1981), Segal (1991), and Barnes-Gutteridge (1993).
† In the United Kingdom, the Mental Health Act Commission describes inner city mental hospitals as "crumbling madhouses" (*The Times*, 11 December, 1993). In Australia the failure of hospital care and of community provision for the severely mentally ill has been branded a national disgrace (*British Medical Journal*, 6 November, 1993).

defining a coherent mental health policy, in the United Kingdom at least, has not been achieved, despite political proclamations to the contrary. This contradictory situation prevents successive governments, public servants, and the public themselves from recognizing and understanding what is needed to provide the best treatment and care of the mentally ill. It is not only psychotic patients who suffer from an underfunded, strategy-starved, and increasingly impersonal mental health service. Psychiatrists, psychologists, nurses, and social workers often work under tremendous handicaps in their attempts to assist psychotic patients, being required to meet unrealistic expectations using inadequate resources. Psychiatrists frequently spend more time in administration than talking with patients. "Burnout" is common and serious among staff, and a proportion of psychiatrists make no secret of their regret at having chosen psychiatry as a career. Beneficial advances in the knowledge of neurobiology and pharmacology can, if misused, lead to adverse, iatrogenic consequences for patients and clinicians. For example, where inadequately trained or hard-pressed psychiatrists confine their first contact with a psychotic patient to completing checklists of symptoms, making a diagnosis, and prescribing the appropriate medication, the patient is receiving second-rate care and the clinician learning very little. Similarly, the value of psychiatric diagnostic classifications varies entirely according to the aims of the user. The relentless pursuit of greater diagnostic precision, and of concern with form at the expense of content, can distract from recognition of the *meaning* of disturbed experience, processes, and behavior, and its interpersonal consequences, which may be crucial for the outcome of treatment. Lest I, the author, appear overly partisan in my advocacy of psychotherapy, it needs to be said that psychotherapists remain by no means beyond reproach where matters of clinical rigor are concerned. Psychotherapists may have something to learn from the intellectual discipline of traditional descriptive psychiatry—the so-called "medical model"—and the painstaking application of phenomenology to clinical work, if they are to shake off a reputation for imprecision.* Considering the complexity of the material confronted by the clinician, especially in psychosis, it is not surprising that the formulations of psychotherapists can sometimes become vulnerable to loose or confused thinking. This is not, however, an excuse for lack of rigor. Good psychotherapy will always possess an inherent uncertainty in its approach, which is a hallmark of respect for the human mind; yet psychotherapists need to cultivate clarity of thinking, conceptual accuracy, and technical precision as much as any other clinical discipline. A plea should be inserted here for psychiatrists and psychotherapists to never forget the patient's personal history, including the individual's responses to past treatment—if only to avoid a repetition of past

---

* Comprehensive treatment of these topics is to be found in Cawley (1983), Mullen (1989), and Clare (1986).

mistakes and further ineffectual treatment.* At the same time it should be recognized that traditional psychiatric procedures such as history-taking, while essential, can readily be used by a clinician as an intellectual defense against genuine emotional engagement with the patients in front of them. This is an impediment and a danger for all psychiatrists, not only those in their charge who suffer the brunt of inattention.

Although the cases presented in this book appear at times dramatic, such patients are commonly encountered in the daily work of the public hospital service, and offer ample opportunity for mental health workers to increase their understanding of psychotic states. If these patients are approached from a psychoanalytical perspective, as we have done, many issues, theoretical and practical, arise. The advantages to the patient of detection of psychosis, imminent or overt, at the earliest possible moment cannot be overestimated, and a skilled psychodynamic assessment is of enormous help in achieving this. All the patients we have described in this book were chronically ill by the time they were referred to us—a situation that could have been avoided in many cases had an earlier psychodynamic assessment taken place. Recent innovative developments in the work of early intervention teams are achieving success in this respect. Other efforts to help families adapt to the care of schizophrenic relatives have emerged in recent years, notably through education, with impressive results. With only a little psychodynamic knowledge to complement their understanding of the patient's character, families can often make good sense of the schizophrenic condition. It has also been established that high expressed emotion (EE) in the family has an adverse effect on schizophrenic patients, and training of the family in stress management can redress this. However, if, as may happen, relatives are only advised that their child has a disease like diabetes to which they must adapt, and that they should take comfort from the fact that the illness is in no way their fault, the opportunity for deeper investigation of the psychodynamic nature of the stressful emotions evoked in the patient may be lost, and with it the understanding of the patient's psychotic thinking and behavior. Although reassurances can help some families, they are unlikely to resolve the guilt that many relatives feel, often unwarranted, nor will they illuminate the unconscious elements in parent-child relationships that may be more complex than "blame" or "guiltless" imply. As Lehtinen (1993) has remarked, psychoeducational approaches often stress the importance of continuous depot neuroleptics, whereas the Scandinavian need-adapted approach goes further: "[M]edication is not used to cure an illness, but is explicitly prescribed to help a behavioral pattern or experience, and its effect is analyzed in those terms." The same author has made

---

* This injunction does not apply to moments during the course of psychotherapy when it is important that therapists should not be constrained by their knowledge of the patient's past history.

the trenchant observation that when the concept of mental illness or disease is widely overused, as is all too frequent, it may contaminate (in a manner analogous to a computer virus) all subsequent transactions with a schizophrenic patient. Seeing patients as passive victims of a disease process can infantilize them and deprive relatives of better understanding, which may sometimes be superior to that of the professional. The frequent adverse consequences of approaching the patient from an exclusively biomedical point of view were described long ago as "closure, a labeling of the patient by all concerned as totally different from other people" (Scott & Ashworth, 1967). This view of the patient as a passive victim can also serve to conceal the part the patient may be playing, for whatever reasons, in creating and maintaining stressful situations. An interesting comparable approach to this aspect of the problem can be seen in the philosophy of Alcoholics Anonymous. Participants are told that they have an incurable disease from which they will not recover and to which they are or have been innately vulnerable. However, treatment is based on a firm confrontation of their individual responsibility for the management of their condition, and for the cultivation of a lifelong search for increased self-awareness and psychological insight.

At the present time, when many inpatient units are being closed or drastically reduced in size to accommodate brief admissions for rapid neuroleptic medication and early discharge, there is a case for restating the importance of these units—which are increasingly rare—whose work seeks to promote fundamental psychological change in patients leading to enduring benefit. Such a claim does not imply that all patients should have psychoanalytic psychotherapy or necessarily spend a long time in the hospital. However, if a skilled psychodynamic assessment of a patient is made on first contact, it becomes possible to make an informed selection from a range of treatments (if available) most fitted to the patient's disabilities, vulnerabilities, and potential psychological assets. Medication, individual psychotherapy, group, couple and family therapy, and psychosocial, behavioral, and cognitive methods might all be employed at various stages as the individual becomes able to benefit from them. This method, used in recent years in Scandinavia, gave rise there to hospital and community-based psychosis teams able to differentiate with some precision those patients who did not need admission from those who needed brief or long stays. These psychiatrist-led but nonauthoritarian teams offer an improved role for the clinical psychiatrist of the future, and an opportunity to promote a more integrated psychiatry. Many psychiatrists today see their specialized skills undervalued, and some of their roles usurped by other professionals.* Fragmentation of identity and disillusion within the profession would be less

---

* However, with appropriate development, psychiatry could look forward to a robust and attractive future (see Cox, 1991; Cawley, 1991, 1993).

likely to occur if general psychiatrists were encouraged to acquire a deeper, more rounded grasp of the psychodynamic components of severe mental illness. Part of this understanding would involve some form of training in psychodynamics (already mandatory in some countries), as without this psychiatrists will not be properly equipped to fill their unique place among fellow professionals in the mental health services. Although it may seem obvious to psychotherapists and psychiatrists who practice psychodynamic methods that the approach to psychosis I have described is therapeutically potent and economically cost-effective, financial providers remain to be convinced.* Outcome research presents unique difficulties in a field where controlled clinical trials may be misleading or inappropriate,† and individual case studies rarely carry widespread conviction.‡ Much reported work fails to take account of the different levels of skill, experience, and therapeutic ambitions of the psychotherapists involved in the study, of the criteria used in the selection of schizophrenic patients, or of the setting within which work took place. A useful clarification of psychotherapeutic aims differentiated insight-oriented from reality-adaptive supportive psychotherapy and served as a reminder that different patients have different treatment aptitudes and different requirements (Stanton, Gunderson, & Knapp, 1984; Gunderson, Frank, & Katz, 1984). However, impressive results have been recorded (Fenton & McGlashan, 1987; Karon & VandenBos, 1981; Sjostrom, 1985), and many Swedish studies in case finding and in the identification of predictors of good and bad outcome for psychotherapy have been well received (Cullberg, 1991; Cullberg & Levander, 1991; Levander & Cullberg, 1993). In the psychodynamic treatment and rehabilitation of schizophrenic psychoses, the work of the Finnish group is now well established, not least for its outstanding cost-effectiveness (Lehtinen, 1993). The fact that this advanced work is being done in Scandinavia is a reflection of a long history of concern for the individual and the high quality of social welfare systems.§ Changing social trends have forced revision, and a reduction in welfare provision is taking place in Scandinavia, as in all developed countries. The large population of psychotic patients needing long-term treatment and support is potentially at risk, but it is to be hoped that the flexibility and sophistication of the Scandinavian model will minimize this.

---

* Impatience with demands to produce evidence of results is easily generated in psychotherapists who have done successful work: "If one has had the good fortune to observe the raising of Lazarus from the dead, it is foolish to demand a control sample" (Cancro, 1986).

† Certain influential studies of the outcome of individual psychotherapy of schizophrenic patients (May, 1968; McGlashan, 1984) have been erroneously used as evidence of the unsuitability of this form of treatment (see Alanen, Ugelstad, & Armelius, 1994, p. 18).

‡ See Milton (1993) for a critical review of literature relevant to outcome research in psychotherapy.

§ Although such countries have the advantage of small populations and prosperity, their admirable attitude of concern towards psychotic and other vulnerable people is not simply a consequence of relative affluence.

The devastating impact on families who receive little or no support in their care of a chronic schizophrenic member is gradually being recognized, following many years of psychosocial research.* Undoubtedly, the quality of overall care for the psychotic patient will only be improved by increased financial resources; however, the quality of clinical care by the individual practitioner is largely independent of financial considerations. *All patients should have the right to tell their life story from the first time of contact if possible*, and the practitioner has an obligation to encourage them to do so and to learn to listen with as high a degree of understanding as possible. For example, a genuine but noncolluding interest in the content of a psychotic patient's delusions can offer entry into the nature of the patient's preoccupations and their place in the patient's life history. Simple comments like, "How has it come about that you now believe that you are Hitler?" "What was happening in your life at the time?" "What do you think it might mean that you are experiencing spiders crawling round inside your head?" or "I wonder what it must be like for you to be uncertain whether you are a man or a woman," can lead to relief and often useful developments, and enable patients to feel you are on their side. If no other interest is taken in delusional content than to establish a diagnosis, crucial opportunities are lost. If we do not discover why patients need delusional explanations for their distress, it is unlikely we shall ever succeed in helping them find better, more realistic ones. Public interest in psychodynamic understanding and psychological disturbance has grown over the years. Indeed, the "talking therapies" have burgeoned, an ironic development when viewed against the decreased opportunities for individuals with psychosis to talk about their difficulties. In the United Kingdom, the major psychoanalytic training bodies offer public lectures in the concepts of psychoanalysis and on individual topics of special interest. Presentation in the media of the nature of psychosis varies from occasionally excellent to staggeringly naïve. Tragic cases of self-damaging, violent, or bizarre behavior are often portrayed as mere failures in care by the community, with no interest in the origins and meaning of the psychotic behavior. The conclusion drawn from these tragedies tends to be that patients should receive more supervision to ensure they take their medication. This may be needed in many cases, but it cannot be taken for granted that the treatment these patients have received has been based on an accurate, skilled assessment of their mental state and psychological needs.

It may take time before the treatment pendulum, which has swung in recent years in the direction of biology, will come to rest at a point where

---

* The work of Leff and his colleagues (1982) has been largely responsible for this advance. Such a psychoeducational orientation can have drawbacks if applied within a purely biomedical view of the nature of schizophrenia. See Alanen et al. (1994, p. 20) for a critical commentary.

collaboration between biological, psychosocial, and psychoanalytical thought is achieved. Integrating the treatment modes available to help the severely mentally disturbed patient would create a welcome complementarity. This would not mean equivalence. The relevance of each treatment would need to be assessed according to its power to increase understanding of psychotic patients, reduce distress, improve the quality of their life, and stimulate mental growth processes. Applied sensitively, conditions for improved object-relationships and a more integrated sense of self would be created. This objective is neither utopian nor beyond the capacity of daily psychiatric practice to achieve. Even if the necessary resources do not exist, we are obliged to provide the best treatment we can. The approach presented could make considerable improvements possible in ordinary circumstances, given some integrated planning by collaborating professionals. Psychiatry today is an extremely demanding discipline. Its practitioners carry a heavy burden of responsibility for difficult and often potentially dangerous decisions, and they are obliged to do good work each day in the face of psychotic and psychopathic behavior. Psychiatrists are under pressure from many quarters, not least from the effects of inadequate resources and unrealistic expectations. The perspectives I have brought to bear might suggest that there exists a large-scale failure in psychiatric provision for psychotic patients, a failure that has not been properly realized. Some would argue this is the case. My aim in this book was to demonstrate how the present difficult situation can be improved by those people with an immediate opportunity to effect change—clinicians themselves. If the dimension of unconscious mental processes and the inherent meaning of psychotic experiences can be taken into account in our daily work, then much psychiatry, including research into the outcome of treatment, will no longer run the risk of lacking substance. The care of psychotic patients may suffer immeasurably if attention is restricted to diagnosis, symptom control with medication, return to the community, and time-limited stress counseling for relatives. Where concern is absent for the relevance of delusional experience and its unconscious formation, and a developmental approach not acknowledged, a grasp of the psychotic patient's world is unlikely to be acquired. Understanding the meaning of psychotic experience and behavior permits the clinician to bring to the psychotic individual the depth of understanding all human beings, normal or psychotic, need and deserve, and without which life is impoverished and, at worst, meaningless. The proper application of psychoanalytical concepts to psychotic patients in a contained, well-managed setting yields profound benefits we ignore at our patients' cost.

I have described the setting in which the work I presented was carried out and how the work represents the application of psychoanalytical principles within the context of general clinical psychiatry. I have drawn attention to centers in Scandinavian countries where these principles have been applied with a high level of sophistication and encouraging results. Such work has not received the attention it deserves outside Scandinavia, and I believe it offers both a cost- and treatment-effective way forward for the care of psychotic patients. If the motivation and the resources exist, beneficial changes in patients will not be difficult to achieve. In addition, the use of experienced psychotherapists, medical or nonmedical, as members of hospital and community teams could make a major contribution to treatment (see Hobbs, 1990). At the very least an experienced psychotherapist should be on hand at the assessment stage. Nurse training in psychodynamics could revive interest in a creative career in psychiatric nursing, an interest sadly declining in the public sector. A psychodynamic perspective on psychopharmacology would improve the quality and sensitivity of prescribing, and maximize the potential of these essential, potentially dangerous, and often misused drugs. I do not suggest that all mental health professionals become psychodynamic psychotherapists, but I believe they should acquire some understanding of what this knowledge is, and of its potential contribution to hospital and community psychiatry. Education can be acquired in different ways, at different levels. The most important single item in any psychotherapy training is a period of personal psychotherapy. This can be recommended to all interested workers, as there is little to match firsthand experience of the process. If it proves successful, perhaps even profound, it provides the worker with a unique deepening of sensitivity to the pain and suffering experienced by a high proportion of patients, a recognition of the fact that "normal" people also have psychotic characteristics, and what it is like to experience questioning of painfully acquired mental defenses. An invaluable consequence of successful personal therapy for the mental health worker is a heightened capacity to understand the experience of *countertransference*. For example, it is easy to feel irritation, even flashes of hatred, towards a difficult or impossible patient. This can be a countertransference reaction. In an inpatient setting staff have to cope with such feelings every day. Only by distinguishing which feelings originate and belong to the patient (and are perhaps being unconsciously forced into another person), and which to oneself, is it possible not to take these emotional assaults personally in a way that inhibits work. When psychotic patients have the good fortune to meet such a sensitive, psychodynamically informed professional helper, their experience of the treatments subsequently made available to them, not to mention the clinical encounter itself, is likely to be a very different and more valuable one. I hope that this book will contribute to the search for a comprehensive model for the understanding and treatment of psychotic individuals and be of some value to those engaged in a personal and professional search for a more integrated perspective.

REFERENCES

Alanen, Y. O., Ugelstad, E., & Armelius, B. (1994). *Early treatment for schizophrenic patients*. Oslo: Scandinavian University Press.

Barnes-Gutteridge, W. (1993). Imagination and the psychotherapeutic process. *British Journal of Psychotherapy*, 9(3), 267–279.

Cancro, R. (1986). General considerations relating to theory in the schizophrenic disorders. In D. Feinsilver (Ed.), *Towards a comprehensive model for schizophrenic disorders*. Hillsdale, NJ: The Analytic Press.

Cawley, R. H. (1983). The principles of treatment and therapeutic evaluation. In M. Shepherd (Ed.), *Handbook of psychiatry, vol. I: General psychopathology*. Cambridge: Cambridge University Press.

Cawley, R. H. (1991). The psychiatrist of the 21st century. *British Journal of Psychiatry*, 157, 174–181.

Cawley, R. H. (1993). Psychiatry is more than a science. *British Journal of Psychiatry*, 162, 154–160.

Clare, A. (1986). The disease concept in psychiatry. In R. Hill, R. Murray, & A. Thorley (Eds.), *The essentials of post-graduate psychiatry*. London: Grune & Stratton.

Cox, J. L. (1991). A psychiatry with beds: Evolution and evaluation of socio-therapy on an acute admission ward. *Psychiatric Bulletin*, 15, 684–686.

Cullberg, J. (1991). Recovered versus non-recovered schizophrenic patients among those who have had intensive psychotherapy. *Acta Psychiatrica Scandinavica*, 84, 242–245.

Cullberg, J., & Levander, S. (1991). Fully recovered schizophrenic patients who received intensive psychotherapy. *Nordic Journal of Psychiatry*, 45, 253–262.

Falloon, I. R., Boyd, J. L., & McGill, C. (1984). *Family care of schizophrenia*. New York: Guilford Press.

Fenton, W. S., & McGlashan, T. H. (1987). Sustained remission in drug-free schizophrenic patients. *American Journal of Psychiatry*, 144, 1306–1309.

Gabbard, G. (1992). The decade of the brain. *American Journal of Psychiatry*, 8, 991–998.

Grotstein, J. S. (1981). *Splitting and projective identification*. Northvale, NJ: Jason Aronson.

Gunderson, J. G., Frank, A. F., & Katz, A. M. (1984). Effects of psychotherapy of schizophrenia: Comparative outcome of two forms of treatment. *Schizophrenia Bulletin*, 10, 564–598.

Hill, D. (1970). On the contribution of psychoanalysis to psychiatry: Mechanism and meaning. *British Journal of Psychiatry*, 117, 609–615.

Hill, D. (1978). The qualities of a good psychiatrist. *British Journal of Psychiatry*, 133, 97–105.

Hobbs, M. (1990). The role of the psychotherapist as consultant to in-patient psychiatric units. *Psychiatric Bulletin*, 14, 8–11.

Karon, B. P., & VandenBos, G. R. (1981). *Psychotherapy of schizophrenia: The treatment of choice*. New York: Jason Aronson.

Killingmo, B. (1989). Conflict and deficit: Implications for technique. *International Journal of Psychoanalysis*, 1, 65–79.

Leff, J., Kuipers, L., & Berkowitz, R. (1982). A controlled trial of social intervention in the families of schizophrenic patients. *British Journal of Psychiatry*, *141*, 121–134.

Lehtinen, K. (1993). Family therapy and schizophrenia in public mental health care. *Annales Universitatis Turkuensis ser D. Medica-odonotologica*, 106.

Levander, S., & Cullberg, J. (1993). Sandra: Successful psychotherapeutic work with a schizophrenic woman. *Psychiatry*, *6*, 284–293.

Lewis, A. J. (1967). *The state of psychiatry*. London: Routledge & Kegan Paul.

Lewontin, R. J. (1993). *The doctrine of DNA: Biology and ideology*. London: Penguin.

Matte-Blanco, I. (1988). *Thinking, feeling, and being*. London: Routledge.

May, P. R. (1968). *The treatment of schizophrenia*. New York: Science House.

McGlashan, T. H. (1984). The Chestnut Lodge follow-up study. *Archives of General Psychiatry*, *41*, 587–601.

McNeil, T. F., Cantor-Grace, E., Nordstrom, L. G., & Rosenlund, T. (1993). Head circumference in "preschizophrenic" and control neonates. *British Journal of Psychiatry*, *162*, 517–523.

Milton, J. (1993). Presenting the case for NHS psychotherapy services. *Psychoanalytic Psychotherapy*, *6*(2), 151–167.

Mueser, K. T., & Barenbaum, H. (1990). Psychodynamic treatment of schizophrenia: Is there a future? *Psychological Medicine*, *20*, 253–262.

Mullen, P. (1989). The mental state and states of mind. In R. Hill, R. Murray, & A. Thorley (Eds.), *The essentials of post-graduate psychiatry*. London: Grune & Stratton.

Pao, P.-N. (1983). Therapeutic empathy and the treatment of schizophrenics. *Psychoanalytic Inquiry*, *3*, 145–167.

Pylkkanen, K. (1989). A quality assurance program for psychotherapy. *Psychoanalytic Psychotherapy*, *4*, 13–22.

Rubin, P., Karle, A., & Moller-Madsen, S. (1993). Computerized tomography in newly diagnosed schizophrenic and schizophreniform disorder: A controlled blind study. *British Journal of Psychiatry*, *163*, 604–612.

Rycroft, C. (1968). *Imagination and reality*. London: Hogarth Press.

Scott, R. D., & Ashworth, P. L. (1967). Closure at the first schizophrenic breakdown: A family study. *British Journal of Medical Psychology*, *40*, 109–415.

Segal, H. (1991). *Dream, phantasy and art*. London: Routledge.

Sjostrom, R. (1985). Effects of psychotherapy on schizophrenia: A retrospective study. *Acta Psychiatrica Scandinavica*, *71*, 513–522.

Stanton, A. H., Gunderson, J. G., & Knapp, P. H. (1984). Effects of psychotherapy in schizophrenia: Comparative outcome of two forms of treatment. *Schizophrenia Bulletin*, *10*, 520–563.

Tienari, P. (1992a). Implications of adoption studies on schizophrenia. *British Journal of Psychiatry*, *18*(Suppl.), 52–58.

Tienari, P. (1992b). Interaction between genetic vulnerability and family environment. In A. Werbart & J. Cullberg (Eds.), *Psychotherapy of schizophrenia: Facilitating and obstructive factors* . Oslo: Scandinavian University Press.

Index

A

anorexia nervosa, 47
anticipation of fulfillment, 73
art
    incubation process, 174
    insanity, kinship with, 174
    ordinary thinking, link to, 174
    psychosis, use in healing, 179–180
auditory hallucinations, 123–124
autonomy, 154

B

binocularity, 17
borderline personality disorder
    Ms. B, case of, 10–12, 16–17
    sexuality, confused, 126
bricoleur, 164–165

C

case studies, clinical. *See* clinical case
    studies
Cawley, Robert, 1
central phobic position
    Alec, case of, 200–201
    associative process in treatment,
        185–188
    autoerotic activities, 188
    effects of, 186
    Gabriel, case of (*see* Gabriel, case
        of)
    generalization, 198
    Mr. X, case of, 201–204
    overview, 183, 184
claustro-agoraphobia, 47, 130–131

clinical case studies
    James (incorporation of invasive
        object), 4–10
    Ms. B (incorporation of invasive
        object), 10–12
Cluster A personality disorders
    countertransference in, 102
    demographics, 85
    description of, 85–86
    overview, 85–86
    paranoid personality disorder
        (*see* paranoid personality
        disorder)
    psychotic anxieties in, 101–102
    regression in, 102–103
    schizoid personality disorder
        (*see* schizoid personality
        disorder)
    schizotypal personality disorder
        (*see* schizotypal personality
        disorder)
    self-esteem issues, 102
    transference difficulties, 87–88
    treatment of, 86–87, 103
countertransference
    Alec, case of, 32, 45
    Cluster A personality disorders, in,
        102
    Gabriel, case of, 192–193
    schizotypal patient, in, 100–101

D

desymbolization, 122–123

E

ego
    fantasy dimension of, 3–4
    fragmentation, 199
    internal objects, negotiations with,
        80–81
    splitting, in schizoid personality
        disorder, 93
Eliot, T. S., 81

F

Foucault, Michel, 150–153, 156
fractal objects, 14
Freud, Anna, 17
Freud, Sigmund
    homosexuality, focus on as
        pathogenic factor, 124
    ineffectiveness of psychoanalysis,
        criticisms of, 211
    infantile fantasies, theories of, 174
    influence of, 207
    lying, accusations of, 210–211
    methodology, 209–210
    obsessional neurosis theories,
        220–221, 224–225
    paranoia, theories on, 89–90
    personal correspondence, release of,
        207
    Rat Man case (see Rat Man case)
    topographical mind model, 221
    unscientific, criticism of as,
        208–210
fundamentalism in psychoanalysis,
    197–198

G

Gabriel, case of
    analyst's listening skills, 189, 190
    anxieties, 194
    associative process, 185–187, 188,
        189–190, 192, 196–197, 199
    countertransference, 192–193, 194
    insanity, fear of, 185–186
    mother, 190–191
    resistance, 192
    symptomatic behavior, 184
    transference, 185, 194–195
Grunbaum, Adolf, 207

H

heterogeneity, 4

I

idee fixe, 48
improvisation
    masks, afforded by, 162, 163, 164
    trauma, after, 168
infants
    fulfillment, anticipation of, 73
    invasive objects, incorporation of, 3,
        14–15, 17–18
institutional psychiatry, 151
intersubjectivity, 17
intrusive objects, 15
invasive objects, incorporation of
    description of, 15–16
    infants, in, 3, 14–15, 17–18
    intrusive objects, versus, 15–18
    James, case study of, 4–10, 16
    Ms. B, case study of, 10–12,
        16–17
    overview, 3–4
    projection, 13
    self, influence on the, 12–13
    treatment of, 17–18

J

Jackson, Murray, 1

K

Klee, Paul, 178–179

L

Lewis, Aubrey, 227
Lorenz, Paul. See Rat Man case

M

madness
    art, kinship with, 174
    defining, 148–150
    externally generated, 157
    Foucault's influence on treatment
        and contemporary view of,
        150
    historical overview, 149–150

institutional psychiatry, 151
internally generated, 157
therapies for, 154–155
Western society's view of, 147–148,
  157–158
masks
  bricoleurs, 164–165
  common links between, 163–164
  cultures that foster, 165–166
  improvisation, 162, 163, 164
  primitive mental life, 162
  psychoanalytic view of, 161–162,
    163–164
masochism, 52
  debate over, 43–44
  narcissistic injury in, 43–44
  passivity, associated with, 44
mental health definitions, modern,
  156–157
Milner, Marion, 5
mimesis, 169
modernism, 153
Ms. B, case of
  analysis, 51–57
  anorexia, 62, 64, 67
  anxiety, 51, 54, 56–57, 58
  borderline personality, 64
  career choice of, 48, 66–67
  co-existence of personalities, 59
  depression, 47, 60–61, 63, 64
  Director, 10, 12, 16, 53, 56, 57–66,
    68
  double-identification, 66–67, 68
  dreams of, 55–56, 59, 60, 62–63
  fantasies, 11–12, 48–49, 50–51, 63,
    67
  father, hatred of, 62, 64, 65
  grief, 64
  loneliness, 47
  marriage, 50, 53
  medication, 56
  mother, contempt for, 63
  mother, identification with, 66
  narcissism, 52
  overview, 47–48
  paranoid psychosis, 10–12, 57,
    58–59, 60
  patient history, 48–51
  sadomasochism, 50, 53
  sexual abuse of, 49–50, 53, 60
  sexual issues, 16, 60, 61–62
  suicide attempt, 61

symbolic thinking, 65, 66

N

narcissistic states
  equilibrium, 28
  equivalence statements, 28–29
  James, case of, 161, 166–168
  masochism, in, 43–44
  Ms. B, case of (*see* Ms. B, case of)
  Nash, John, in (*see* Nash, John)
  psychotic anxieties underlying,
    32–33
  rage states, 25–26
  submissiveness, related to, 42–43
  thick- *versus* thin-skinned, 22–23,
    36, 45
Nash, John
  anti-Semitism, 125–126
  auditory hallucinations, 117–118,
    123–124
  biographer's views on, 111–112
  biological vulnerability, 136–137
  birth, 110
  bisexuality, 126
  case presentation approach, reasons
    for, 109–110
  childhood, 140
  claustro-agoraphobia, 130–131
  Cold War, 110–111
  delusions, 124–125
  depression, 131, 138
  desymbolization, 122–123
  discontinuation of the antipsychotic
    medication, 108, 118, 127
  double-life strategy, 121
  employment, 110–111
  father's death, 120–121
  film treatment, 112–115
  grandiosity, 129–130
  homosexual behavior, 111, 120
  medications, 108, 116, 118, 127
  narcissism, 114, 115
  Nobel Prize, winning of, 119
  numerology, 125
  overview, 107
  paranoia, 131
  pathogenic conflicts, 119–122
  psychosis, 115, 116
  recovery, 132, 137–138
  remissions, 127–129, 132–133

repentingness oscilloscope,
    126–127
self-cure, 118–119
superego, 138–139
theories on conflict, 110–111
underlying mental processes,
    108–109
Nietzche, Friedrich, 72, 152
nihilism, 152

O

Oppenheimer, Robert, 121
oral frustration, 13
oral stage, 15–16

P

paranoid personality disorder. *See
    also* Cluster A personality
    disorders
    characteristics, 88
    differentiation of, 89
    medications for, 89
    object-relations crisis in those with,
        90–91
    projective identification in, 90–91
    psychoanalytic therapy, 91
    vignette therapy example, 88–89
Popper, Karl, 208
projection, 33
projective identification
    Alec, case of, 33
    fixations, 47–48
    paranoid personality disorder, in,
        90–91
    Rat Man case, 224
Proust, Marcel, 72
psyche-soma
    infants, of, 17–18
    trauma to, 4
psychiatric diagnosis classifications,
    237
psychotics. *See also* specific types of
    psychotic disorders
    anxieties, 156, 159
    funding for treatment, 236–237
    hospitalization, 236–237, 239
    imagination, recovery of the,
        235–236
    James, case of, 5–10, 16
    Ms. B, case of (*see* Ms. B., case of)

psychoanalytic theories of, 135–136
recovery of, 2
Scandinavian model of treatment,
    238–239, 240
suffering of, 229
treatment, 134–135, 234–235

R

rape, dynamics of, 16–17
Rat Man case
    clinical exploration, 214–217
    Father Complex, 219
    Freud's assessment, 217–219
    girlfriend, 217–218
    obsessional neurosis, 220–221,
        224–225
    oedipal anxieties, 216
    overview, 213–214
    projective identification, 224
    transference, 215–216, 218,
        222–223
reflective function, 17
regression
    Cluster A disorders, in, 102–103
    malignant, 102–103
    psychotic, 170
repetition-compulsion, 81
repression, of child abuse, 43
Rey, Henri, 1, 47

S

schizoid personality disorder
    analytic vignette, 94
    anxiety in, 95–96
    characteristics, 92
    clinical complications of treatment,
        95–96
    differentiation, 96–97
    ego splits in, 93
    internal defense strategies, 96
    intervention and interpretation,
        two-step treatment model,
        94–95
    overview, 92
    psychic reality of, 92–97
    suffocation-isolation, 97
schizophrenia
    aftercare programs, 230
    brain pathologies, 231–232

burden of, on families, 135–136,
        241
controversies, 229–230
medications for, 230–231, 239
misleading nature of term, 134
psychotherapeutic treatments, 231
remissions, 127–129
self-awareness, 233–234
stigma, 133
treatment, 135–136, 230, 233, 242,
        243
schizotypal personality disorder
anxiety, 99–100
characteristics of, 97–98
countertransference in, 100–101
genetic link with schizophrenia, 98
treatment, 99–101
self
development of, 14–15
incorporation of in invasive
        object (see invasive objects,
        incorporation of)
lack of sense of, 160
sexual confusion, 35
sexual fantasies
transference, in case of, 41–42
unconscious, 13–14
sexual identity, confused, 43
shamans, 164
splitting
Alec, case of, 31–32, 33
ego, 93
mental functioning, impact on, 33
paranoid personality disorder, in,
        90
primary, in psychosis, 79
time, influence on concept of, 76–77
Steiner, John, 227–228
suicidal ideation, 4
superego
abnormal, 16
humanizing, 138–139
overdeveloped, 91–92
paranoid personality disorder, in,
        91–92
symbolic functioning
capacity for, 160–161
disturbances in, 3
incorporation of an invasive
        object (see invasive objects,
        incorporation of)

James, case of, 173, 175, 176,
        177–178
masks (see masks)
poetry exploration, 172–173

T

time
anxious patients, disturbances in,
        75–76, 77
borderline patients, disturbances in,
        75, 77–78
chronological, 71
conflation of, 72
first recorded awareness of, 71
Freud's view of, 73–74
human preoccupation with, 82–83
memory, link to, 72
neurotic disorders, disturbances in,
        74–75
omnipresent nature of, 82
psychological, 71
psychotic patients, disturbances in,
        78, 79–80
quasi-present, 75
transference, 21. See also
        countertransference
Alec, case of, 26, 31, 40–41,
        41–42
Cluster A patients, in, 87–88
Gabriel, case of, 185, 194–195
James, case of, 9
maximum tolerance for, 34
physical pain, relationship to,
        40–41
Rat Man case, 215–216, 218,
        222–223

U

unconscious
early theories of, 153, 155
Freud's studies of, 209
maladaptive, 153–154
significance of, 145–146
temporal perspective, lack of,
        73–74
unimaginable storms
metaphor of, 235–236
overview, 227–229

W

wish fulfillment, 175
withdrawn patient, analysis of
    analysis sessions, 24–30
    depressed session, 39–40
    distressed session, 36–39

overview of case of Alec, 21–23
patient history, 23–24
physical pain, caused by
    transference, 40–41
Wolfli, Adolf, 179